T0391490

COSMOLOGY AND POLITICS IN PLATO'S LATER WORKS

Knowledge of the structure of the cosmos, Plato suggests, is important in organizing a human community which aims at happiness. This book investigates this theme in Plato's later works, the *Timaeus, Statesman* and *Laws*. Dominic J. O'Meara proposes fresh readings of these texts, starting from the religious festivals and technical and artistic skills in the context of which Plato elaborates his cosmological and political theories, for example the Greek architect's use of models as applied by Plato in describing the making of the world. O'Meara gives an account of the model of which Plato's world is an image; of the mathematics used in producing the world; and of the relation between the cosmic model and the political science and legislation involved in designing a model state in the *Laws*. Non-specialist scholars and students will be able to access and profit from this book.

DOMINIC J. O'MEARA is Professor Emeritus in the Department of Philosophy at the Université de Fribourg, Switzerland. His numerous publications on the history of Platonism include *Pythagoras Revived* (1989) and *Platonopolis* (2003). He is a founding member of the Academia Platonica Septima and a recipient of the Prince of Liechtenstein Prize.

COSMOLOGY AND POLITICS IN PLATO'S LATER WORKS

DOMINIC J. O'MEARA
Université de Fribourg, Switzerland

CAMBRIDGE
UNIVERSITY PRESS

University Printing House, Cambridge CB2 8BS, United Kingdom

One Liberty Plaza, 20th Floor, New York, NY 10006, USA

477 Williamstown Road, Port Melbourne, VIC 3207, Australia

4843/24, 2nd Floor, Ansari Road, Daryaganj, Delhi – 110002, India

79 Anson Road, #06–04/06, Singapore 079906

Cambridge University Press is part of the University of Cambridge.

It furthers the University's mission by disseminating knowledge in the pursuit of
education, learning, and research at the highest international levels of excellence.

www.cambridge.org
Information on this title: www.cambridge.org/9781107183278
DOI: 10.1017/9781316869581

© Dominic J. O'Meara 2017

This publication is in copyright. Subject to statutory exception
and to the provisions of relevant collective licensing agreements,
no reproduction of any part may take place without the written
permission of Cambridge University Press.

First published 2017

Printed in the United Kingdom by Clays, St Ives plc

A catalogue record for this publication is available from the British Library.

Library of Congress Cataloging-in-Publication Data
NAMES: O'Meara, Dominic J., author.
TITLE: Cosmology and politics in Plato's later works / Dominic J. O'Meara,
Universite de Fribourg, Switzerland.
DESCRIPTION: New York : Cambridge University Press, 2017. | Includes
bibliographical references and index.
IDENTIFIERS: LCCN 2017012149 | ISBN 9781107183278 (alk. paper)
SUBJECTS: LCSH: Plato. | Cosmology. | Political science.
CLASSIFICATION: LCC B395 .O44 2017 | DDC 184–dc23
LC record available at https://lccn.loc.gov/2017012149

ISBN 978-1-107-18327-8 Hardback

Cambridge University Press has no responsibility for the persistence or accuracy of
URLs for external or third-party internet websites referred to in this publication
and does not guarantee that any content on such websites is, or will remain,
accurate or appropriate.

Contents

List of Illustrations	*page* vi
Preface	vii
Acknowledgements	xi
Prologue. The Future of the Past in Plato's Work	1
PART I THE WORLD OF THE TIMAEUS	11
1 A Feast for the Goddess	13
2 The World-Maker	25
3 The Model of the World	41
4 The Beauty of the World	65
Interlude	83
PART II THE CITY OF THE STATESMAN AND THE LAWS	85
5 The *Statesman*: A New Robe for the Goddess?	87
6 The Legislators of the *Laws*	105
7 The Order of the City of the *Laws* and Its Model	117
Epilogue	135
Bibliography	141
Index locorum	149
General Index	155

v

Illustrations

1 The *peplos* scene, central block, Parthenon east frieze. Photo courtesy of the Trustees of the British Museum. *page* 12
2 Reconstruction of the central scene, Parthenon east pediment. Courtesy of Olga Palagia. 24
3 The Parthenon. Photo courtesy of Frédéric Möri. 40
4 Architectural planning sketch, temple of Athena at Priene. Courtesy of Wolf Koenigs. 64
5 Hagia Sophia, Istanbul. View of the central dome from below. Photo Wikimedia commons/Myrabella. 81
6 Athena defeating Encelados. Black-figure vase, Rouen Museum. From a lithograph by Kaeppelin (1864). Photo New York Public Library digital collections. 86
7 Gortyn law code, Crete. Photo Wikimedia commons/Afrank99. 104
8 Plan of the paradigm state of the *Laws*. 116

Preface

The purpose of this book is to examine the relation between the order of the world and the order of what would be a good human community, as this relation was explored by Plato in his later writings. Among these writings may be counted the *Timaeus*, the *Statesman*, the *Philebus* and the *Laws*. The *Timaeus* will be discussed here, to the extent that its cosmology might relate to the conceptions of a good human community proposed in the *Statesman* and in the *Laws*. Some attention will also be given to the *Philebus*.

All four of these works of Plato have experienced a sort of renaissance in contemporary studies. The *Timaeus* has always fascinated. But a narrow perspective in the English-speaking world, in particular an anti-metaphysical stance, has distorted the way in which it was read, a prejudice that has happily given way in recent years to a wealth of work open to the many dimensions (and difficulties!) of Plato's text. Similarly, the *Statesman*, long overshadowed by an exclusive concentration on the *Republic*, has come into its own right and has been explored in detail and discussed in its possible relation to the *Republic* and *Laws*. Finally, the *Laws*, also long neglected, if not dismissed as the expression of disillusion and decline in Plato's final years, has more recently become the object of serious, sympathetic and detailed investigation.

In the vast sea of studies published on Plato, the theme of the relation between cosmology and politics, as this relation may be suggested in Plato's later works, is not absent. For example, André Laks, referring to earlier work by Glenn Morrow,[1] reports:

> He [i.e. Morrow] drew a parallel between the divine Demiurge of the *Timaeus*, who is responsible for the organization of the universe, and the legislator of the *Laws*, who is responsible for the organization of the city – that is, of the city as it should be, as opposed to the universe as it is.

[1] Morrow (1954).

viii   *Preface*

The parallel, which assumes some kind of structural similarity between the political and the cosmic processes, is philosophically promising. One might expect this common structure to give us some clues about the 'political' aspects of Plato's cosmological theory as well as about the 'cosmological' aspects of this political theory. Furthermore, the cosmo-political parallel might be founded upon a more general metaphysical scheme that could explain some fundamental features of Plato's political philosophy.[2]

Laks goes on to point out, however, that Morrow did not pursue the cosmological-political parallel very far. I believe the same is true of more recent work on Plato's later dialogues. Attention has been called to the political purpose of the cosmological story told in the *Timaeus* and to the idea that the order of the world may serve as a model of political order,[3] but this suggestion has not been developed by means of an investigation of Plato's political theory in the *Statesman* and *Laws* which would show in more detail how, in particular, the cosmological-political parallel might work. Connections have been explored between the cosmology of the *Timaeus* and the ethics of the *Philebus*, with some attention being given to the political implications of the cosmological myth of the *Statesman* and of the cosmological argument of *Laws* Book X, but a discussion of the wider political theory of the *Statesman* and of the *Laws* is not undertaken.[4] It is my hope, in this book, to pursue the topic further, by means of a more extensive comparison between the cosmology of the *Timaeus* and the political theory of the *Statesman* and *Laws*.

The approach adopted in this book is singular in some respects. I will *not* attempt to make direct contributions to what have recently become mainstream topics in English-language discussions of Plato's later works. Rather, working outside this framework, I will draw attention to the cultural, religious and technical contexts in which Plato's writings live, contexts which are often neglected, if not completely ignored, in modern discussions. Plato's interest in the many technical skills and arts (*technai*) of his time is evident to his readers. And some note has been made of the presence of the great Athenian festivals in his work. Indeed it was during these festivals that the finest achievements of classical Greek expertise and art were on display. At the Panathenaic festival, a splendidly woven new robe for the goddess Athena was carried, for all to see, in a great procession

---

[2] Laks (1990), 209–10.
[3] Pradeau (1997), Part III.B; Schäfer (2005). Rudolph (1996) includes work by A. Laks and A. Neschke-Hentschke published elsewhere (Laks 2005; Neschke-Hentschke 1995) in versions to which I will refer.
[4] Carone (2005).

which went up to the Acropolis, now filled with magnificent new buildings, among them the Propylaia and the Parthenon, masterworks of architecture, sculpture, metalwork, painting and other arts. And at the City Dionysia, the Athenian population could admire and judge the very best of choral singing and dancing, of tragedy and comedy. In this book I will treat these festivals and these artistic and technical skills as connected, as they were at the heart of the life of the Athenian citizen and as they constantly nourished Plato's thought.

Attention will also be given in this book to the analogical way in which Plato often thinks, a method which allows him to detect similar structures in diverse contexts and on different levels, be it, for example, in the world, in the city, or in the soul. To shift contexts, to move from politics to cosmology, from cosmology to politics, serves, as Laks suggests in the passage quoted earlier, to reveal what is essential to both.

In approaching ancient philosophical texts such as those written by Plato, we can explore them by argumentative elaboration which seeks to tease out the theoretical structure and implications of the text. But we can also make new observations, pointing to aspects and connections which are not noticed, bringing into focus things which are not clearly grasped, throwing light, from a new angle, on features which would otherwise remain in the shadows. It is this latter method which I propose to follow in this book. It is my hope that such an approach might lead us to notice some unfamiliar connections, unsuspected aspects, in Plato's later work, a complement thus to excellent work recently done in the field.

This book has two parts, corresponding respectively to cosmology and political theory. In Part I, I examine the cosmology of the *Timaeus*. I attempt to bring out the importance of the dramatic setting of the dialogue, the Panathenaic festival, for the interpretation of the speeches which are recalled, held and promised in the *Timaeus*, as speeches in praise of Athena. I locate Timaeus' speech about the making of the world in this context, investigating the architectural concepts which Timaeus uses in describing how god made the world. In particular, I will try to show that if we take the trouble to consider the methods and terminology of classical Greek architecture, we will be in a better position to recognize and understand the concepts and language Plato uses in describing the construction of the world in the *Timaeus*. The use Greek architects made of models (projects) and detailed plans will throw new light, as I hope to show, on the way in which Plato conceived of the model of the world and the way in which he described the world as constructed following this model. In Part II, I examine the political theory of the *Statesman* and the *Laws*. I suggest a Panathenaic context for the image of weaving used in the *Statesman* to describe political science. Weaving, as an image of political science, has implications for Plato's conception of political science, in particular the use made in weaving of models (patterns). I also discuss the relation between political science and legislation, a topic I take up again in relation to the *Laws*, where, I argue, Plato elaborates the model (in the form of a constitutional and legislative order) for a good city, not the plan of a particular political enterprise. I suggest the presence of another religious festival within this model, the City Dionysia, reformed and re-appropriated: the arts involved here are those of dancing and music. In both Part I and Part II, I will attempt to draw attention to structural analogies, to political ideas in Plato's cosmology and to the function of cosmology in politics.

This book begins with a Prologue, in which some general suggestions are made as to why Plato situates his dialogues in the past: a recent past, a distant past or even a past forgotten by his contemporaries and first readers. In the Epilogue, I return to this theme, to the extent that this past, I propose, speaks to the present and the future, in particular the political present and future of Plato's readers, those of his day and even those of today.

No attempt will be made in this book to extend the discussion of cosmological and political themes to texts Plato composed earlier in his life, for example the *Republic*. Nor will I venture into other domains of interest – for example, epistemology – which he also explored in his later writings, or into the much disputed field of attempted reconstructions of what Plato's oral teaching in the Academy might have been. To shed some new light on some aspects of Plato's later work is already ambition enough!

Acknowledgements

Ideas developed in this book were first presented in talks given over the years in a number of places, in particular in seminars given at the University of Fribourg, Switzerland; Eötvös Loránd University, Hungary; and the University of Novosibirsk, Russia. I hope to have learned enough from the comments, suggestions and criticisms offered by my hearers on these occasions in order to improve the work, which was completed during a stay as a visiting scholar at the University of Tübingen, Germany. I am very grateful to László Bene, Eugene Afonasin and Irmgard Männlein-Robert for providing me with these opportunities. The readers for Cambridge University Press offered comments which were of considerable help in strengthening some of my arguments. Chris Bobonich kindly sent me detailed suggestions and useful references and Filip Karfík was also of great assistance on many points when I was revising the book, which (under the provisional title 'Festivals of Life. Cosmology and Politics in Plato's Later Works') also benefitted from comments made by Cinzia Arruzza, Chad Jorgenson, Mitch Miller, Luca Pitteloud and Euree Song. The deficiencies which remain in the book are of course mine. More generally, the publications of Myles Burnyeat have been a rich source of inspiration for me in working on Plato. Olga Palagia kindly allowed me to reproduce her reconstruction of the central scene of the east pediment of the Parthenon and Wolf Koenigs generously helped me on matters concerning Greek architecture. I am grateful also to Marc Bayard for technical help and to Nicolas D'Andrès, who prepared the indices.

Earlier versions of parts of this book were published as follows. Prologue: 'Plato's Open Philosophizing: The Presence of the Future in the Past', *Horizons (Seoul Journal of Humanities)* 1 (2010), 345–55; parts of Chapter 1: 'Éloge d'une déesse. Note sur le thème du *Timée* de Platon', in: *Aglaïa. Autour de Platon. Mélanges offerts à Monique Dixsaut*, ed. A. Brancacci, D. El Murr, D. Taormina, Paris 2010, 397–402; parts of Chapter 2: 'Who Is the Demiurge in Plato's *Timaeus?*', *Horizons* 3 (2012), 3–18; parts of

xi

xii   *Acknowledgements*

Chapter 4: 'The Beauty of the World in Plato's *Timaeus*', *ΣΧΟΛΗ* (*Novosibirsk*) 8 (2014), 10–19; parts of Chapter 5: 'A New Robe for the Goddess in Plato's *Statesman?*', in: *Plato's* Statesman. *Proceedings of the Eighth Symposium Platonicum Pragense*, ed. A. Havlíček, J. Jirsa, K. Thein, Prague 2013, 151–61 and in 'Remarks on the Relation between Philosophy and Politics in Plato', in: *Art, Intellect and Politics: A Diachronic Perspective*, ed. G. Margagliotta, A. Robiglio, Leiden 2013, 169–75; parts of Chapter 7: 'Religion und Musik als politische Erziehung in Platons Spätwerk', in: *Platon und die Mousikê*, ed. D. Koch, I. Männlein-Robert, N. Weidtmann, Tübingen 2012, 104–14.

PROLOGUE

The Future of the Past in Plato's Work

In recounting the story of Plato's life, Olympiodorus, a professor of philosophy in Alexandria in Egypt in the sixth century AD, told his students this anecdote:

> Having been loved by many and helped many, Plato, when he was dying, saw himself in a dream as a swan, moving from tree to tree, thus giving much trouble to the hunters. Simmias the Socratic interpreted the dream in this way: Plato [could not] be caught by those who came after him and wished to interpret him. For interpreters who try to capture the thoughts of the ancients are like hunters. But Plato cannot be caught, for one can understand him in a physical, ethical or theological way, in short in very many ways, just like Homer. For the souls of both [Homer and Plato], it is said, contain all harmonies. So it is possible to understand them in all sorts of ways.[1]

The swan was associated in ancient Greece with the god Apollo, a god with whom philosophers also were associated. It was Apollo's oracle at Delphi, for example, which encouraged Socrates in his philosophical quest. Swans appear in many stories about Plato's life, but in this story a swan serves to show how Plato's writings, after his death, became the object of interpretation: Plato's interpreters are hunters of swans.[2] The story tells us that the interpreters never succeed in capturing the swan: there will be many interpretations of Plato's writings and none will be final. The swan will never be caught.

This story can lead us to formulate two questions:

(1) Why do Plato's writings call for *interpretation*, and call for it unceasingly?
(2) Why do Plato's writings provoke a *multiplicity* of interpretations, never definitive, never final?

---

[1] Olympiodorus *In Alcib.* 2, 155–65 (my trans.). Part of this passage is quoted by Tigerstedt (1977), 9.
[2] Swans were hunted and eaten in antiquity.

I

2   The Future of the Past in Plato's Work

Olympiodorus, in the passage quoted here, reports Simmias the Socratic's answer to the second question. Simmias, a young friend of Socrates who is present while Socrates awaits his death in Plato's *Phaedo*, thought, supposedly, that it was because Plato's soul contains all harmonies and so his writings can be read in many ways.[3] I will not attempt to examine Simmias' answer, for this would involve us in difficult discussions about the constitution of Plato's soul! Rather, on the threshold to a reading of Plato's later works, I would like to propose answers to the two questions formulated here to the extent that these questions concern Plato's *writings*. No attempt will be made to show the obvious: that Plato will always be interesting and intriguing. Rather, what I wish to discuss is the following: *what is it* in Plato's writings that creates the need to interpret them, and to interpret them in ever-renewed ways? What is it, in this work, a work which belongs to the past, which allows it to carry with itself its future? To deal with these matters, I would like to follow three paths.

1   **Three Temporalities in Plato**

A first path is indicated by the literary structure of Plato's writings. A start may be made on this path by recalling some well-known facts. Plato, we know, wrote his texts as if they were scenarios, dramatic scenes of dialogues usually between Socrates and his contemporaries or of exchanges of speeches between them. We also recall that Plato himself is absent from these scenarios: he is never one of the figures in the play, even if, sometimes, we might feel his presence in the wings. We are also aware that if we read Plato's dialogues, we become involved as readers in the dialogue, as if we were actually present to it, as if we had become members of it, and are provoked by it to think, to dialogue in our minds, to react.

One might draw attention to the following particular feature of this complex literary situation. The situation involves what we might call different temporalities, or times:

T 1: the time in the past when the scenario is supposed to be taking place, the time of Socrates' discussion with others, what is usually called the 'dramatic date' of the dialogue;

---

[3] Simmias appears, according to this late report, to be applying the theory of the mathematical structure of the soul of Plato's *Timaeus* (see Chapter 4, section 3) to Plato himself. Various works were attributed to Simmias in later antiquity, including a work on music (Diogenes Laertius, *Lives of the Philosophers*, 2, 124).

1 Three Temporalities in Plato

T 2: the time when the text was actually written by Plato, Plato's present as he was writing the text, the date of composition of the work;

T 3: the time when the reader reads the text. This time is the present of the reader and may be any time between the time when Plato's contemporaries first read his texts up to *our* present, as we read Plato now.

One might describe the relations between these three temporalities[4] as follows.

Even if **T 2** is the same as **T 3**, that is, even if the reader reads the text just when Plato wrote and published it, **T 1** is already in the past, as compared to the present of **T 2/T 3**. The past, we might say, is *written into* the text. But this past is brought by the text into relation with the present of the reader, to the extent that the reader becomes involved in the dialogue *as if* it were the reader's present. The reader then becomes part of a system of relations. The present time of the reader – the reader's cultural milieu, experience, interests – becomes part of the system of relations and affects it correspondingly. Since the present time is the future of the past, and since the present time of the reader is the present of any future, Plato has integrated the future into the texture of his work. And since the present time of potential readers is multiple and open, so is the text in its interpretations open. In their very past, Plato's works provoke our present, as his readers, and the variety of our presents gives a corresponding variety of interpretations.

However, might one not say this is true of *any* text portraying the past and read by later readers? For example, Thucydides, in his history, or Aeschylus, Sophocles and Euripides, in their tragedies, recount the past, including the mythical past, in a way which would not have failed to appeal indirectly to the preoccupations of their contemporaries (and ours). The system of relations I have sketched here is not unique, then, to Plato's work.

But it need not be and we need not claim any exclusivity for him in this respect. Yet among the various ways in which texts recounting the past can provoke our interest, Plato's writings, by including the future reader as an

---

[4] Further temporalities might be discerned in dialogues where the main conversation with Socrates is reported within other, later conversations (as in the *Phaedo*, or in the *Symposium*, the *Parmenides* and the *Theaetetus*). But I think that these further temporalities have to do especially with the fictionality of the dialogue involving Socrates (**T 1**), whose literary plausibility is constructed by the intermediate stages when it was reported and through which it supposedly can reach us. On this question, see Johnson (1998). On the fictional transmission through stages of the story of Atlantis in the *Timaeus*, see Chapter 1, section 3.

4 The Future of the Past in Plato's Work

(albeit silent) interlocutor and participant in philosophical enquiry, are uniquely effective in provoking the reader to *philosophize*, at any time. Plato's writings can be said to be dramas (dramas directly taking place, or dramas reported by others),[5] but they are dramas in which *we* as readers are invited to join the *dramatis personae* in philosophizing, to think about problems Plato situates in the past as they affect us in our present and call us to respond.

One might take some concrete examples in order to see how this open system of relations, with the wide interpretative possibilities it allows, actually works. My choice of examples is not intended to be systematic or final: the analysis could well be extended to other dialogues of Plato.

Chronological chart[6]

	Dramatic date (T 1)	Date of composition (T 2)	Date of reading (T 3)
Phaedo	399 BC	ca. 383	ca. 383 → ...
Republic	ca. 412	370s	370s → ...
Parmenides	ca. 450	after 370	after 370 → ...
Timaeus	late 430s	360s	360s → ...

As a first example we might take Plato's *Phaedo*. The *Phaedo* represents a discussion which Socrates is portrayed as having with his friends (including Simmias) on the day of his death. The dramatic date of the dialogue (**T** 1) is therefore 399 BC. It is probable that Plato wrote the *Phaedo* (**T** 2) around 383, about twenty years after the death of Socrates.[7] There is thus a distance of about twenty years between **T** 1 and **T** 2, a difference of one generation. Let us suppose now that **T** 2 is **T** 3, that we are reading the text when Plato first published it. What had happened since the time of Socrates' death? Athens had continued to attempt to recover from the losses suffered in its defeat in the war with Sparta. Plato himself had gone to Sicily, met Pythagoreans there, returned to Athens in 387 and founded the Academy. The *Phaedo* was written probably not long after. How, then, does what Socrates says on his last day appear to us in the retrospective light of this present time (if **T** 2 = **T** 3)? In the *Phaedo*, on the day of his death, Socrates exhorts us to have confidence in reasoning (*logos*), not to despair of

---

[5] See Erler (2007), 71–5, for a survey of this theme.
[6] The dramatic and compositional dates of Plato's works are much debated in some cases. For a review of dramatic dates, see Nails (2002), 307–30, and, for compositional dates, see Ledger (1989), 224–5.
[7] See Dixsaut (1991), 28.

1 Three Temporalities in Plato

the value of argumentation. For knowledge is the goal of the philosopher who will lead a good and admirable life, like the philosophical life exemplified by Socrates on his last day. In a curious way, these ideas, if seen in relation to **T 2/T 3**, provide support for the present work of Plato's newly founded Academy. The meaning and value of the philosophical work begun in Plato's Academy receive strong support from what Socrates tells us, speaking to us from the past. Plato, of course, does not refer explicitly in the *Phaedo* to the Academy, and what Socrates says can have a wider application. If **T 3** is not **T 2**, if our present as readers of the *Phaedo* is distant from Plato's present, as founder of the Academy, we can also think again, as we read the *Phaedo*, about what we want to do, and why, in *our* academies, why knowledge is important to us and how it relates to a good life for humans. As **T 3** is open-ended and can be the present of any future reader, the past of Socrates can speak to any future, as long as there are humans who can read Plato.

A second example might be provided by Plato's *Republic*. Here, as regards **T 1**, Socrates is younger, in his forties or fifties (he was seventy when he died).[8] The *Republic* was written by Plato (**T 2**) after the *Phaedo*, perhaps somewhere around 380 or later, in the 370s. This gives us a greater distance between **T 1** and **T 2**, perhaps a gap of about forty to fifty years, two generations. **T 1** is situated in the past of Athens, almost a decade (or perhaps more) before its defeat in 404 BC in the catastrophic war with Sparta, a past which is now (**T 2**) long gone, a distant memory. The Academy now is well established and successful in its endeavours. What does Socrates recommend to us in the *Republic*? He imagines (two generations before the Academy) a project for an ideal system of the sciences and of education. He speaks of a utopia which is based on scientific knowledge put in the service of the human good. We can suppose that all of this would have surprised and amused the members (**T 2**) of Plato's Academy. Imagine! Socrates, a long time ago, already saw the Academy! But the considerable temporal distance Plato put between the time when Socrates is supposed to be speaking (**T 1**) and Plato's present (**T 2**) has its importance, I think. Putting what Socrates says in a distant past has the effect of making this something far removed, not immediately present, describing projects which have not now been fulfilled and are not to be attempted, as such, right now, but which indicate, in their past, what

---

[8] In the chronological chart proposed earlier, 412 is given as the **T 1** of the *Republic*, a date which is proposed by Notomi (2010). Others have argued for an earlier date for **T 1**; for a survey, see Nails (2002), 324–6.

6   The Future of the Past in Plato's Work

could be aimed at and reached in a possible future, in relation to which present efforts can be orientated.[9] This applies, I would suggest, not only to Plato's first readers, when they read the *Republic*, but also to us now, his present readers, and to his readers of the future.

A third example might be Plato's *Parmenides*. Here Socrates has become *much* younger. Plato insists, in the scenario, on just how young Socrates is by comparing his youth and immaturity with the old age and maturity of his partner in the discussion, Parmenides. If Plato wrote the *Parmenides* after about 370, as seems likely, then a very long gap in time separates **T** 1 from **T** 2, about eighty years, almost four generations. For the first readers of the *Parmenides* (**T** 2 = **T** 3), the effect of this gap must have been startling. For there, in the dialogue, in a discussion between the young Socrates and the old Parmenides, a very long time ago, difficult metaphysical problems were discussed which were actually, in the present (**T** 2), being hotly debated in Plato's Academy (perhaps Aristotle was already there as a young student).[10] This technique of consigning to a very distant past debates actually taking place at present has the effect, I would like to suggest, of allowing the reader to take some distance, to detach and free herself or himself from the immediate present, opening the debate to new perspectives. Even today, when we are so far from such debates, when **T** 3 is so far from **T** 2, we can still be fascinated by the text and cannot but read it in relation to our present metaphysical interests.

A last example might be provided by Plato's *Timaeus*. Here also, the time gap between the time of the scenario and the time of composition, between **T** 1 and **T** 2, is very great, about as great as in the *Parmenides*, perhaps nearly seventy years.[11] And within the text Plato creates an even greater distance in telling how a figure in the discussion, Critias, could recount the long-forgotten story about the war between Athens and Atlantis. This story is so old that the Athenians (**T** 1 and **T** 2) have forgotten it entirely (*Timaeus* 21d, 23b). Only the Egyptians, thanks to their ancient records, kept its memory and could tell it to Solon, the source of Critias' story. The story is about the heroic deeds of a good city, similar to the utopia of Plato's *Republic*. Through the story, the utopia is projected back into a distant past, beyond the limits of the history that Athenians knew. And this very distant past is itself introduced by a speech, given by

---

[9] Notomi (2010), 117, comments: 'The *Republic* shows the tension between the hope of realizing the best possible city in the time of Socrates (412 BC) and the difficulty of changing the severe reality in Plato's maturity (the 370s BC).'

[10] For a possible resonance of the *Statesman* with the Academy, see Chapter 5, n. 2.

[11] For the **T** 1 of the *Timaeus*, see Chapter 1, n. 19.

2 The Complexity of Socrates

the figure Timaeus, about the beginning of the world. We leave here the realm of human history, Athenian or even Egyptian, and find the birth of cosmic order, which no human could have witnessed, a cosmic order which would inspire the long-forgotten ancient Athenians, victors of Atlantis, to create a good state and live a good and virtuous life. In this mythical past, the real Athenians of the present (**T 2**), whose more recent history rather resembles that of Atlantis and its destruction, could imagine another Athens, a good city, as a promise in a hypothetical, distant future.[12] And we, today, even further removed from the mythical past than Socrates' and Plato's contemporaries, can also try to imagine what it would be like for human society to live in harmony with the world and with nature.

2 The Complexity of Socrates

A second path might be followed in describing how Plato built the future into the past, how his works are written so as to call for interpretation and interpretations that are never final. This path might be made somewhat shorter than the first path. It has to do, not with the particular literary structure of Plato's writings, but with the ways in which he portrays Socrates in these writings. At first, probably, Plato wanted to preserve in writing the memory of Socrates after Socrates had died. But Socrates stays on as a figure throughout Plato's long career as a writer, and it seems as if the figure of Socrates evolves with the evolution of Plato's thinking, as if Plato never ceased to think about the reasons for Socrates' life, his action and his death.

It is precisely this continuing, evolving presence of Socrates in Plato's writings that creates a tension between what we may suppose was the historical reality of Socrates, what he actually was,[13] and his changing appearances in Plato's writings, appearances changing with Plato's preoccupations. We have already seen examples of this tension, when Socrates appears to foresee the founding and the work of the Academy. Of course there is not only the tension which Plato creates between Socrates at **T 1** and Socrates as anticipating **T 2**; there is also the tension between these and the Socrates of much later readers (**T 3**), the Socrates of Nietzsche, of Kierkegaard, of Plato's readers today. Decidedly belonging to a past long gone, Socrates also speaks to the reader's present and acts as a challenge for the future.

---

[12] See Chapter 1, section 4.   [13] On this, see Kleve (1987), 123–37.

8 The Future of the Past in Plato's Work

The tensions which Plato creates, with the figure of Socrates, our doubts about the historical reality of Plato's Socrates are symptomatic, I believe, of Socrates' role in Plato as a figure of the past announcing the future. I would like to note two aspects of this symptomatic doubt:

(i) In Plato, Socrates is sometimes a hero who is almost too perfect: he shows, in Plato's *Apology*, complete integrity, courage, freedom without compromise, responsibility for himself and for others, a life completely given to self-examination. But how could such a man really have existed? Is this figure not rather an appeal to us in the imperfection of our present, a call for a better future?

(ii) Yet Socrates, in Plato's dialogues, can sometimes appear, in some dialogues, to be a complex, problematic figure. He can give the impression of cheating in arguing with others. He says that he knows nothing, but seems to know enough to be very sure about himself, about what he is doing and why he is doing it, to the point of dying for it. He presupposes a number of claims, in particular claims about what it takes to lead a good life. These apparent presuppositions worry us (after all, we are Socrates' children), drive us to think about them, and to think, through them, about our own life ideals, in their assumptions.

Under both aspects, Socrates is a part of the past, conjured up by Plato as a figure of a possible future to our present. Socrates is Plato become a swan!

3 Plato's Open Philosophy

It might suffice here for the moment to signal, very briefly, a third path, by means of some general remarks about the ways in which Plato presents his ideas about philosophical method and his doctrines, since, in the following chapters, we will be examining these matters in much more detail. Philosophical methods and doctrines, as Plato presents them in his works, can have the character of a past which opens the way to the future. They are presented by him often as sketches, projects, to be rethought and reshaped by the reader in his or her present. In this sense Plato's philosophizing is 'open'.[14] Let us take first what Plato tells us about philosophical method.

---

[14] Clay (1988), 19–24, describes the *Republic* as an 'open dialogue'; see also Erler (2007), 87 ('Offenheit der Dialoge'), with further references.

3 Plato's Open Philosophy

Plato indicates in his works that the method he applies and follows is provisional, inadequate, compared to what would be the best method.[15] Accordingly, the results of an exploration conducted by means of such an imperfect method can only be provisional. They await, in their provisional past, a more adequate future. And when Plato tells us what an ideal method might be like, he leaves his account very open. For example, when Plato writes about the highest kind of knowledge at the end of *Republic* Book VI, what he calls 'dialectic' (511bc), he leaves the sketch he gives of it very incomplete, imprecise, seemingly vague, so much so that we have great difficulty if we try to find out exactly how dialectic works. I think this lack of precision, this vagueness in Plato, is not proof that Plato is an imprecise and confused thinker. The vagueness is an openness to the future, to what could be a perfect method permitting the systematic, unified and complete organization of knowledge.[16] Plato's vagueness is the vagueness of our future, of our expectations in regard to scientific method.

When we turn to the doctrines we find in Plato's works, we find here too, I believe, that they carry the mark of a past which speaks to the future. Thus, for example, the political utopias which Plato sketches in the *Republic* and the *Laws* are not, I believe, intended to be concrete plans to be realized in the here and now. Rather they are projects to be interpreted and modulated in relation to different times and places, the result being, in each case, different. The utopia of the *Republic* appears again in the *Timaeus* as an ancient and long-forgotten Athens, situated in a mythic past prefiguring what could be in a distant future, some time very far from the present reality of Socrates' Athens. The good city elaborated in Plato's *Laws* is also born, in the discussion, in a quasi-legendary atmosphere, far from Athens, in Crete. Socrates is not there, but a citizen of Athena's city (*Laws* 626d), Socrates' city, is. It is clearly indicated that the good city of the *Laws* is not to be realized as such (746bc): it requires adaptation, changes, in relation to particular circumstances.[17]

Finally, if we come to Plato's most famous (or notorious) doctrine, his metaphysical 'Theory of Forms', or, as it is sometimes called, the 'Theory of Ideas', here also we struggle with lack of precision, vagueness, incompletion, when we try to find out what exactly these 'Forms' or 'Ideas' are. Here, I think, it would be a mistake to think that Plato has an established, definitive doctrine. Rather, Plato is giving us pointers[18] to what *would* be

---

[15] See, for example, *Phaedo* 107b, *Republic* 435d, 504bd, *Timaeus* 48cd; Ferber (2007), 25–7, 32–41.
[16] See Ferber (2007), 25–7. [17] I return to these themes in more detail in Chapter 6.
[18] See Ferber (2007), 63–4.

the content of a true knowledge of things. What are these pointers? What expectations do they express regarding such a knowledge?

Here I must be very brief. A fuller treatment will require a journey, a rather long journey. However, anticipating what could be found on such a journey,[19] I believe one can say that Plato's Forms or Ideas point us to the possibility of a knowledge of the functional laws allowing every and any complex entity, be it a soul, a city-state or the world, to function harmoniously, efficiently, in a way beneficial to all of its parts and to the whole. In a political system this means knowledge of the laws allowing a society to live in peace for the good of each and every part of the society, without exploitation of one part of society by another part, a society where the causes of evil and of war are reduced to a minimum. This, I propose, is what Plato's swan sings to us.

[19] See Chapters 3 and 4.

PART I

The World of the Timaeus

Figure 1 Left half of the stone carrying the scene of the *peplos*, at the centre of the east frieze of the Parthenon. The scene is framed on the left by Zeus (shown here) and on the right by Athena.

CHAPTER I

A Feast for the Goddess

In writing the *Timaeus*, Plato told a story about the making of the world and of man, a story which would become one of the fundamental documents in the history of philosophical and scientific cosmology. But this story, for Plato, is just part of a larger story, much of which he did not write or has not survived. In this chapter I would like to describe aspects of this larger story, so that an appropriate context can be identified for reading the cosmological account of the *Timaeus* and for appreciating its purpose and wider implications. Plato gives us many indications at the beginning of the *Timaeus* concerning the larger story, indications which are of some importance, as I hope to show, not only in approaching the cosmological account, but also in relating this cosmology to Plato's political philosophy.

1 A Feast of Speeches[1]

The dramatic setting of the *Timaeus* is the festival organized every year at Athens in honour of the city's patroness, the goddess Athena (21a, 26e3). Every four years this festival, the Panathenaea, was celebrated on a very grand scale, lasting days, involving athletic and artistic competitions which attracted people from all of Greece.[2] It included a procession by night of the youth, followed the next day by a mass procession along the Panathenaic way, bringing a new robe (the *peplos*) for the goddess in her temple, the Parthenon, high on the Acropolis (see Figure 1). Sacrifices were made, sacrificial meat distributed, and the whole city must have been full of people, Athenians and foreign visitors, dancing, drinking, singing, feasting, performing, watching, for days. The festival took place at the height of the summer,

---

[1] I borrow this expression from S. Slaveva-Griffin (2005).

[2] See Parke (1977), 33–50. In the *Ion*, Socrates meets a rhapsode contending for victory in a competition in the greater Panathenaic festival (530b). Nagy (2002) emphasizes the Panathenaic context of the *Timaeus* and the connections of the text with the festival.

14   A Feast for the Goddess

when the dead heat would have done its bit in the elevation (and exhaustion) of the participants.

During these festivities Socrates and another citizen of Athens, Critias, meet their foreign guests, Timaeus and Hermocrates. A third foreign guest (he seems to be a companion of Timaeus, 17a) is not feeling well and is absent.[3] The guests had come from afar, from southern Italy and Sicily, to see the Panathenaea. We can suppose that it was for the quadrennial festival, by far the most interesting and impressive of these festivals. It is difficult to identify the period in Socrates' life when, roughly, Plato intends us to think that Socrates met his friends (T 1), since no indications are given. Socrates seems to be of mature age, receiving the deference of his foreign guests. He is not the young man of the *Parmenides* who once had rushed to see another distinguished foreign visitor come from southern Italy to see the Panathenaic festival, Parmenides. That was (in the scenario of the *Parmenides*) in about 450. The meeting of the *Timaeus* must be seen, then, as having taken place a good deal later. But one does not feel any sign (yet) in the *Timaeus* of the disaster that Athens would suffer in finally being defeated by Sparta in the Peloponnesian War (431–404). If, as will be suggested later, the story of Atlantis to be told by Critias and Hermocrates prefigures the Athenian empire and its destruction, then, as a prophetic criticism of contemporary Athens, it would imply that the meeting of Socrates and his friends is taking place in a city of Athens still at the height of her imperial power, before or perhaps in the earlier stages of the war during a period of truce.

Socrates is received by his guests, as he had received them the day before. In fact, Socrates and his friends are continuing an entertainment that had started (with the third foreign guest) the day before, a feast of hospitality and reciprocal gifts taking place over several days in the context of the Panathenaic festivities surrounding them and in some of which they themselves presumably also took part. On being greeted by Socrates,

---

[3] This missing guest, as a companion of Timaeus, probably came like him from southern Italy, as was remarked in antiquity by Atticus (Proclus, *In Timaeum* I, 20, 20–7). If the dramatic date for the *Timaeus* proposed later (n. 19) is correct, a possible name for the missing guest (proposed by Ritter [1910], 174, 181–2, and Burnet in Taylor [1928], 25) would be Philolaus, a contemporary of Socrates, a Pythagorean Plato may have met on his first trip to southern Italy and who is named in Plato's *Phaedo*. In the *Phaedo*, it is Plato who is missing, as not being well (*ésthenei*, 59b10) – and yet he is very much present – just as the missing guest of the *Timaeus* is absent as not being well (*astheneia*, 17a4), yet perhaps also present, in the Pythagorean speech of his friend Timaeus. (A further link is suggested by the ancient report that Philolaus taught Plato's Pythagorean friend Archytas [DK 44 A3].) It may be on the basis of such allusions and associations that Plato's early critics could fabricate the accusation that Plato's *Timaeus* was copied from a book by Philolaus (see Huffman [1993], 12–13).

1 A Feast of Speeches

Timaeus recalls this feast within a feast in which Socrates, Critias and their foreign guests are sharing:

> Yesterday you entertained us with the hospitality due to foreign guests (*xeniois*) and it would not be fair if the rest of us were backward in offering you a feast in return.[4]

Socrates refers shortly afterwards to the entertainment he had offered the others the day before, discourse (*logoi*) about what seemed to him to be the best state (*aristê politeia*) and its citizens (17c). Now, today, the others, Timaeus, Critias and Hermocrates, will reciprocate, offering each in turn a discourse. The feast is thus a feast of discourse, begun by Socrates the day before and continued now by the others. Socrates already had this sequel in mind when he spoke the day before:

> Accordingly this was in my mind yesterday when I was so ready to grant your request for a discourse on the state (*politeia*): I knew that, if you would consent to supply the sequel, no one could do it better; you would describe this city (*polis*) engaged in a war worthy of her. . . . So after fulfilling my part, I set you, in my turn, the task of which I am now reminding you. You agreed to consult among yourselves and to requite my hospitality today, in this feast of speeches (*ta tôn logôn xenia*). So here I am in full dress for the entertainment, which I am most eager to receive. (20bc)

The others discussed the evening before, while returning to Critias' house – the foreign guests were staying with Critias – how they would return Socrates' gift of discourse and now propose their plan to Socrates for his approval (20d).

Before looking at their proposal, we should note the formal structure of the feast to which Plato is alluding: it is a feast of discourse, spanning two days, in which each participant offers in turn a speech and in which the sequence of speeches is directed by one of the members who assigns (*epitattein*, 17b5, 20b6, 20d2, 26d6) the tasks to be carried out by each speaker in relation to what is appropriate (*epitêdeios*, 20d3). We can recognize here, and the terminology confirms it, the formal structure of a banquet[5] in which each participant contributes a discourse and in which the sequence of discourses is directed by a 'banquet master', the 'symposiarch'. Plato's *Symposium* is, of course, the most familiar example

---

[4] *Timaeus* 17b. I use Cornford's translation (Cornford [1935]) here and in what follows, with slight modifications.

[5] Note the terminology of *hestiasis* and *xenia* (17b2–3, 20c1, 27a2, 27b8), on which see Schmitt Pantel (1992), 126–30, 164–5. See Regali (2012), 13–16, for a detailed discussion of the literary genre of the *Timaeus-Critias* as a banquet.

16 A Feast for the Goddess

of this structure in Plato's work, and Plato also describes the good symposiarch in his *Laws* (640b–641a): he should be sober and wise! In the *Symposium* it seems that the proceedings are poorly directed: the symposiarch, Eryximachus, does not manage things well and the party ends in drunkenness and confusion.[6] In the *Timaeus*, Socrates takes on the role of symposiarch and we may assume that his approval of the sequence of discourses proposed by the others will be correct. He will approve of what is 'appropriate'. But appropriate in what way?

In the *Symposium*, the banquet of speeches is a feast of discourse in honour of Eros, the son of Aphrodite. Each speaker in turn praises Eros. We may consequently wonder if the banquet, of which the *Timaeus* represents the beginning of the second day, is also in honour of a divinity or superior being and if the sequence of discourses is intended (as it is in the *Symposium*) as praise of such a being. Critias provides us with an answer which we could in any case easily find in reminding ourselves of the dramatic background of the *Timaeus*:

> Greatest of all was one [story] which it will now suit our purpose to recall, and so at once pay our debt of gratitude to you [Socrates] and celebrate the goddess, on her festival (*panêgurei*), with a true and merited hymn of praise. (20e6–21a3)

The speeches to follow, in and beyond the *Timaeus*, are thus presented as speeches in honour of the goddess Athena.[7] But in what way, we will ask, do these speeches actually praise the goddess? How is Socrates, as symposiarch, to judge of their appropriateness? Luckily, Plato gives us some indications concerning these questions in the preliminary pages of the *Timaeus* which will bring us further. But first, before coming to the question of appropriateness, we should consider the overall sequence of speeches that Socrates' friends have planned as a sequel to his discourse of the preceding day.

2 The Sequence of Speeches

The plan they submit for Socrates' approval is the following. Socrates had spoken, the day before, of the best state and its citizens. He now recalls the main points (*kephalaia*, 19a8) of what he had said (17c–19a) and expresses

---

[6] *Symposium* 176e–177d, 214a7–c5; Dover (1980), 11. For the terminology of assigning speeches (*epitattein*) in the *Symposium*, see 214b8, 214c3.

[7] See Garvey (2008). This crucial point is not taken into consideration by Johansen (2004), 180–4, in his discussion of the speeches of the *Timaeus-Critias* as exchanged speeches of praise (*encomia*).

2 *The Sequence of Speeches* 17

the wish to see this best city (*polis*) in motion, acting, showing her value in relations with other cities, in war or otherwise (19c). Now it turns out that Socrates' discourse about the best state corresponds in many respects, by some wondrous chance (25e4, *daimoniôs ek tinos tuchês*), to what Critias says he had heard about a city of Athens that had once existed, in a very distant past, and of which no memory now survives. Critias, as a child, had heard the story of this ancient Athens from his grandfather. He in turn had it from Solon, the legendary lawgiver of Athens, who had gone to Egypt and been told the story there by a priest of Sais, where the story of ancient Athens and its victory over Atlantis had been preserved. Critias therefore proposes to tell the full story of ancient Athens and its victory over Atlantis, which he has just summarized (*en kephalaiois*, 26c6), as a way of bringing into action (in a long-forgotten past) Socrates' best state. But before this, Timaeus will tell the story of the making of the world and of man. And after Critias, Hermocrates will continue the story of the victory over Atlantis.[8] The complete plan of the banquet is thus the following (I bracket the parts of the plan for which no corresponding text survives; only the beginning of Critias' speech survives):

> 1. [Socrates]; 2. Timaeus; 3. Cr[itias]; 4. [Hermocrates]

From this it can be seen that the surviving texts, *Timaeus* and *Critias* (incomplete), are but the torso of a larger body of work of which significant parts are missing. This has its importance for the interpretation of the function and meaning of the cosmological story told in the *Timaeus*.

Some commentators, ancient and modern, have thought that the first part of the sequence does survive – it is the *Republic* – since Socrates' summary of the main points of his discourse at the beginning of the *Timaeus* (17c–19a) includes selectively some of the doctrines presented in the *Republic*.[9] However, we should distinguish carefully between the literary and doctrinal levels of Plato's work. If there are some doctrinal correspondences between Socrates' summary of his discourse at the beginning of the *Timaeus* and what Socrates proposes in the *Republic*, this does

---

[8] Although Timaeus, Critias and Hermocrates take turns in covering the various parts of their common plan, it is not the case that their contributions are just parts of one speech; their speeches reflect their different interests and competences and they vie with each other (see Critias' remarks about Timaeus' speech at *Critias* 106c–108a), as the speakers vie with each other (but even more so) in the *Symposium*.

[9] Proclus is an important representative of this view, on which see Festugière's notes (1966), I, 55, n. 1, and 121, n. 2.

18 A Feast for the Goddess

not mean that the *Republic*, as a literary *work*, represents Socrates' discourse of the day before the scene depicted in the *Timaeus*.[10] On the contrary, this seems impossible, since the dramatic framework of the *Republic* is *another* sacred feast, that of Bendis, which took place, in the Piraeus, months before the Panathenaea.[11] Furthermore, Socrates' speech of the day before, as the first part of the sequence, could hardly have been like the (very long) dialogue of the *Republic*, but would have corresponded more, in style and size, to the speeches of Timaeus and Critias (or of Socrates in the *Symposium*), more in the way of a continuous speech (not necessarily excluding elements of dialogue, as in Socrates' speech in the *Symposium*) and less extensive than the ten books of the *Republic*. It is possible that Plato did not write, or indeed did not feel the need to write, the first part of the sequence, Socrates' discourse: the summary given at the beginning of the *Timaeus* may have sufficed, and could recall more generally some of (the more notorious of) Plato's political ideas (for example, about community of goods, women and children). As for the last parts of the sequence, Plato may not have got around to (or may even have lost interest in) finishing the *Critias* and writing the *Hermocrates*.[12] He had other very large-scale projects to complete in his later years, the sequence constituted by the *Theaetetus, Sophist, Statesman* and (probably) the (unwritten?) *Philosopher*, and the enormous *Laws* (in twelve books).

3 Praising the Goddess

Returning to the feast of speeches of the *Timaeus*, we may consider now the question raised earlier of the appropriateness of these speeches as praises honouring the goddess Athena. Since Socrates is given the role of symposiarch whose approval is requested by the others as they describe their plan to him, we may hope to find indications as to the reasons why he would approve of the proposed speeches, in what sense they are considered appropriate.

---

[10] Compare the 'summary' at the beginning of the *Philebus* (11b1–2), which fairly clearly does not refer to something written by Plato.

[11] Clay (1997), 50–1; see Parke (1977), 149. The dramatic date of the *Republic* also appears to be later than that of the *Timaeus* (see p. 4). In the *Republic*, Socrates leaves Athens and goes down to the Piraeus to watch the new festival of Bendis, where he is received as a guest by Polemarchus and Cephalus, whereas Timaeus and his friends have come up, in the *Timaeus*, to Athens to see the Panathenaea, and are the guests of Socrates and Critias.

[12] On this matter, see the review of the debate in Nesselrath (2006), 34–41. The fact that the *Critias* suddenly breaks off might mean that Plato did not manage to go further in composing the *Critias*, which would mean that he never got around to beginning work on the *Hermocrates*.

3 Praising the Goddess

(i) To take first the clearest case, the *third* speech of the sequence, we can see that Critias' story of ancient Athens is a speech in praise of Athena in that it is Athena who founded ancient Athens, who gave it its favourable location (*topos*), its institutions and sciences, nourishing it and educating it (23d5–e2, 24c4–d6).[13] Thus the exploits of ancient Athens, in manifesting its value, are to the credit of the goddess as source of this value. Critias' speech can also be described as appropriate, as a speech in praise of Athena, in the sense that Critias is eminently competent[14] to tell the story of ancient Athens in that the story has been carefully preserved by himself and by his ancestors,[15] brought to them and supported by the authority of a great lawgiver, Solon, and of an ancient Egyptian priesthood and ancient Egyptian monuments where records of a long-forgotten past are preserved. It was in the city of Sais in Egypt that Solon heard the story, a city also (strangely) similar in structure to Socrates' best state and to ancient Athens, a city founded by the Egyptian Athena, Neith (21e, 24a–d).[16] Plato is insistent on the continuity linking Critias through his ancestors and Egypt to the history of ancient Athens, responding in this way, on the surface of the text at least, to readers' possible scepticism about a story of which contemporary Athenians seem to be ignorant.[17] But this initial improbability, even thus mitigated, and the heavy emphasis on the distance in the past of the events described in the story (they took place 9,000 years ago, 23e4–5) may have the effect of placing the story of ancient Athens outside real history, in the sort of a past where such an excellent city might indeed have existed.[18]

(ii) The *fourth* and last speech of the day, to be given by Hermocrates, was to carry on Critias' story, dealing or continuing to deal with the war between ancient Athens and Atlantis and the victory of ancient

---

[13] Garvey (2008), 384. In the *Critias* (109c) Athena is joined in this by her brother Hephaistos. The Panathanaic procession passed the temple of Hephaistos (and Athena) on the way to the Acropolis.

[14] For the theme of speakers' competence in the *Symposium*, see 177d7–e3. Socrates is competent to speak of Eros thanks to the teaching he received from Diotima (201d).

[15] Critias invokes the divine aid of Memory (*Mnemosyne*) at the beginning of his speech (*Crit.* 108d).

[16] Sais, when Solon visited it, was the seat of the twenty-sixth dynasty ruling Egypt.

[17] Critias suggests later (*Crit.* 109d–110b) that traces of the ancient past remain in the names of Cecrops, Erechtheus, Erichthonius and Erysichthon. He even suggests (110bc) that the statue of Athena as warrior goddess goes back to ancient Athens when men and women shared in warmaking!

[18] See the suggestive discussion in Johansen (2004), 44–7. Broadie (2012), 129–32, describes the Atlantis story as 'pseudo-history'.

20 A Feast for the Goddess

Athens over Atlantis. We do not have the corresponding text, but we can suppose that Hermocrates' contribution is appropriate in the way that Critias' is, as a discourse in honour of Athena, since the military exploits of ancient Athens go to the credit of the founding goddess. If the figure of Hermocrates is intended to evoke a real person, the Syracusan leader who contributed to the serious defeat suffered by the Athenians in Sicily in 415–413, then it is possible that Hermocrates' military competence fits him for the role of telling a story of war and victory.[19] This possibility evokes further hypotheses: could Hermocrates be recounting this story to his Athenian hosts at a time subsequent to his victory over the Athenians? Perhaps this is not absolutely impossible. But if the scene of the *Timaeus* is to be seen as taking place before these events, then, in describing the defeat of Atlantis, might Hermocrates be referring to the future defeat of the imperial city which celebrated the goddess on that day?

(iii) The *first* speech of the sequence, Socrates' offering of the day before, may be relevant to the praise of Athena through its connection to the city in action described by Critias and Hermocrates. Since the best state described by Socrates corresponds to ancient Athens, and since the qualities of ancient Athens, its education, institutions and sciences, are due to Athena, then the goddess, as the source of what makes a state good, is celebrated in the account of the best city. Yet Socrates declares (19d1–2) that he is not able (*dunatos*) to praise his city and its citizens sufficiently (*hikanôs*). Nor does he think that poets or sophists are in a position to do this: the poets, since they just imitate the life in which they have been brought up and will have difficulty in imitating something else; the sophists, since they travel from one city to another, do not have a place of their own and will not grasp what philosophers and statesmen would do in war. But he does hope that his three guests, since they are both philosophers and statesmen, will be able to carry out this task (19d–20b). The point seems to be that Socrates lacks the competence to say what his best city would actually *do*, in action, in

---

[19] Hermocrates seems to be a good deal younger than Timaeus and Critias: the political experience and distinction of the latter are emphasized, whereas Hermocrates' nature and education (only) are mentioned (20a; see Taylor [1928], 14). If the figure of Hermocrates is intended to evoke the (future) Syracusan general (see Nesselrath [2006], 50–4), then this would be an indication of a dramatic date for the *Timaeus* in the late 430s. Later, in 424–423, Hermocrates would give a speech at Gela to the Sicilians persuading them to unite against Athenian imperialism (Thucydides IV, 59–64). In the *Critias* (108c), Critias uses a military image, putting Hermocrates in the rear, in the protection of the front lines (which suggests that Hermocrates, if young, is old enough for military service), as Hermocrates' speech, coming after, is protected by Critias' present speech.

war. The others can do this, through the memory of the past, but also, it seems, through their political experience and skills. Yet Socrates must have some competence to have been able to speak as he did of the best state, even if, given his lack of political experience and skills, this does not *suffice* as praise and requires the contributions of the others.[20] But what then is his particular competence? Perhaps it is that of a philosopher who enquires into what it is that would make a good life for humans, a philosopher who can sketch a model city 'in heaven' in the *Republic* (592b2–3), a philosopher who, as Socrates says in Plato's *Apology* (31d–32a), stays out of real politics.

(iv) There remains to consider the *second* speech of the sequence, which follows Socrates' discourse and which indeed is the only speech to survive as a whole, the cosmological story told by Timaeus that constitutes by far the greatest part of the *Timaeus*. Again we may ask: in what way does Timaeus, with his story, contribute to the praise of Athena? And what are his competences for this task? The question of Timaeus' qualifications for speaking about the making of the world and of man is handled by both Socrates and Critias: Timaeus is an eminent statesman, philosopher (20a), mathematician and keen enquirer into the nature of the universe (27a). But if Timaeus is so well qualified for his task, in what way will his speech about the world and man contribute to the praise of Athena?

This question will require a more extended enquiry, which will be undertaken in the next chapter. To anticipate what I will propose there, it will emerge that Timaeus' story of the making of the world contributes to the praise of Athena, not only in that it describes a good and beautiful world in which the good city once founded by Athena, ancient Athens, could prosper, but also in that the god who made such a world can be related to the goddess who founded such a city: his praise will contribute to hers.

4 Athens and Atlantis

The story of Atlantis is part of the story of ancient Athens.[21] Plato's picture of Atlantis has so captured popular imagination that the rest of the story has been neglected, all the more so in that future discoverers of lost Atlantis read

---

[20] A speech of praise includes not only praise of the nature and education of the object of praise, but also of its acts (*erga*); cf. Erler (1997).

[21] See Vidal-Naquet (1981), 344.

only part of Plato's text, selectively and out of context, or, better (if they really want to find Atlantis), do not read the text at all. The incompletion or loss of the speeches of Critias and Hermocrates has also contributed to the exclusive attention given to the Atlantis part of the tale. But we have seen already that the primary purpose that Critias and Hermocrates have in mind is to praise the goddess Athena by recounting the great exploits of the city which she founded in the distant past, ancient Athens, in particular the exploit in defeating Atlantis. Atlantis thus appears as a foil to ancient Athens, the representation of a morally corrupt state, driven by material desires to ever-extending conquests and domination over other states, until defeated by its contrary, a virtuous state living by its founding principles, ancient Athens. Ancient Athens and Atlantis are the contrasting images of the best and the corrupted state: these images are linked.

The tale of Atlantis, as recounted by Critias in the *Critias*, begins auspiciously enough. Under the patronage of the sea god Poseidon (113c, Athena's rival for the patronage of Attica, shown on the west pediment of the Parthenon), Atlantis possessed great natural resources and was ruled by kings who were virtuous, despite their wealth and power. These kings' absolute power was limited by divine laws to which they were bound by elaborate religious ceremonies (119c–120d). However, in time, the moral virtue of the kings became corrupted through excessive greed (*pleonexia*) and power (120e–121b). Atlantis become an imperial regime which sought to extend its enslavement of other states further and further, until at last stopped by its contrary, a virtuous state, ancient Athens.[22] Then the world suffered a cataclysm which destroyed both Atlantis and Athens and the memory of their deeds. Only Egypt survived, preserving in its monuments of legendary antiquity a record of the story that would be handed down to Critias. How ancient Athens defeated Atlantis, how its virtue allowed it to do this and thus become manifest, we do not know. Critias' tale describes the happier beginnings of Atlantis and the first signs of the moral decline and corruption that would lead to the war with Athens, but goes no further.

What would Athenian contemporaries of Socrates and Critias have thought about this story had they heard it (say, in the late 430s)? What would Plato's contemporaries have thought as they read the text when he wrote it, roughly in the 360s (about seventy years after the date when the feast of speeches is supposed to be taking place)? The Athenian contemporaries of Socrates (**T** 1) might be supposed to have thought of the great victory of their city over the Persian empire, when they freed the Greeks

---

[22] *Timaeus* 25bc.

from Persian slavery. But this victory became the start of Athenian domination over other Greek city-states, an increasing power and prosperity of the city that would lead in the end to the war with Sparta and to defeat. The first readers of Plato's *Timaeus* (**T 2**) lived in the defeated Athens and could perhaps wonder if the city celebrating the goddess, when Socrates and his friends exchanged speeches, was not (or no longer) the city that had defeated the Persians, but another city that was becoming more like its contrary, Atlantis.[23] What city is this which is celebrating Athena while Socrates and his friends speak? Is this celebration worthy of the goddess? Socrates and his friends honour Athena appropriately in describing her as the founding goddess of a quite different city, a virtuous city that had disappeared 9,000 years ago and is now unknown to those who, outside, celebrate the goddess.

5   Conclusions

Considered in the literary context to which it belongs, the account of the making of the world in the *Timaeus* is part of a larger whole, to which it contributes: the praise of Athena through the story of an excellent state founded by her in a forgotten past, ancient Athens, as it showed its value in action, in the victory over Atlantis. If, in literary terms, this means that the cosmological account is subordinate to the political story told in the three other speeches making up the whole, this does not mean, of course, that the world is itself subordinate. But it does mean that the story of the making of the world and of man, as told by Timaeus, is intended to lead to the story of an excellent state and of its exploits. We should then enquire into the way in which Timaeus' speech actually contributes to the story told by Critias and Hermocrates. How does Timaeus' speech relate to the main theme of the feast? In what way does it prepare the appearance of an excellent state? In the following chapters, I will attempt to answer these questions. The next three chapters will concern Timaeus' cosmological speech. Since we cannot read the speeches of Critias (apart from the first pages) and Hermocrates, in order to bring out more fully the implications of Timaeus' cosmological account for the concept of an excellent state, I will then attempt in Chapters 5–7 to make use of other texts written by Plato probably after the *Timaeus*, the *Statesman* and the *Laws*, to the extent that they might offer something like a substitute.

---

[23] On this see especially the discussion in Vidal-Naquet (1981), 335–60, and (2005), 23–42 (reviewing other, more recent studies); see also Pradeau (1997), 76–7, 102–8.

Figure 2 The lost central scene of the east pediment of the Parthenon, as reconstructed by Palagia (1993), 18 and 27–30. The figures of Athena and Zeus are purely conjectural. This reconstruction takes account of the technical constraints involved in building the cornice and refers to the scene after Athena's birth as described in the second Homeric *Hymn to Athena* (II, 7–16). Cuttings for metal clamps and dowels preserved in the stones remaining from the cornice are also represented.

CHAPTER 2

The World-Maker

The scene has been set at the beginning of the *Timaeus*. Socrates' speech of yesterday has been recalled and a preview given of the feast of speeches to follow. Timaeus can now begin his contribution to the banquet. He regales the company and us, his readers, with a wonderful discourse, full of amazing ideas and wild imagination, frequently very amusing, dealing with nothing less than the origin of the world, as an ordered universe, and the origin of man. Dominating the story, at its beginnings, is the figure of a rational god who is not named, a god who made the world, a 'demiurge'[1] who produced cosmic order and who used for this purpose the best of 'models', of which he made the most beautiful image, the world in which man came to be. The theoretical complexity and imaginative richness of Timaeus' story is matched by the perplexity with which it has been met by its readers, from its first readers to Plato's readers of today.

Plato's first readers were puzzled by the image of a divine world-maker and some of them rejected it as a way of describing how the world is organized. These debates about Plato's world-maker have continued up to today and no doubt will continue on.[2] The issues concern not only the interpretation of Plato's text, but also fundamental questions about how to explain the world and the status of such explanations. How are we to read Plato's story of the divine world-maker or demiurge? Are we to take it literally, as if there really were a god who made the world? How could he have 'made' it? By planning things and putting them together, just like a human craftsman who produces something? The Epicureans made fun of such a toiling god, unworthy of the perfection involved in the notion of the divine. Aristotle also thought that natural causality was to be distinguished from, and not reduced to, the workings of human craftsmanship. He rejected in any case the implication of Plato's story, as he saw it, that the world had a beginning in time.

---

[1] The meaning of this term will be discussed in section 5.
[2] For clear and useful surveys, see Karfík (2007); Ferrari (2010).

26 The World-Maker

But if we protest and say, like Plato's pupil Xenocrates, that we should not read Timaeus' story literally, then we are faced with the problem of saying how the divine demiurge is to be interpreted. If this god does not operate like a craftsman, how then does he operate? If he did not begin his work in time, then how is this 'beginning' to be understood? What is the demiurge's relation to the model, or paradigm, which he uses? Is the model something different from him, or in some way part of him, for example as being in his thinking? How does the demiurge relate to other primary causes mentioned elsewhere by Plato, for example the 'Form of the Good' which appears in Plato's *Republic*? If the story of the making of the world in the *Timaeus* is not to be taken literally, do we really still *need* the divine demiurge, once the story is read otherwise?

In this chapter I would like to focus on a much more modest question, which, as it will turn out, is not without relevance when it comes to dealing with the more fundamental issues: how does Timaeus' speech fit into the sequence of speeches given in honour of the goddess Athena? Dealing with this will involve answering another question concerning Timaeus' divine world-maker, a question which might strike modern readers of Plato as peculiar or old-fashioned, certainly not one often asked today: who is the demiurge? I hope to show that this question is reasonable and that it is worth pursuing. The Platonists of late antiquity would readily have given an answer: the demiurge is Zeus. But what 'Zeus' meant to these Platonists is itself a complicated issue involving their very elaborate metaphysical system.[3] Here I would like to concentrate on the question as it relates just to Plato and the *Timaeus*.

1 A Speech in Honour of Zeus?

The complete scenario to which Timaeus' speech belongs, as I have described it in the previous chapter, is the following. It is a banquet of speeches in praise of the goddess Athena: Socrates spoke the day before of the best state, Critias will speak today of its founding by Athena 9,000 years ago, and he and Hermocrates will show how ancient Athens showed its value in defeating Atlantis. But what of the main part of the surviving work, the speech Timaeus gives about the making of the world and of man, a speech which is complete, following Socrates' (missing) speech of the day before and preceding Critias' (incomplete) speech about the founding of ancient Athens? How does Timaeus' speech about the world fit into the

---

[3] Proclus, *In Timaeum* I, 303, 24–317, 20 provides a survey.

1 A Speech in Honour of Zeus? 27

sequence of speeches about the best state? How does his speech relate to the celebration of the goddess Athena?

A first answer to these questions would be that Timaeus' speech about the making of the world and of man sets the stage for the founding of ancient Athens, as recounted by Critias. Not only does the description of the making of the world and of man introduce the story of ancient Athens. We are also told that it is by imitating the order of the world, described by Timaeus, that man can lead a good life (90cd), a good life which, we may suppose, is led in a good city. Already in the ancient Egyptian city of Sais, where the story of ancient Athens was preserved and which resembled ancient Athens, being founded by Neith, the Egyptian Athena, the study of the cosmos was essential (24bc).[4] It thus seems that there is a strong connection between knowledge of the cosmic order and the goodness of a city, such that Timaeus' speech about the making of the world is not just a prelude to Critias' tale of ancient Athens: it also provides the cosmic foundation for the possibility of a good city and of human happiness. Timaeus' speech can thus be seen as contributing in an important way to the sequence of speeches in praise of the goddess Athena. This answer, which I believe to be correct, will require, if it is to be complete, a detailed comparison of the cosmic order described in the *Timaeus* with the order of what would be a good city, a comparison which will be elaborated step by step throughout the following chapters of this book.

For the present it will suffice for our immediate purpose to introduce the following considerations. Athena, daughter of Zeus, was often associated with her powerful father at Athenian festivals, for example at the annual feast of Apaturia, a feast when Critias' grandfather heard the story of ancient Athens.[5] At the Panathenaic festival, the great procession made its way up to the Acropolis, where one could see, on the Parthenon,[6] on the east pediment, the birth of Athena (she was born from her father, Zeus; see Figure 2) and, on the east frieze, Zeus framing with his daughter a representation of the robe, or *peplos*, to be presented to the goddess by the procession (see Figure 1). The association of Athena and Zeus would then have been an easy and natural one to make in the context of the Panathenaic festival. Thus, when Timaeus refers, in his speech, to the demiurge of the world as 'father' (28c3), this reference, which for the Greeks usually designates Zeus,[7] could

---

[4] 90cd and 24bc are quoted in section 5.
[5] More generally on the special and very close relationship between Zeus and Athena, see Neils (2001), 191–3.
[6] Finished in 432 BC, in a period to which corresponds, I propose (Chapter 1, n. 19), the dramatic date of the *Timaeus*.
[7] See later at note 16.

28   The World-Maker

easily be taken to identify the demiurge as Zeus. Following up these associations, we could say then that Zeus is praised in Timaeus' account of the beautiful world he made, just as Athena is praised in the story of the good city she founded in this world; the praise of Zeus fits naturally into a feast of speeches in honour of his daughter, just as her founding of a good city fits into a beautiful world.

But is the god who makes the world in the *Timaeus* really Zeus? We have seen that there are reasons for thinking this.[8] But we can also see that there are differences between Timaeus' demiurge and the 'father' of men and of the gods of the Greeks. In particular Zeus, as one of the traditional Greek gods, appears by name *later* than the demiurge in the story of the making of the world, as subordinate, as generated with the production of the world (40d–41a). It thus looks as if, to borrow some words of Heraclitus (fr. 32), Timaeus' demiurge 'does not wish and wishes to be called by the name of Zeus'. I would like therefore to examine this situation in more detail, starting with the way Timaeus describes the demiurge, comparing this with Greek conceptions of Zeus, and seeking to explain why, for Plato, the maker of the world both is and is not Zeus.

2   Timaeus' Description of the Demiurge

Timaeus begins his speech (27cd) with the reminder that at the beginning of any enterprise, small or large, we should invoke, if we have good sense (*sôphrosunê*), the divinity. And so must he, intending to speak of the universe, invoke the gods and goddesses and pray that what he says is acceptable to them and (consequently) to us. He then (A) formulates a distinction between 'what is always', the object of intelligence, and what is subject to generation and destruction, the object of opinion with sense-perception. He then affirms (B) that all that which is generated is necessarily generated by a cause. Then (28a6) – without preparing us in any way for this – Timaeus tells us (C) that 'the demiurge, therefore', if he looked to eternal being as a model, would have produced a beautiful whole, but if he looked to a generated model, a whole that is not beautiful. Timaeus thus mentions the demiurge for the first time very abruptly, without introduction, preparation or explanation, as if the demiurge were presupposed, as if we were

---

[8]   Further support for this might be found in Plato's *Philebus*, where the cosmic rational ordering power (*dêmiourgoun* 27b1) is named Zeus (30cd). This power is identified with the demiurge of the *Timaeus* by Menn (1995), 9–10. See also *Sophist* 265c (*theou dêmiourgountos*). In Chapter 7 (section 6), I discuss the question of Plato's attitude to the gods of traditional Greek religion.

2 *Timaeus' Description of the Demiurge* 29

already thinking of a god who makes the world.[9] But what justifies this presupposition, if we, as Greeks, have other stories, told both by poets and by philosophers, about the origins of the world?

As if applying then the principles he has just formulated, Timaeus draws the conclusions which they entail: the world, as a body, the object of sense-perception, is something generated (A). Therefore it must be generated by a cause (B). Then Timaeus immediately says, presumably speaking of this cause:

> The maker (*poiêtês*) and father of this universe it is a hard task to find, and having found him it would be impossible to declare (*legein*) him to all mankind. (28c3–5)

That this ineffable god is the demiurge (C) becomes immediately clear, since Timaeus decides that the maker of the universe (*ho tektainomenos*) used the best model, because the world is most beautiful and the demiurge is good and the best of causes. To say otherwise would not be right (*themis*, 29a4).

Having got this far, however, Timaeus quickly relativizes the ambitions of his account. In speaking of the world as object of the senses, itself made in the image of eternal being, Timaeus finds himself on the level of opinion rather than knowledge, of belief rather than truth:

> If then, Socrates in many respects concerning many things – the gods and the generation of the universe – we prove unable to render an account at all points entirely consistent with itself and exact, you must not be surprised. If we can furnish accounts no less likely than any other, we must be content, remembering that I who speak and you my judges (*kritai*) are only human, and consequently it is fitting that we should, in these matters, accept the likely story and look for nothing further. (29cd)

Without going into the difficult modern debate about the truth-status of Timaeus' story,[10] we might at least note how much is unknown, both of the divine cause of the universe and (scientifically) of the world. And what *human* could possibly tell the story of the generation of the universe? At most we can talk about what it would (or must) have been like, in the light of the little that

---

[9] Sedley (2007), 102, speaks as if the introduction of the divine craftsman is justified in the text. But Timaeus gives *no* explanation of the transition from saying that what is generated must have a cause to saying that the demiurge must have used a good or bad model. It is simply presupposed that the cause is a demiurge using a model. This is pointed out very clearly by Ebert (1991), 52. However, I do not agree with Ebert (as will become clear in the following) that the presupposition is an 'Argumentationsfehler'. Johansen (2004), chapter 4, elaborates a speculative argument to fill the apparent explanatory gap in the text. A demiurge of the heavens had been mentioned in the *Republic* (530a4–6), but this does not suffice to explain his sudden introduction at the beginning of Timaeus' speech.

[10] See Hadot (1983); Burnyeat (1995); Rowe (2007), 258–64; Sedley (2007), 110; Broadie (2012), 33–52.

30   The World-Maker

we might know or suppose. Timaeus does appear to know or suppose some things, and it is from these that he can develop his speech.

Timaeus knows that he who constituted (*sunistas*) the universe was good, therefore free of any jealousy (*phthonos*). It is because he is good that he constitutes the universe, wishing it to be like him: this is what one would correctly accept from men who are wise (*phronimôn*, 29e–30a). Then, as if rethinking the ways in which the god would have thought, Timaeus has him wanting (*boulêtheis*) all to be good, and nothing bad, as far as possible, bringing the confused and disorderly visible mass to order, thinking (*hêgêsamenos*) that this would be entirely better. Insisting again that the best can only do what is most beautiful, Timaeus has the demiurge think further, reasoning and finding that the best world would be an ensouled world endowed with intelligence. So therefore one should say, according to the probable account, that the world is a living and intelligent cosmic animal generated by the providence of the god (30b).

So does Timaeus' account develop. He continues considering possible options in the making of the world and decides for options implied by the goodness of the maker. Thus the model of the world used by the demiurge must be complete, a totality; the world must be unique; as visible it is made up of four elemental parts (fire, air, earth and water) linked by mathematical proportions so strong that only the maker can dissolve them (32c2–3). Timaeus replays the cosmological decisions the demiurge would have taken, given his goodness:[11] it is almost as if Timaeus himself is the demiurge,[12] thinking in his place, choosing in his speech (55d7 *logôi*; *Crit.* 106a4 *logois*) the right things for the demiurge to do in constructing a most good and beautiful world.

Having made the soul of the world, the demiurge joined it to the body of the world, and

> When the father who had begotten it saw it [the world] set in motion and alive, an image brought into being of the everlasting gods,[13] he rejoiced and being well pleased he took thought to make it yet more like its model. (37c6–d1)

This involved the making of time, as the moving image of the eternity of the model. As reasoned by the demiurge (38c3), this meant the organization of the movements of the heavens through the movements of the sun, moon and other stars so as to mark day and night, month and year (38c–39d). The stars are themselves living bodies, travelling in orbits without

---

[11] See Sedley (2007), 109.   [12] See Osborne (1996).
[13] For this correction of Cornford's translation, see Karfík (2004), 123–6.

2 *Timaeus' Description of the Demiurge* 31

interruption, the most perfect of the denizens of the world organized by the demiurge. They are indeed, in the perfection of their lives, visible gods (40d4) made by the maker of the world.

Timaeus then turns, very briefly, to the question of the origins of the traditional gods (40d6–41a2), as if in an aside. Curiously, he says that this matter is beyond him (yet he has been able to speak of the ineffable god and his making of the world) and that one should believe what is told by those who say they are descendants of the gods: they ought to know about their family ancestors! What follows is a mere few lines of a theogony reminding us, for example, of that told by the poet Hesiod,[14] i.e., a genealogy of the gods going from Gê and Ouranos, through their offspring, to Zeus, Hera and their kin and offspring. But Timaeus does not seem very concerned with these traditional gods. They seem, here, to be inferior to the visible astral gods, being produced after them and not directly by the demiurge, and are somewhat marginalized in not being part of Timaeus' own story, relegated as they are to the stories told by others.

Once both the visible astral gods and the traditional gods (they who show themselves 'as they wish', 41a4) are generated, the maker of the world addresses them in a speech:

> Gods among the gods and works whereof I am the maker and father,[15] those which are my own handiwork are indissoluble, save with my consent. Now, although whatsoever bond has been fastened may be unloosed, yet only an evil will could consent to dissolve what has been well fitted together and is in a good state; therefore, although you, having come into being, are not immortal nor indissoluble altogether, nevertheless you shall not be dissolved nor taste of death, finding my will (*boulêsis*) a bond yet stronger and more sovereign. . . . Now, therefore, take heed to this that I declare to you. (41a7–b7)

The demiurge then goes on to explain to these 'young' gods (42d6) that he is assigning them the task of making the lower living beings in the world, in what is mortal in them, the creatures of the air, earth and water, combining it with what is immortal, which he provides. This delegation of tasks preserves a vital difference between the young gods, who are immortal by will of the demiurge, and the other, mortal living beings in the world. It also allows the demiurge to withdraw from lower tasks, since, once he had given his instructions in his speech, he 'stayed in his proper mode' (*emenen en tôi heautou kata tropon êthei*), while his children obeyed him and proceeded with their assigned work, imitating their maker (42e5–8).

---

[14] See Pender (2010), 225.   [15] For this translation, see Karfík (2004), 87–148.

32   The World-Maker

3 A Comparison with Zeus

Allowing the demiurge to retire from his work for the moment, we might now
ask ourselves to what extent he can be identified, as he is described by
Timaeus, with Zeus, in what sense, through him, Timaeus' speech may
function as a praise of Zeus. There are many features of the demiurge which
would lead Plato's contemporaries to associate the demiurge with Zeus in
their minds, but also features which would dissociate them. In the following
I would like to mention these associating and dissociating features with a view
to clarifying the relation Plato makes between Timaeus' demiurge and Zeus.

The most obvious Zeus-like feature of the demiurge is his designation as
'father'. The Greeks ordinarily referred to Zeus as 'father' of men and the gods,
a father both in the sense of a paterfamilias and in the sense of the king who is
head of the community.[16] Zeus exerts absolute supremacy, so that the other
gods and, of course, all mortals must bend to his will. Such is the supremacy of
Zeus that he can become in effect *unnameable*, an awesome divinity eliciting
religious respect.[17] Zeus' will (*boulê*), mind (*nous*), and thoughts are often
mentioned in Homer and Hesiod. Zeus deliberates and decides. Things
happen as he wills. He sometimes addresses the assembled Olympian gods
in a speech, communicating his decisions, giving them instructions, assigning
different tasks to the different gods, as he had assigned gods to different parts
of the world.[18] Zeus could also then retire to his proper place[19] (as does
Timaeus' demiurge after his speech). The absolute universal rule exerted
over gods and men by Zeus had been imposed through war, at first through
war with the Titans and then with the Giants,[20] wars won with the vigorous
help of Zeus' daughter Athena and of the other Olympian gods. Through
these victories, order was made out of disorder (as Timaeus' demiurge brings
order to disorder). The rule of Zeus ensured justice and peace, of sorts.[21]

---

[16] See, e.g., Homer, *Iliad* I, 544; IV, 68.
[17] Aeschylus, *Agamemnon*, 160–1; Euripides, *Trojan Women*, 884–8; see *Philebus* 12c1–3 for Socrates'
      fear with respect to the *names* of the gods.
[18] For some of Zeus' speeches, see Homer, *Iliad*, VIII, 5–27; XX, 20–30; Hesiod, *Theogony*, 644–53; for
      assignments see also *Theogony*, 885; Aeschylus, *Prometheus Bound*, 229–31. The last remaining words
      of the *Critias* describe a very Homeric assembly of the gods convoked by Zeus, who wishes to address
      them on the subject of Atlantis. But the text stops just as he starts to speak (121c5). See also
      Symposium 190cd. Regali (2012), 167–75, provides an interesting comparison between the Zeus of
      Hesiod's *Theogony* and *Works and Days* (1–10) and the demiurge of the *Timaeus*.
[19] *Iliad* VIII, 49–52; XX, 22 (*emenen*). Blondell (2005), 46, n. 90, refers to *Iliad* VIII, 49–52, in relation
      to Plato's *Statesman* (272e5, on the god's vantage point).
[20] The gigantomachy was represented on the metopes on the east side of the Parthenon and on the
      peplos of Athena (Chapter 5, section 1); it is criticized as unworthy of the divinity in *Republic* 378bc
      and amusingly adapted as a conflict of metaphysical positions in the *Sophist* 246ab.
[21] Lloyd-Jones (1971).

These various features of Zeus reappear, we can see, throughout Timaeus' descriptions of the demiurge. It is as if Timaeus were constantly reminding us, in his references to the demiurge, of Zeus. If, as I have suggested, associating Athena with her mighty father would come easily in the context of a festival and a sequence of praises in honour of Athena, then Timaeus' friends could easily have assumed that he was speaking of Zeus when, at the beginning of his speech, he refers to the demiurge without explanation, taking him for granted, so to speak, and simply speculating about how he might have made the world. Zeus needs no introduction! Later, when Timaeus moves to another part of his speech, dealing with the mysterious, obscure, chaotic milieu which the demiurge brings from disorder to order, he invokes again the divinity, the aid of the 'saviour' (*sôtêr*, 48d4–e1), an epithet of Zeus (for example in Plato's *Republic*, 583b2–3), who, in this passage, can hardly be anything other than the demiurge.[22]

At the same time, however, Timaeus' demiurge does not always correspond to Zeus, the most obvious indication being that Zeus appears *by name* in Timaeus' speech (41a1) as a somewhat subordinate, indirect product of the demiurge. We need then to take stock of what differentiates Timaeus' demiurge from Zeus so as to understand better their relationship and its significance. I will first consider how Timaeus' demiurge represents a reformed image of divinity, and then take up the idea that this divinity 'made' the world.

4 Zeus Reformed

The emphasis in Timaeus' description of the demiurge is very much placed on the demiurge's goodness: the god is good and wishes only to produce the good, as far as possible; he suffers from no envy. This emphasis reminds us of the educational project of Plato's *Republic*, Book II, where the poets' stories about the gods are criticized in that they give an unworthy and immoral image of the gods. Socrates advocates a reform of these stories, since they deeply influence and can corrupt the moral education of children. These stories should be reformed so that they will portray the god as good, therefore as the cause (*aition*) of good, not of evil (379b), even if people think the god is the cause of all things, both of good and of evil (379c).[23] A further correction must be made in the stories about the gods, when they have the gods make

---

[22] See Karfík (2007), 139.
[23] Plato refers to Homer's Zeus as the cause of good and evil (379de); see also *Euthyphro* 5e–6a. On Hesiod's Zeus as 'bad', corrected by Plato's demiurge as the cause only of good, see Capra (2010), 210, Pender (2010), 227 and (2007), 25–6 ('Plato's alternative creation myth').

34 The World-Maker

appearances, here and there, at will (380d2–3), like the gods to which Timaeus refers after the astral gods, who show themselves 'as they wish' (*Timaeus* 41a4). This behaviour, for Socrates in the *Republic*, makes the divinity into a deceiving magician. No! The divinity must not leave its own form (*Rep.* 380d5–6), as Timaeus' demiurge stays in his own condition (*Timaeus* 42e5–6). Finally the gods should not be represented as responsible for morally reprehensible acts or as taking bribes (*Rep.* 390e). In short, the gods, in our stories, should represent moral models, the good, so as to influence in a positive way the education of children. In the *Laws* Plato describes an educational system which concerns not just children, but the population at large. And here again, it is important to get the representation of the gods right.[24] Elsewhere, Plato insists on his reform of Greek divinity: divinity is good and, as such, can be the cause only of good.[25]

It thus seems that Timaeus' demiurge is a reformed divinity, not the Zeus of the poets denounced by Socrates in the *Republic*, but a Zeus who is morally and metaphysically perfect.[26] Is Timaeus then telling, as if he were a poet following Plato's educational guidelines, a morally edificatory story about the divine demiurge? Timaeus' story is hardly for children. But his 'song' (*nomon*, 29d5–6), as if the song of a poet recited in a theatre (as in a Panathenaic competition?), delighted his audience, Socrates says in his verdict as symposiarch of the banquet (*Critias* 108b3–5). Is Timaeus' audience just the other three members of the festive group? Has he a wider audience?[27]

5 Why a 'Demiurge'?

Coming back to the idea of a divine demiurge, we should note that the maker of the world is not a creator: he does not 'create' the world in a Christian theological sense, but makes a world, a cosmos, in the sense that he gives order, goodness and beauty to a pre-existent disorderly chaotic milieu. To speak of the generation of the world as if it were a 'creation' could be misleading: the god, as good, is cause of that which is good only; he is not the cause of everything, good and bad. Nor is the making of the world in the *Timaeus* like the mythical cosmogonies sung by poets such as Hesiod.[28] In the poets' stories, Zeus does not make the world. The world emerges in the context of a divine

---

[24] See below, p. 128. [25] See *Phaedrus* 246a7–b1; *Theaetetus* 176a5–7.

[26] See Vlastos (1975), 26–8. In Chapter 7, section 6, I discuss how Plato might have seen the Zeus who appears among the 'young', traditional gods generated by the demiurge of the world.

[27] See Chapter 7, n. 41, for a suggestion in this regard.

[28] In his *Hymn to Zeus* (fragments in Pindar, *Nemean Odes*, 229–37), Pindar also seems to have recounted a mythical cosmogony; see Snell (1980), 84–9.

5 Why a 'Demiurge'?

genealogy in which primitive deities such as Gê and Ouranos, through a history made up of sexual shenanigans, conspiracies, skulduggery and violence, produce the reign of Zeus who sees, hears and knows all from his high vantage point, controls everything with his will, and on occasion uses his thunderbolt (like a guided missile!) to annihilate the recalcitrant. Timaeus' divine demiurge has no such ancestry and no such modus operandi.[29] Here too, Zeus must be reformed. How then, as Timaeus' demiurge, does he act?

The first question Timaeus asks in his story, we have seen, is that concerning the model used by the demiurge: which model did he use? The question surprises us, as I have suggested, to the extent that we are not prepared for it by an introduction of this demiurge prior to the posing of the question. If we assume that Timaeus is praising Zeus, albeit a reformed Zeus, in his speech, perhaps the surprise is less great. But why refer to this Zeus as 'demiurge' and why raise this question as to the choice of models?

It has been noted that the term *dêmiourgos* has a wide range of meanings covering a variety of activities in the public service (*dêmios*).[30] *Dêmiourgos* can mean a magistrate who acts for the people. The political sense of the word can lead to the question of political models.[31] Timaeus' demiurge frequently acts like a statesman, lawgiver, founder of cities: he deliberates about what to do, seeks the best option, gives speeches to his subordinates, gives instructions, delegates tasks, exercises persuasion, legislates.[32] Timaeus himself was a magistrate in Locri, a Doric city known for its good governance (*eunomia*, see 20a2) where the word *damiorgos* could have had this sense. And perhaps Timaeus' friends would have seen this image of a statesman when he referred to his Zeus as demiurge.

But the term, as becomes clear almost immediately in Timaeus' words (28e6), also designates a craftsman, an artisan, who also produces by looking to a model. Models are used in crafts, for example in making couches or shuttles.[33] The imagery and language Timaeus uses to describe the demiurge's work cover a wide range of crafts such as metallurgy, pottery and weaving.[34] It is as if the variety of professions and trades – magistrates, architects, supervisors, the many

---

[29] See Kahn (2013), 159–60, for some precedents to the cosmic demiurge of the *Timaeus*.

[30] See Bader (1965), 133–41; Balansard (2001), 71–82, who provides a semantic study of Plato's use of the term. In the *Republic* (389d), Plato quotes Homer *Od.* XVII, 383–4, where the diviner, the doctor and the carpenter are referred to as *dêmiourgoi*. In (2016), I describe other professionals providing public services to whom Plato refers as 'demiurges'.

[31] See *Laws* 739ce. On political models, see Chapter 3, section 2.

[32] See, for example, 42d2–3 and section 3 earlier in this chapter.

[33] *Republic* 597ad; *Cratylus* 389b.

[34] See Brisson (1998), 36–54, 88–92, for a full collection of the evidence in the *Timaeus*, with sources for the term *dêmiourgos* as designating a magistrate in Greek cities.

36   The World-Maker

metalworkers, stonemasons and subsidiary trades – which had filled Athens during the great period of the reconstruction of temples[35] had left their mark on Timaeus' speech. And of course the goddess being honoured while Timaeus speaks, Athena, was not only the founding goddess of ancient Athens. She was also the patroness of crafts (*erganê*), such as weaving and pottery, and as such closely associated with her brother, the craftsman god Hephaistos,[36] in myths, in festivals (at the Chalkeia,[37] when the weaving of the *peplos* for the Panathenaea was begun) and in buildings, on the Parthenon's east frieze and in the Hephaistaion overlooking the Panathenaic way.

But if these different senses of *dêmiourgia*, political and artisanal, give Timaeus' god a way of acting differently from that of the traditional Zeus, in their very variety and differences they do not seem to make for a coherent and plausible picture of the god's action: how can he be both statesman and blacksmith of the world, or even either?

The point of Timaeus' speech, I would like to suggest, is rather this: to show what it is that makes this world good and beautiful, a living perceptible god, image of the intelligible, 'supreme in greatness and excellence, in beauty and perfection, this heaven single in its kind and one' (92c6–9), as Timaeus describes the world in the last words of his speech. Zeus is praised by Timaeus through showing the goodness and beauty of his work.[38] What matters is the craft, legislative or artisanal, which produces the order of the world, rather than the craftsman.[39] It is this craft, this skill, this rational competence as manifested in the order of the world, which can provide the conditions for the emergence of a good city.

In Chapters 3 and 4, I will describe in more detail how political and artisanal *dêmiourgia* can help in identifying what it is that makes the world well-ordered, beautiful, good, a cosmos. Zeus is praised by Timaeus by showing the goodness and beauty of his work. And this fits with the praise of Athena, founding goddess of ancient Athens, since what makes a city such as ancient Athens good, as I will argue in Part II, is the rationality

---

[35] See Plutarch's vivid account, *Pericles* 12. The Parthenon was finished in 432 BC as part of this programme of reconstruction, necessitated by the Persian devastation of Attica in 480 BC, and financed by funds taken from the Delian League.

[36] *Laws* 920de.   [37] See Parke (1977), 92–3.

[38] As inspired in this regard by Timaeus' prose hymn to the demiurge we might mention the Stoic Cleanthes' *Hymn to Zeus* and the Christian Boethius' hymn 'O qui perpetua mundum ratione gubernas' in his *Consolation of Philosophy*, III, 9. Pernot (2007), 177–7 and 186, suggests that prose hymns represent a reform, in terms of clarity, precision and truth, in relation to poetic hymns. See also Garvey (2008), 389.

[39] For the merging of the demiurge with his craft, see Johansen (2004), 83–6.

manifested in the goodness and beauty of the cosmos. The idea is indicated towards the end of Timaeus' speech:

> These, therefore, every man should follow, and correcting those circuits in the head that were deranged at birth, by learning to know the harmonies and revolutions of the world, he should bring the intelligent part, according to its pristine nature, into the likeness of that which intelligence discerns, and thereby win the fulfilment of the best life set by the gods before mankind, both for this present time and for the time to come. (90d1–7)

It is through knowing the divine in the cosmos that we can attain the good, happy life (68e7–69a5). The idea, as applying to a city, is already present at the beginning of the *Timaeus*, where the law of the city of Sais, a good city comparable to ancient Athens, is said to have been based on the study of the cosmos:

> Again, in the matter of wisdom, you see what great care the law has bestowed upon it here [in Egypt] from the very beginning, both as concerns the order of the world, deriving from those divine things the discovery of all arts applied to human affairs, down to the practice of divination and medicine with a view to health. ... All this order and system (*diakosmêsin kai suntaxin*) the goddess had bestowed upon you earlier when she founded your city, choosing the place (*topon*) in which you were born (*gegenêsthe*), because she saw that the well-tempered climate would bear a crop of men of high intelligence. (24b7–c7)

In his speech Timaeus also discusses, among many other things, prophecy and medicine (71e–72b, 87c–89c), matters which, as we can already see in the case of Sais, will be of importance to ancient Athens.

6   A Birth to the World?

The world has no end, since it is held by bonds that the demiurge, because he is good, would not wish to dissolve. But a debate arose among Plato's pupils and successors around the question of the world's beginning. Aristotle, for his own polemical reasons, thought that Plato, in the *Timaeus*, gave the world a beginning in *time*, a logical and physical absurdity (for Aristotle, time, as such, can have no beginning). Xenocrates, on the other hand, thought that Plato spoke of the generation of the world in a manner of speaking, as a pedagogical device for showing the constitution of a world with no beginning in time. It is significant that the question divided Plato's first readers, who were also his students and colleagues: the matter was not that clear.

The World-Maker

Against the idea that the world was made in time it has been argued that since time is part of what is generated, the product of the organization of the movements of the heavens, then the world cannot be generated *in* time. However, Timaeus himself repeatedly speaks of the world as 'generated' (*gegonen*, 28b7). Could there then have been, 'at the beginning', an inaugural act of making the world, willed by the demiurge? But he ordered a pre-existent chaotic milieu: was this milieu in some sort of pre-cosmic time? But pre-cosmic time is, for the *Timaeus*, a contradiction in terms.[40] What does 'beginning' mean? The expression 'generated' in Plato's text can simply mean that the world, as a body which changes, as bodies which are born and die, requires a cause. The heavenly bodies change in that they carry out celestial movements eternally, whereas lower, mortal things in the world are born and die: all require a cause, as Timaeus tells us at the beginning of his speech.[41] I believe myself that this is indeed the sense in which the world is 'generated'. But, in the light of the approach to the *Timaeus* followed in this chapter, it is possible to add further observations as regards the question as to what Timaeus might have had in mind when he spoke of the world's genesis, observations which, as far as I know, have not yet been made.

In his speech Timaeus describes this genesis in a curious way: he does not follow a strict chronological order in his account, a chronology of the making of the world,[42] but an axiological order, the order of value of the causes involved in this making. So he begins with the highest cause, the demiurge, and the demiurge's model. As if to emphasize this order, Plato has Timaeus actually forget it at one point, when he speaks of the making of body before that of soul. Timaeus realizes his mistake and quickly corrects himself: he should have spoken *first* of soul and then of the body (34b10–35a1)! Only after having dealt with the higher, divine causes of the world does Timaeus pass to the lower causes, which he describes as 'necessity': this is also constitutive of the world; without this 'necessity', the world would not be made. The order of value represented in the order of Timaeus' account brings out what is most valuable in the making of the world, what makes the world good, as well as what contributes otherwise to this making. The story of world genesis is thus also a story of

---

[40] Carone (2005), 34; Kahn (2013), 178. See Chapter 4, section 3.

[41] See Baltes (1999), 303–25, whose arguments, I think, are decisive; I am not persuaded by Sedley's argument (2007) for a 'past act of creation' (102–3). The text from the beginning of the *Critias* 106a3–4 which he cites (102) as clinching evidence contrasts the antiquity (*palai*) of the genesis of the world as a reality with the present 'birth' of the world in Timaeus' speech; but this does not entail an act of 'creation' in the past. On the question, see also Broadie (2012), chapter 7.

[42] See Baltes (1999), 307.

genesis in the sense of birth as pedigree[43], a noble birth in the case of the 'father' (the demiurge), mixed with that from the 'mother', necessity:

> Now our foregoing discourse, save for a few matters, has set forth the works wrought by the craftsmanship of intelligence; but we must now set beside them the things that come about of necessity. For the genesis of this universe is a mixed result of the combination of necessity and intelligence. Intelligence overruled necessity by persuading her to guide the greatest part of the things that become towards what is best; in that way and on that principle this universe was fashioned in the beginning by the victory of reasonable persuasion over necessity. If, then, we are really to tell how it came into being (*gegonen*) on this principle, we must bring in also the wandering cause. (47e3–48a7)

The mixed 'birth' of the world, offspring of a noble father and a needy mother,[44] prefigures the birth of the ancient Athenians from divine parents, Hephaistos and Athena, children of Zeus, and from the earth of Attica, as recounted by Critias in his speech, following that of Timaeus:

> But Hephaistos and Athena, as they had one nature, being brother and sister by the same father, and at one, moreover, in their love of wisdom and craft, so also obtained one lot in common, this our land, to be a home meet for virtue and understanding. They produced from the soil (*autochthonas*) a race of good men and taught them the order of their polity.[45]

Critias omits the story of Hephaistos' rebutted attempt to have sex with his sister and the fall of his seed to earth. (Here too, presumably, divinity must mend its ways.)[46] What matters is not the sexual engendering, but what makes the birth of the ancient Athenians noble[47]: their divine 'parents', sources of wisdom, craft and political order. So also does the world have a mixed 'birth', deriving its value from divine causes which make it noble, which give it order and beauty.

---

[43] Compare Aristotle, *Athenaion politeia* 42, 1 (on the qualifications of eligible citizens): *ei eleutheros esti kai gegone kata tous nomous*. The same sense of *gegone* as indicating pedigree is used of the (mixed) birth of Eros from Poros and Penia in Plato's *Symposium* 203c2–3. See also *Theaetetus* 173d6. Taylor (1928), 247, indicates the sense of *genesis* as pedigree (giving further references) in his note on the genealogy of the traditional gods at *Timaeus* 40c.

[44] See 50d2–3: 'And we may liken the receiving principle to a mother, and the source or spring to a father, and the intermediate nature to a child.'

[45] *Critias* 109c6–d2, trans. Taylor (1929). For the relation between the theme of autochthony and the Panathenaea, see Loraux (1990), 48.

[46] See Garvey (2008), 386.

[47] See Plato *Menexenus* 237a6: 'they [the Athenians] were good as growing (*egenonto*) from good [parents]' (Athenian autochthony was also celebrated in the official funeral speeches in memory of the fallen dead at the Ceramicus).

Figure 3 The Parthenon.

CHAPTER 3

The Model of the World

At the beginning of his speech about the making of the world, Timaeus asks which model (*paradeigma*) it is that the demiurge used in making the world, and he answers that it must be the best model, the eternal (28a6–b2, 28e5–29a6). In the previous chapter I noted that Timaeus' description of a world-maker, the demiurge, has political and craftsmanly aspects (models being used in both cases) and that the conception of a demiurge helps to show what it is that makes the world good and beautiful. In this chapter I would like to explore this further by examining in more detail the notion of a 'model' as part of the craft involved in making something good and beautiful. Craftsmen can use models in producing something, for example in making a couch or a shuttle.[1] But so can founders of cities, as we will see. Indeed the two aspects, models in crafts and in political action, can come together. By examining in more detail in this chapter the function of a model in the making of the world, I hope to show in particular what it is that makes the world 'good'. In Chapter 4, I will continue the investigation by discussing the way in which this model is applied in the making of the world in such a way as to make the world into something 'beautiful'.

Timaeus introduces the question as to the model of the world as if it were basic, as if it were the first question that we would raise if we, sharing in the feast of speeches of the *Timaeus*, are to assume that the world has a maker. Timaeus concludes that the demiurge, being good, must use the best model so that he may make a world that is beautiful. This model, what 'always is', appears to correspond to the 'Forms' found in Plato's earlier works, for example in the *Phaedo* and in the *Republic*. But if the Forms are the model of the world, does the model include all the Forms, or just some of them? Which Forms are concerned? Does the model constitute a structure of Forms? What structure? In what way does the demiurge use the Forms in making the world and in what sense are the world and its contents

[1] Chapter 2, n. 33.

42 The Model of the World

'imitations' of the Forms? What is the relation between the demiurge and the Forms? Are they in some sense to be identified with each other, or are they different (and in what way)? Speaking of the model as including Forms seems correct, but does this really help us very much, since Plato's Forms are themselves just as obscure to us, or even more obscure, than the world's model? The text of the *Timaeus* provides limited help in dealing with these questions and it will be useful to bring in what we find elsewhere in Plato on the subject of models in order to make some headway.

1   A Traditional Interpretation in Exotic Disguise: Bardesanes

A traditional way of dealing with the questions raised by Plato's demiurge and his model is given vivid expression in a story told by a Syrian philosopher of the late second century/early third century AD. I summarize the story since it illustrates, as if in a caricature, the sort of reading of the model of Plato's *Timaeus* which, I will argue, is misleading. The caricature, it must be admitted, has its own fascination.

Bardesanes, who taught philosophy in Emesa, on the eastern fringe of the Roman empire, reports, in one of his works,[2] on what he had been told by some Indians about a large cave situated in a very high mountain in the centre of the earth. In this cave was to be seen a statue about six meters high. The statue was of a standing figure, arms outstretched. It was male on the right side, female on the left, with no visible transition between them. On the statue were carved the sun on one breast, the moon on the other, a multitude of angels, heavens, mountains, the sea, rivers, 'all' plants and animals. (It is not clear if all individuals or just all the various types of plants and animals is meant.) The Indians told Bardesanes that the statue had been given by the god to his son, when his son made the world, so that 'he would have a model (*paradeigma*) he could contemplate'. The statue, then, was nothing less than the model of the world, made by the god for the convenience of his world-making son. And this model of the world could still be seen in a cave in India.

Research has discovered statue-types, in India and China, corresponding to what Bardesanes seems to be describing, statue-types which portray Shiva or the cosmic Buddha, but with meanings quite different from that which Bardesanes gives. The statue of the cosmic Buddha, for example, shows his vision of the world, not a model he would have used in making

---

[2] Our source is Porphyry, fragment 376 Smith, translated and discussed by Castelletti (2006) as fragment 7.

the world.[3] In fact, Bardesanes interprets the statue as illustrating an interpretation of Plato's *Timaeus* characteristic of Platonists of the Roman imperial period. According to this interpretation, a first god inspires a second, subordinate god who is the demiurge of the world. This demiurge uses a model, which is simply a replica of the world, or rather the world is a replica of the model: all the contents of this world are found in its model, which is just another world that the demiurge copied. Bardesanes' story of the statue illustrates in a very concrete and material way this reading of Plato's cosmic model, whereas it was often thought in Platonist circles of his time that the model was conceptual, rather than material, that it existed in the thought of the demiurge. In what follows I will try to show that this way of seeing the demiurge's model, as simply a replica in reverse of the world, is not adequate.

2   Political Models

More can be learnt about the demiurge's model in the *Timaeus*, I would like to suggest, if we look elsewhere in Plato's work, in places in particular where he describes the use of models in politics. We are encouraged in this, not only by the political meaning of the term 'demiurge' (as magistrate), but also by Timaeus' description of his demiurge as a reformed Zeus who thinks, deliberates, seeks to achieve the best, gives speeches, delegates, persuades, legislates.[4]

An example of a political model can be found in Plato's *Republic*, Book VI. Socrates is describing the action of the rulers of his good state, the philosopher-kings:

> [...] no city could ever enjoy happiness unless its lineaments were traced by painters who used the divine model (*paradeigmati*) ... They [would] take the city and the characters of men, as they might a tablet, and first wipe it clean ... and then they would sketch the figure of the constitution ... and then, I take it, in the course of the work they would look frequently in either direction, at the just in itself, the beautiful, the moderate and all these sorts of things, and alternately at that which they were trying to reproduce in mankind, mingling and blending from various pursuits that hue of flesh, so to speak, deriving their judgement from that likeness of humanity which Homer too called ... the image and likeness of the divine.[5] (500e2–501b7)

---

[3] Castelletti (2006), 253–62.   [4] See Chapter 2, section 2 and *Timaeus* 42d2–3.
[5] Translated by P. Shorey, slightly modified.

The rulers of the good city are compared to painters, who are inspired by a divine model, 'the just in itself, the beautiful, the moderate' and so on, and seek to produce in the citizens of the city a likeness of this divine model. The models of Socrates' philosopher-kings, we may suppose, are the Forms of Justice, Beauty, Moderation and other unspecified Forms. By making the city into a painting of this model, they make it like the divine model they use.

Socrates' comparison of philosopher-kings to painters who use models, which they reproduce in their painting, helps to explain how the demiurge of the *Timaeus* could have been thought by its readers to be producing (like an artist) a cosmic replica of his model, as in Bardesanes' story. But the passage does not take us very much further in understanding political models, apart from suggesting an analogy between artistic (craftsmanly) and political production, and pointing to particular Forms (Justice, Beauty, Moderation) as having the function of models.

Justice is already described earlier in the *Republic* Book V (472c4–d7) in terms of its function as a model (*paradeigma*) to which one should look in dealing with matters of happiness and what it might be to be just or unjust. And earlier still, at the end of Book IV, Socrates defines justice as 'to do that which is one's own' (*to ta hautou prattein*, 433b4, 443b1–2). What this means, as regards the structure of the soul, is that each part of the soul carries out the function proper to it, and, as regards the city, that each part of the city carries out its proper task. The result, in both city and soul, is inner peace, friendship, harmony, unity (443d–444b). Justice, we can conclude, is a principle according to which, in a complex of parts, be it soul or city, each part realizes the function proper to it as being what it is and as a part of a whole. To 'paint' an image of this principle would then mean, for the philosopher-king, to bring what he orders by his actions to function according to this principle.

More can be learnt about political models from Plato's last writing, the *Laws*, to which I now turn. The *Laws* is a vast work in which Plato has three elderly gentlemen, an unnamed guest and citizen of Athena's city (626d), Megillos (a Spartan) and Cleinias (a Cretan) discuss, on a leisurely walk in Crete, a plan for a new city to be founded in Crete. In Chapter 7, I will come back to this plan in order to discuss its organization in more detail, but for present purposes we can limit ourselves here to noting aspects of the conception of a political model (*paradeigma*) that is described in some passages in the work.

In order to introduce these passages, we should recall first the strong emphasis Plato places in the *Laws* on the relation between the finality or

2 Political Models
45

aim (*skopos*)[6] of a city-state and its organization. City-states may be organized in relation to various aims and these aims are reflected in the way the city-states are structured. Thus states such as the Cretan and Spartan states are organized for the purpose of making war.[7] However, such objectives are criticized in Book I of the *Laws*. A state organized for the purpose of war divides, separates, discriminates against and destroys, not only others, but also, ultimately, itself. Such an objective is thus self-destructive in the long run. It is argued that other objectives should be sought, objectives which include peace, harmony, friendship, liberty (no sector of the state should be enslaved by another), intelligence and the virtues which make possible a harmonious whole.[8] These objectives of a state indeed are one and the same:

> One should always consider that a state ought to be free and wise and enjoy friendship with itself, and that this is what the lawgiver should concentrate on in his legislation. It ought not to surprise us if several times before now we have decided on a number of other aims and said they were what a lawgiver should concentrate on. . . . When we say that the legislator should keep moderation or wisdom or friendship in view, we must bear in mind that the aim (*skopos*) is the same, not different. Nor should we be disconcerted if we find a lot of other expressions of which the same is true.[9]

These aims, as one aim, are the 'best, for the sake of which' (*tou aristou heneka*) laws are made (628c).

If what is best is the aim (*skopos*) to be achieved in a state, then the way (*tropos*) in which this aim might be reached, the means whereby it might be attained, would appear to be the way in which the state is organized, what legislation it is to be given as directed to achieving the aim.[10] The question thus arises as to the organization needed by a state for it to be able to attain 'the best'. It is in this context that the notion of a political model is introduced in two interesting passages which merit quotation. The first passage reads as follows:

> You'll find the first state and constitution and the best laws where the old saying 'friends' property is genuinely shared'[11] is most put into practice throughout the entire state. Now I don't know whether in fact this situation – a community of wives, children and all property – exists anywhere

---

[6] *Laws* 693c, 962ab ; cf. 701d and 705e (for the image of the archer).
[7] 626ab. Plato links the unlimited search for wealth with war, in that the former creates the need for the latter, in *Republic* 373de; see also *Phaedo* 66c5–7.
[8] 688a, 693bc, 701d, 715ac, 962a; see Bobonich (2002), 119–23.
[9] 693bc, translated by T. Saunders (1970), slightly modified.   [10] 962b; see 705e.
[11] A Pythagorean saying (references collected in O'Meara [2003], 92, n. 20).

46 The Model of the World

today, or will ever exist,[12] but at any rate in such a state the notion of private property will have been completely eliminated . . . the laws in force produce the greatest possible unity in the state – and you'll never posit a better or truer criterion of an absolutely perfect law than that. It may be that gods or a number of the children of gods inhabit this kind of state: if so, the life they live there, observing these rules, is a happy one indeed. And so men need to look no further for their model (*paradeigma*): they should keep this state in view and try to find the one that most nearly resembles it as far as possible. This is what we've put our hand to, and if in some way it could be realized, it would come very near to immortality and be second-best in unity.[13] Later, God willing, we'll complete a third best. (739ce)

The political model described here is that of a state which reaches a maximal degree of unity and happiness through legislation which abolishes private property and family, a feature characteristic of the ruler group in the good city of the *Republic* and of the city Socrates describes in his speech of the day before the day of Timaeus' speech (*Timaeus* 18bd). In the passage it is also suggested that such legislation, applying to the city as a whole, may be beyond human possibilities: it might take (Platonic!) gods or children of gods (ancient Athenians?[14]) to be part of such a state.

However, the good city of the *Laws*, as we will see in more detail in Chapter 7 (section 3), allows for a limited amount of private property (providing for some inequality, but preventing extremes) and regulates family life, as if in consideration of the human needs and limitations of its future members. This 'second-best' state is also a model, even if it is less ambitious than the first or highest model of a state, as is indicated a little later in the work:

> This as a whole is never likely to find such favourable circumstances that every single detail will turn out precisely according to plan. It presupposes men who won't turn up their noses at living in such a community, and who will tolerate a moderate and fixed level of wealth through their lives, and the supervision of the size of each individual's family as we've suggested. Will people really put up with being deprived of gold and other things which, for reasons which we went into just now, the legislator is obviously going to add to his list of forbidden articles? What about this description of the city and countryside with houses at the centre and in all directions round about? He might have been relating a dream, or modelling a state and its citizens out of wax!

---

[12] *eite pou nun estin eit'estai pote*; almost the same phrase is used of the model in *Republic* 592b4: *eite pou estin eite estai*, as is noted by Schöpsdau (1991), 140.

[13] I follow here the Greek text as defended by Schöpsdau (2003), 314.   [14] See Chapter 2, section 6.

2 Political Models   47

These things [i.e., objections] impress well enough, but they must be reconsidered as follows. The legislator will again say this to us: 'My friends, in these talks we're having, don't think it has escaped me either that the point of view you are urging has some truth in it. But I believe that in every endeavour for the future, when you are displaying the model (*paradeigma deiknunta*) such as ought to be that which is being put into effect, the most correct procedure is to spare no detail of absolute truth and beauty [in this model]. But if you find that one of these details is impossible in practice, you ought to put it on one side and not attempt it: you should see which of the remaining alternatives comes closest to it and is most akin to your policy, and arrange to have that done instead. But you must let the legislator finish describing what he really wants to do, and only then join him in considering which of his proposals for legislation are feasible, and which are too difficult. You see, even the maker (*dêmiourgon*) of the most trivial object must make it internally consistent if he is going to get any sort of reputation.'[15]

These two passages are found in Book V of the *Laws*: they come at the beginning of the development of a legislative code for a good city which extends from Book V to Book XII. We can regard this code and the various dispositions proposed for the structure of the city as constituting a *model* which is to be elaborated as fully and as perfectly as possible, prior to its use when founding a *particular* city, in a particular place with particular citizens, where adjustments of various sorts might be required.[16] The *Laws*, we can say, presents us with the political model of a good state, in the form of a legislative and administrative order, which is then to be used and adapted, as circumstances require, when founding a new state.[17]

The main steps of the whole procedure, as described so far, might be summarized as follows:

(i)   The aim or goal to be achieved in a city (unity, harmony, peace, etc.) is to be fixed.

(ii) A model showing the organizational means (in particular legislative order) whereby this goal might be attained is to be elaborated. This will represent an order for the life of a city and its citizens which does not take into account the particular limitations entailed, for example, by establishing the city in a particular place (with specific geographical

---

[15] 745e–746d; compare *Republic* 472cd.

[16] The distinction between the model city elaborated in the discussion in the *Laws* and the use of this model in founding a particular city, for example the city to be founded by Cleinias in Crete, is clearly drawn by Schöpsdau (1991), but otherwise generally ignored, as far as I can see, in modern studies.

[17] See also Chapter 6, section 2. Schöpsdau (1991), 145, identifies the 'third' state mentioned in the passage from *Laws* 739ce quoted previously as that which is realized on the basis of the model proposed in the *Laws*.

48   The Model of the World

features) and populating it with particular citizens (with various back-
grounds and characters).

(iii)   Once the model is elaborated in full, one may then proceed to the
founding of a particular city, following the model. Here specific circumstances may require changes in various dispositions in the model.

As regards the second step, we might add that the political model of the *Laws*
is 'displayed' in the text: it is the legislative and administrative order elaborated
as a whole and subjected to scrutiny in the discussion between the three elderly
speakers of the *Laws*. The model exists in their thinking and discussion.

3   Architectural Models

The passage just quoted from the *Laws* suggests a comparison between the
model developed by the legislator and the practice of an architect or city-
planner who elaborates, as part of his building project, a model out of wax.
The comparison with an architectural model is exploited by the early first-
century Jewish author Philo of Alexandria, who, in the context of explain-
ing the model used by the god in making the world, compares this with
architectural practice:

> Having observed both the favourable climate and location of the site,
> he [a trained architect] first designs within himself virtually all the parts
> of the city that is to be completed – temples, gymnasia, public offices, market-
> places, harbours. . . . Then, taking up the imprints (*tupous*) of each object in
> his own soul, as if in wax, he carries around the intelligible city as an image in
> his head . . . he begins, as a good builder (*dêmiourgos*), to construct the city
> out of stones and timber, looking at the model (*paradeigma*) and ensuring
> that the corporeal objects correspond to each of the incorporeal ideas.
> The conception we have concerning God must be similar to this, namely
> that when he decided to found the great cosmic city (*megalopolis*), he first
> conceived its outlines (*tupoi*). Out of these he composed the intelligible
> cosmos, which served him as a model (*paradeigma*) when he completed the
> sense-perceptible cosmos as well.[18]

Philo goes on to insist that the model exists only in the soul of the maker, in
the divine Logos which organized it: the intelligible city is nothing but the
calculation (*logismos*) of the architect who is planning to found the city of
the world (24–5). Philo's text, which may be inspired in part by the passage
quoted earlier from Plato's *Laws*,[19] encourages us to look further into actual

---

[18] Philo, *De op. mundi* 17–19 (trans. Runia [2001], slightly modified).
[19] See also Philo, *De vita Mosis* II, 49–51 and 76. On Philo's use of Plato's *Laws*, see Annas (2010), 80–4.

3 Architectural Models

49

Greek architectural practice, in particular as regards the use made of models (*paradeigmata*) in building projects. In the following I would like to summarize information on this subject that can be found, not only in literary texts, but also in inscriptions which have been found on building sites, in particular those of the sacred island of Delos.[20]

At the beginning of a building project, for example the building of a temple, the city, or perhaps a rich patron, would consider architectural proposals for the building. These proposals might be made by different architects in competition with each other,[21] or perhaps a local architect would be solicited. The city, or rather the commission or body representing the city,[22] would consider these proposals, which the architect could make by means of an oral description (*logos*) and by showing a *paradeigma*.[23] The *paradeigma* could be a sketch made on a tablet or it could be a model of the building to be constructed.[24] In either case, wax could have been used, a model made of wax, or perhaps shapes traced on a tablet coated with wax.[25] At any rate, these descriptions, sketches or models would have been quite general, merely giving an overall idea of the styles and general proportions to be used in the projected building. This was possible in the classical period, when the standardization of architecture made it relatively easy to visualize a future building on the basis of a few specifications. Full-scale models came into use after the classical period, with the increasing complexity and variety of building projects.

When contracts for the work were established and construction begun, the architect would supervise the work as the building progressed,[26] establishing detailed measured plans for the builders[27] and providing

---

[20] The evidence drawn from these inscriptions is very usefully collected and analyzed in Hellmann (1992), who also presents (1999) a selection of architectural inscriptions drawn from a variety of sites.

[21] Plutarch, *An vitiositas ad infelicitatem sufficiat*, 498EF. For a detailed survey (with further bibliography) of the various stages of a building project in classical Greece see Koenigs (2012), largely taken up again in Koenigs (2015), 151–3.

[22] Aristotle, *Ath. pol.* 49, 3, identifies the body which judged submitted *paradeigmata* at Athens as the Council (*Boulê*). On this text see Chapter 5, section 1. See also Plato, *Protagoras* 319b.

[23] Plutarch, *loc. cit.*   [24] Hellmann (1992), 317.

[25] It is not completely clear in the passages of the *Laws* and in Philo which is meant; see also Gregory of Nyssa, *In Christi resurrectionem Or.* III, 665D: the architect (*mêchanikos*) prepares first with 'a little wax' shapes and *tupoi* of great buildings.

[26] Plato describes this in *Statesman* 259e–260a.

[27] Some examples of these plans have survived, in particular in the temple of Apollo at Didyma and in the temple of Athena at Priene (mid-fourth-century BC, attributed to the architect Pytheos in Vitruvius); see Figure 4; Koenigs (1983a), (1983b), (2015), 44; Haselberger (1980), (1983); Hellmann (1992), 320–1; Senseney (2011), 49, 119. In speaking of a detailed planning sketch found at Priene (Figure 4), Koenigs (1983b, 168) comments: 'The sketch confirms the observation made already at Didyma, that work continued on the project even while actual building was proceeding. Thus the project ["Konzept"] assigned at first to the architects and contractors can only have been general.'

50   The Model of the World

paradeigmata for particular parts or features of the building, exemplars
which the craftsmen could replicate, for example models for roof tiles or for
capitals of columns.[28] Thus we need to distinguish between two kinds of
models, or *paradeigmata*: the general sketch or overall model of the initial
project, and the detailed exemplar to be reproduced by workers in making
a particular part or feature of the building.[29]

The actual building that was constructed could, of course, turn out to be
somewhat different from what had been initially envisaged: the architect
could make changes in his detailed plans in response to practical contin-
gencies, money could run out, the work drag on, magistrates, architects,
builders change, and so on. Herodotus (V, 62) tells the story of a temple
built in Delphi that was even more beautiful than its *paradeigma*, thanks to
the additional funds provided by its sponsors. This sounds like it was
a surprise, an exception compared to what must have been the more usual
experience.[30]

4 The Cosmic Model of the *Timaeus*

Returning to the story of the making of the world in the *Timaeus*, I would
like to show that we can make good use of these conceptions of political
and architectural models in the interpretation of the model of the world
in Timaeus' story.[31] As in the case of the political model of the *Laws*, in
the *Timaeus* we can distinguish between the objective, or goal, sought by
the divine demiurge; the model he chooses in order to realize this goal;
and the producing of the world according to the model, in a place. I will

---

[28] Hellmann (1992), 317. Some of these can still be seen, for example a marble *paradeigma* for a roof tile.
[29] For this important distinction in Greek architecture, see especially Käppel (1999), 85–6 (who distinguishes between *paradeigma*, as 'Entwurfsplan', and 'Prototyp'). Perl (1999), 357–8, notes this distinction in Plato. Yet another, third type of *paradeigma* can be found in Plato's works, in particular in the *Statesman*, and is discussed by Goldschmidt (1947) and Kato (1995). In brief, it is an example taken from familiar experience which makes it easier to grasp wholes and relationships in another, less easily understood domain. The example in the *Statesman* is weaving, which helps to show what political science is (see Chapter 5). This illustrative *paradeigma*, although different, can be compared with the *paradeigma* of the initial project of the architect to the extent that both show wholes and general proportions or relationships in these wholes. Goldschmidt distinguishes (93–5) this (third) kind of *paradeigma* from that described in Aristotle's *Rhetoric* 1.2.1356b5–16, 1357b27–36, which is a familiar example used as a means of persuasion by a speaker in relation to a comparable, but less familiar case.
[30] Hellmann (1999) presents a useful selection of inscriptions concerning competition between architects for projects, their models (*paradeigma*), adjudications of projects, detailed contracts (*suggraphai*), exemplars (*paradeigmata*) of building elements, accounts, etc.
[31] Senseney (2011) suggests comparisons between Plato's Forms, Vitruvius' 'ideas' and architectural *paradeigmata* (cf. 16–17, for example). However, his analysis of Plato remains at a somewhat general level.

4 The Cosmic Model of the Timaeus

therefore follow these three procedural steps, as distinguished previously (section 2), first discussing briefly the fixing of the aim or goal of the making of the world, then moving to the model to be used in order to reach this goal. This second step will require a fairly long and detailed investigation. Finally, in the next chapter, I will take up the third step, the realization of the model in the world.

The *goal* at which the demiurge aims is clearly stated by Timaeus. The demiurge is good, indeed the best of causes (29a3 and 6). As good, the demiurge suffers no envy and can only want to make everything as good as possible, thus similar to himself (29d7–30a2). The goal of the demiurge can then be described as the good. He produces a good world, the best of worlds, in that it is a world which is characterized by unity, harmony, friendship,[32] a world which is a 'felicitous god',[33] a most perfect or complete (*teleôtatos*) world.[34] The goal of the demiurge, we may note, corresponds to that of the legislator of Plato's *Laws*.

Although Timaeus does say some things about the *model* used by the demiurge in making the world, it is very difficult to reach a view of this model which is full and precise enough to provide answers to the many questions we might have about it, as they are formulated at the beginning of this chapter. At the outset one should consider that Timaeus is perhaps not able or willing to say very much about the model of the world. Already the divine demiurge, for him, is 'hard to find' (28c2–4) and he describes the participation of the things of this world in the Forms as 'difficult to say' (50c6).

We will indeed find some indication a little later that Timaeus is not willing to say much directly about the model. This is perhaps why, having established that the demiurge must use the best of models (therefore an eternal model, not one that is generated), he next speaks of the model by approaching it indirectly, from below, as it were, i.e., from the world which is made according to it. Thus Timaeus (or rather the demiurge) decides that this world, to be the best, must have intelligence (*nous*) and, to have intelligence, it must have soul (30b). The world must therefore be a rational ensouled being, a rational animal. This being established, Timaeus then asks 'in the likeness of what animal' was the world constituted (30c2–3) and concludes that it must be in the likeness of a 'complete' (*teleos*) animal, complete in the sense of including all animals, just as our world includes all animals (30c4–31a1). It thus seems that Timaeus thinks that the model of the world must be an all-inclusive (intelligible) animal, because this is what

---

[32] *Timaeus* 32c2, 33a1 and 7; 34b4–9; 46c8; Burnyeat (2000), 74–5.   [33] 34b8.   [34] 92c8.

52 The Model of the World

the world must be, if it is to be the best of worlds, and it is this as being in the likeness of its model. He is thus making inferences, from what this world should be (if it is to be the best of worlds), to what the model of such a world must be. But what could an all-inclusive intelligible animal possibly be?

Timaeus comes back a little later to the all-inclusive model animal:

> He [the demiurge] thought that this world must possess all the different forms that intelligence discerns contained in the [model] animal. And there are four: one, the heavenly race of gods; second, winged things whose path is in the air; third, all that dwells in the water; and fourth, all that goes on foot on the dry land. The form of the divine kind he made for the most part of fire. (39e7–40a2)

From this passage we can infer that the model is all-inclusive, not in the sense that it includes all animals (a Bardesanes version of the model), but in the sense that it includes all the main animal genera.[35] To these genera correspond four genera in the world, genera differentiated in terms of the four types of elements in which they live: fire, air, water and earth. But how are the genera differentiated in the model? Is it also in terms of four types of elements?[36] If not, then how are they differentiated? If so, does this mean that the four types of elements are also to be found in the model? Are there Forms of fire and of the other elements in the model?

In making the world, the demiurge starts first with two elements, fire (which makes things visible) and earth (which makes things tangible). Then, in order to bind these elements together, he resorts to two intermediary terms, on the grounds that solids require two mean terms to link them to each other. Thus the demiurge places air and water between fire and earth to bind them, the bond (*desmos*) being the structure of geometrical proportion: as A:B = B:C, and B:C = C:D, so is fire to air as air is to water, and air to water as water is to earth. Through geometrical proportion the four elements are linked and the body of the world is unified, made coherent and in 'friendship' with itself, indissoluble by any other than by him who bound it together (31b–32c). Looking further on in the text, we find that the demiurge, in bringing order to a disordered indeterminate moving milieu, found in it what we might call 'pre-elements', to which he gave structure and order, in particular geometrical shapes, built up from

---

[35] See Sedley (2007), 108–9.
[36] There are also different grades of each element in the world, different grades or kinds of fire, air, etc. (58c–61c).

4 *The Cosmic Model of the* Timaeus

triangles, which give the four elements determinate shapes, characteristics and actions and allow them to be transformed into each other (48b, 53b).[37]

It thus appears that the four elements are indeterminate pre-elements structured into determinate bodies by means of a variety of geometrical shapes and bound to each other by geometrical proportion. Geometrical shapes and proportion thus seem to be what constitutes what is determinate in the four elements. These geometrical structures, introduced by the demiurge, seem in turn to have their origin elsewhere:

> This then [geometrical shape] . . . we posit as the origin (*archê*) of fire and the other bodies. . . . But the causes (*archas*) of these from above (*anôthen*), god only knows, and he of men who is the friend of god. (53d4–7)

The causes of the geometrical shapes that constitute the four elements as determinate constituents of body come from 'above'. If we stay within the framework of Timaeus' story, 'above' can be taken most simply as referring to the model of the world.[38] If Timaeus, as a distinguished philosopher, is a 'friend of god',[39] then perhaps he might know more about the model than what he is willing to say here. At any rate, it would seem that the 'causes' of the variety of geometrical shapes which constitute the four elements as determinate entities are to be found in the model of the world. It is perhaps in this very limited sense that we can say that there are what might be described as Forms of the elements in the model.[40]

Returning now to the question of the different genera of animals in the all-inclusive model animal, it would seem that we can conclude that the differentiation between these genera in the model must be other than that which would correspond to the four determinate elements of this world, since these elements *result* from the imposition by the demiurge of geometrical shapes on pre-elements, the shapes themselves having causes which are known only to god and to the 'friend of god'. Furthermore, it seems

---

[37] In Chapter 4, section 3, I discuss these mathematical structures in more detail.

[38] For an overview of various interpretations of this passage, see Karfík (2007), 149, n. 138 (these interpretations make use of Aristotle's reports on Plato's metaphysics; see n. 40).

[39] See *Laws* 716ce, where being a 'friend of god' means becoming like god, the god presumably of the true philosopher (see *Theaetetus* 173d–176b).

[40] Timaeus raises the question as to the existence of a Form of fire and of other Forms at 51b7–c1 and answers with an argument in support of the Forms in general, without specific reference to fire. I come back in section 5 to some passages where Forms of the elements may be thought to be present. An enigmatic report in Aristotle's *De anima* (1.2. 404b19–21) refers to the model animal of the *Timaeus* as being 'out of the Form of the one, of the first length, breadth and depth, and so on for the others'. These items may have to do with the causes of the geometrical shapes mentioned in *Timaeus* 53d, but the Aristotelian report is so obscure that it is more of an *explanandum* than an *explanans*. I will relate 'equality' in mathematical structures (Chapter 4, section 3) to identity in the demiurge's model.

54 The Model of the World

that the lower (non-astral) genera of animals in the world are not simply derived from the cosmic model. For having told us that the demiurge made the astral gods and placed immortal souls in the fiery stars, Timaeus has the demiurge assign lower work to the gods he had made, the 'young gods', as follows:

> Having received the immortal principle [i.e., the soul] of a mortal creature, imitating their own maker, they borrowed from the world portions of fire and earth, water and air ... these they took and welded them together, not with the indissoluble bonds (*desmoi*) whereby they were themselves held together, but welding them with a multitude of ties (*gomphoi*) too small to be seen and so making each body a unity of all the portions. And they bound (*enedoun*) the circuits of the immortal soul within the flowing and ebbing tide of the body. (42e7–43a5)

The young gods in fact construct the human body, including the head which they make spherical in imitation of the spherical shape of the world, to house the divine, immortal part of human nature (44d3–6). The image conveyed in this description is that of craftsmen working under the instructions of the architect, using ties or dowels (*gomphoi*) which contrast with the bonds or clamps (*desmoi*) the demiurge uses to bind together the constituents of soul and of the elements,[41] to make the human body from the elements available in the world and to attach the soul to it. For making the human head the young gods take their model from the spherical shape given the world by the demiurge.[42] Thus the sphericity of the world is a *paradeigma*, in the sense of an exemplar of a part of a building, of the human head. In the case of humans, therefore, the immortal soul is made by the demiurge and the body is made by the young gods, drawing from the elements available in the world and imitating, as regards the head, the world as a model, rather than something *in the model* of the world.

The animal genera are described very rapidly at the end of Timaeus' speech (91d–92c). They appear simply as different types of bodies corresponding to different degrees in the philosophical fall of soul, from its original fiery abode in the stars, to a flighty, naïve faith in sight, an ignorant subjection to the earth (multipeds and reptiles) and ending in submersion in aquatic gloom! The different genera of animals relate then to the different degrees in soul's fall from rational life and the different sorts of

---

[41] For the technical sense of these terms in building, see Hellmann (1992), 85: *desmos* is a clamp linking blocks of stone horizontally, *gomphos* is a vertical dowel. Plato invents, in name if not in reality, an art of making dowels (*gomphotikê*) in *Statesman* 280d. On the binding of soul, see 35b (with Cornford [1935], 67–9).

[42] I am indebted here to suggestions made to me by Gabor Betegh.

4 *The Cosmic Model of the* Timaeus

bodies appropriate to these different degrees. The degrees in the fall of the soul cannot be attributed to the model of the world,[43] and the different types of sub-astral animal bodies occupied by fallen souls relate to these degrees. In the case of man, we have seen that his head is modelled after the shape of the world.

In view of all of these considerations, in what sense then, we may ask, can there be the different animal genera in the model of the world? It seems that we find little left in the model but possibly the causes of the geometrical shapes given to the elements[44] and the requirement that the world be the most perfect animal containing all genera of animals. We might formulate this requirement as follows (I use the form of a hypothetical imperative so as to show the relation between goal and model):

> If the world is to be the best of worlds (the goal), therefore a rational animal, then it should fulfil the following requirement (the model): it must include all genera of animals.

We are encouraged to describe the situation in this way if we take up the question of the cause of the geometrical proportion which serves to bind both soul and the elements in the world.[45] This cause might plausibly be sought in the model (it is the demiurge himself who binds soul and the elements). But geometrical proportion is just one way of expressing a more general structure, what might be called the relation of justice.[46] Justice, as we have found it defined earlier (section 2) in the *Republic*, is the principle which requires that each part of a whole perform the function appropriate to it. Justice means, then, the correct correlation of things with their functions. If things differ in their nature, are unequal in nature, they are the same, equal, if their functions are correctly correlated with their nature. The equality expressed here is that produced by geometrical proportion: not the quantitative equality represented by arithmetical proportion (A-B = D-C), but the equality of ratios expressed in geometrical proportion (A: B = C: D). Thus we may say that the same structural requirement, or law, can find expression in the making of the world (geometrical proportion binding soul and binding the elements), in human society and in the inner

---

[43] See Chapter 2, section 4 (the good does not cause evil).

[44] I discuss the causes of geometrical shapes in the next chapter.

[45] How geometrical proportion serves to structure soul and the elements is described in the next chapter (section 3).

[46] This theme in Plato has been fully discussed by Neschke-Hentschke (1995), who also shows its importance for the history of the concept of natural law.

56   The Model of the World

life of the soul (justice).[47] Plato had indicated these continuities before, in
a passage of the *Gorgias* (507e6–508a)

> Wise men ... say that the heavens and the earth, gods and men, are held
> together by fellowship and friendship, and order (*kosmiotês*) and modera-
> tion and justice, and for this reason they call the sum of things the
> 'cosmos' ... not the world of disorder or riot. But it seems to me that
> you pay no attention to these things ... you are unaware that geometric
> equality is of great importance among gods and men alike, and you think
> we should practice overreaching others (*pleonexia*), for you neglect
> geometry.[48]

We have met geometrical equality (proportion) in the making of the world
in the *Timaeus* and will meet it again, in the same context, in the next
chapter and later, in Chapter 7, in the context of the distribution of
property in the good city of the *Laws*. The source of this order, in its
various manifestations, must derive from the model of the world and might
be expressed as the following structural requirement or law:

> If the world is to be the best of worlds (goal), then it should fulfil the
> following requirement (model): each of its parts must carry out its appro-
> priate function.

To these requirements (all-inclusiveness, justice), we could plausibly
add others. For example, self-sufficiency also seems required: the best
of worlds, if it is to be such, must be self-sufficient. What this means
is that the world must be a curious kind of animal, not depending in
any way on an external environment, neither deriving its food from
outside nor excreting, an animal without limbs, a totally self-recycling
organism made possible by its having been given the geometrical
shape of a sphere.[49] Another requirement seems to be that of perpetuity: the world attains the eternity of the model in that its constituents, soul and the elements, are indissolubly bound and in that the
cyclical movements of the heavens have a numbered order expressing
the unity of the model.[50] All of these requirements (all-inclusiveness,
justice, self-sufficiency, perpetuity) are what go to make the world
good, a 'felicitous god', that which the demiurge seeks to achieve.[51]
   In investigating the way in which the demiurge realizes the model in
making the world, in the next chapter, we will come across more hints as to

---

[47] See also *Laws* 757ad; Burnyeat (2000), 66–7.
[48] Translated by W. Woodhead, slightly modified.   [49] 33ad.   [50] 37d.
[51] We might note that Aristotle lists most of these requirements as characterizing the highest human
good, the highest happiness, in *Nicomachean Ethics* 10.7.1177a27–1178a2; see also *Philebus* 66b2.

4 The Cosmic Model of the Timaeus 57

what else might be included in his model. But for the moment we might conclude our enquiry into the model of the world by saying that this model, to the extent that we can infer anything about it, resembles the preliminary project, sketch or *paradeigma* of the architect, rather than a detailed scale-model, or replica in reverse (the Bardasanes interpretation), of the world.[52] The model gives an overall view, general indications of proportions and styles. In comparison with the political *paradeigma* of the *Laws*, we can say that the model of the world includes general specifications, requirements, laws, which are to be followed if the goal (the good) is to be achieved, if the best of worlds is to be made.[53]

The demiurge, as architect, in making the world, being guided by these general specifications, then draws up detailed plans: we can identify these as the intricate and detailed passages in the *Timaeus* where the mathematical structures of the soul and of the elements are described.[54] The demiurge also assigns lesser work to his craftsmen (the young gods), providing them with models (*paradeigmata* in the second sense, exemplars), in particular the spherical world as a model for the human head.[55] They, and other auxiliaries, execute their various tasks.[56] And

---

[52] This conclusion provides a background and support, I believe, to the position taken by Broadie (2012), chapter 3, that the world's paradigm is a 'recipe' or 'pattern' for the world, rather than the original (of a copy, the world). See also Frede (1996), 53.

[53] Penner (2006) interprets the Forms of the *Republic* as structures, like laws of nature, which are the objects of science. Broadie (2007), 243, compares Plato's Forms to laws of nature or 'commandments'. I suggest here a context in which this way of seeing Forms may be made more plausible. The interpretation of the cosmic model as including requirements or laws can be supported, not only through the comparison with the political *paradeigma* (i.e., code of laws) of the *Laws*, but also by reference to the laws which Socrates formulates for the poets in *Republic* Book II: these 'laws' (god does no evil, god does not deceive) are described also as *tupoi* 'in which' (*en hôi*) the poets should compose (379a5, 380c6–7, 383a2–5; see Männlein-Robert [2010], 116). *Tupos* appears in conjunction with *paradeigma* (see already earlier at n. 25 and at n. 18) in architectural language as designating a model in relief serving as a standard for making or repairing parts of a building (Hellmann [1992], 318–19). In the *Republic* (380c7) the *tupoi* to be used as standards for poets to follow are described as laws, *nomoi*. See also *Laws* 801cd, and *Protagoras* 326c7–8, on laws functioning as models, as a *paradeigma*, a passage quoted by Broadie (2012), 69, n. 14. In the *Laws* (811be), the Athenian proposes his own discourse, in the text, as a *paradeigma* for educational literature for the young.

[54] 35a–36b; 53c–55c; these detailed plans are discussed in the next chapter.

[55] The distinction between *paradeigma* as general project and *paradeigma* as exemplar to be copied might be applied in a controversy which took place in English-language studies (see the review in Kahn [2013], 8–11) about self-predication of the Forms: is a Form an instance of itself (e.g. the Form of Justice is just)? If Forms are taken to be *paradeigmata* in the sense of exemplars to be copied, then Forms are self-predicative, just as the model tile (above n. 28) is itself a tile, to be replicated by tile-makers. But if Forms are taken to be *paradeigmata* in the sense of general functional specifications, as I argue in the case of the *Timaeus*, then they are clearly not self-predicative. See also Broadie (2012), 74–5.

[56] At 46e6 Plato uses the word *exergazesthai*, a term used for finishing work (Hellmann [1992], 142), as well as *apergazesthai* (e.g. 43a4), a term he uses for workers finishing jobs assigned by an architect in *Statesman* 260a7. Brisson (1998), 44, collects further terms relating to construction.

58 The Model of the World

around his heavenly construction the demiurge paints a surrounding frieze.[57]

A further matter concerning the model of the world must be mentioned. In the cases of architectural and political models, the architect or legislator thinks up, describes and perhaps sketches an outline of the project or a code of laws, before proceeding to the work of building a temple or founding a city. Thus these analogies might be taken to imply that the demiurge 'thought up', so to speak, the model for the world,[58] as, for example, Philo of Alexandria's version suggests. Are the Forms (as the model) the thoughts of a god, as later Platonists thought? Yet the model is eternal (27d6).[59]

The metaphysical questions which have traditionally arisen among Plato's readers – did a god think up the Forms? Which god? A transcendent or an immanent god? Are the Forms independent of this god, or subordinate to it? – emerge if we press Plato's image of the world-craftsman beyond the function which it has in Timaeus' speech. Our answer to these questions depends on what we make of Plato's demiurge. If the demiurge is part of a Platonic myth, a story told by Timaeus in honour of a reformed Zeus, a story designed to give expression to meta-physical and ethical/political principles which Plato wishes to defend, then there is perhaps less need to go so far as to draw the conclusion that the demiurge, like the architect and legislator, must have thought up his model. Perhaps it might suffice here, as a minimal answer, to say that each and every complex of parts, be it a world, a city, or a soul, if it is to function well, must do so according to the same general functional principles (the model), which will always be valid.

5 A Difficulty: Are there Pre-cosmic Imitations of the Model?

Thus far we have been investigating aspects of the demiurge's use of a model in turning a disordered chaotic milieu into an ordered universe. However, certain passages in Timaeus' story can give the impression that this disordered milieu *already* contained imitations of the model, prior to the

---

[57] 55c6: *diazôgraphôn*. Plato seems to have invented this word. He may be suggesting a word-play with the term *diazôma*, frieze (see Hellmann [1992], 88), while referring to the zodiac. The Parthenon was the first Dorian temple in Greece to have a continuous frieze.

[58] In the *Republic* 597bd god makes the form of couch.

[59] One might note that this does not necessarily exclude its having a cause. From the claim: 'all that is generated must necessarily be generated from a cause' (28a4–5), it does not necessarily follow that all that is not generated does not have a cause.

5 A Difficulty: Are there Pre-cosmic Imitations of the Model? 59

demiurge's work. In particular, this milieu includes four types of elements ('pre-elements') which would already be imitations of the model, before the demiurge gave them geometrical shape, making them into the elements as they occur in the present world.[60] If this were indeed the case, then we would be confronted with a rather complicated situation in which the ordered world would be the product of *two* sorts and stages of imitation of a model: a pre-cosmic (or pre-demiurgic) imitation of the model in the pre-elements found in the chaotic milieu, and the demiurge's imitation of the model in ordering the chaotic milieu and making the elements. What could this pre-cosmic, pre-demiurgic imitation be? It seems somewhat complicated, not to say excessive, to have two sorts and stages of imitation of the model, first a pre-demiurgic and then a demiurgic imitation.[61] And how would the pre-demiurgic imitation relate to demiurgic imitation?[62] Furthermore, as regards the argument proposed in the preceding section, it would seem to follow that if the pre-cosmic elements are imitations of the model, then the model would contain Forms of which these elements are imitations, for example a Form of fire.

Perhaps we should not press Timaeus too hard on this. He needs some sort of pre-cosmic stuff in chaotic motion so that he can tell his story of the demiurge giving order (the demiurge has to give order to something), even if there never was a pre-cosmic stage in the life of the world. However, it is not clear that Timaeus really maintains that there are two sorts and stages of imitation of the Forms, a pre-demiurgic imitation and a demiurgic imitation. The passage where the elements appear as imitations (*mimêmata*, 50c5, *aphoiômata*, 51a2) of the eternal model has to do with Timaeus' elaboration of the initial dichotomy with which his story started (28a) – that between eternal being (the model) and becoming (the world) – into a trichotomy: that between eternal being (the model); becoming (its imitation); and a third, the place or milieu in which becoming comes to be (48e–49b). Timaeus says that it is extremely difficult to be clear about this third component, which should nevertheless still feature in his story. In order to describe it, he speaks of the elements, imitations of the eternal, as passing through it, without it having itself determinate characteristics

---

[60] The passages are *Timaeus* 50c5, 51a2 and 53b2 in particular. See Mohr (1985), 108–12; Karfík (2007), 140.

[61] The reverse of such a sequence is described in the *Republic*, where an artisan (demiurge) makes a couch, according to the 'form' (*idea*) of a couch (596b), and then a painter makes an image, an appearance, of the couch, as if in a mirror (596ce).

[62] For some recent suggestions on this subject, see Harte (2002), 261–4; (2010), 133–4, 137–8; Broadie (2012), 196–7.

60 The Model of the World

(50be). The elements are described in their *present* state (49b7–e7; 50b4–6) of continual change, in a universe which has already been ordered by the demiurge.[63] Timaeus promises to deal presently (*eis authis*) with the wondrous way in which these elements are such imitations of the eternal (50c6). This promise has puzzled readers who have thought that the reference is to a pre-demiurgic imitation of the eternal and have not found an appropriate place, later in the *Timaeus*, where the promise is fulfilled. However, the reference may simply be to the passage a little further on in the text (53c4 ff.), where the demiurge imposes geometrical shapes on the elements.[64] It would be this, the imposition of geometrical shape, which makes the elements into imitations of the model. So far, then, Timaeus need not be referring to a period or phase prior to the work of the demiurge and so the elements he describes as imitations of the model need not be such, independently of the work of the demiurge.

However, a stage, or phase, prior to the work of the demiurge is described at 53a2 ff.:

> Before [the ordered whole came to be], all these kinds [the pre-elements] were without proportion or measure. Fire, water, earth, and air possessed indeed certain traces of themselves (*ichnê ... hautôn atta*), but were altogether in such a condition as we should expect for anything when deity is absent from it. Such being their nature at the time when the ordering of the universe was taken in hand, the god then began by giving them a distinct configuration by means of shapes and numbers. (53a7–b5)

These 'traces' (*ichnê*) in the pre-elements are not to be identified, I would claim, with the 'imitations' of the model mentioned earlier.[65] The 'traces' are traces *of the elements, not of models of the elements*. It is to these 'traces' that the demiurge gives geometrical structure and thus makes into elements which are imitations of a model. A trace is not yet, or no longer, an image.[66] It would therefore follow that we need to conclude, neither that there are two sorts, or stages, of *imitation* of the model, nor that there are Forms, in the model, of which the pre-elements are imitations.

---

[63] Kahn (2013), 196–7; Kahn thinks, however, that there are pre-demiurgic imitations of the Forms (198, 202).

[64] See Kahn (2013), 204.

[65] The *toutôn* in the expression *mimêmata toutôn* at 51b6 need not refer in particular to Forms (of the elements).

[66] Plato does not use the term *ichnos* for the relation between a particular thing and a Form. Harte (2010), 133, n. 6, provides a list of occurrences of the term in Plato and some discussion of its meaning.

6 The Place of the World

Of course there remains the problem of what the pre-demiurgic 'traces' of the elements might be. Here Timaeus gives us little help. We might suppose that the traces are indeterminate, confused *je ne sais quoi* which the demiurge will work up and give determination and shape. Later, at 69b2–c1, it seems that the pre-elements might have shared to some extent, by chance (*tuchê*), in the order which the demiurge will give them, by anticipation, as it were.

> As was said at the outset, these things were in disorder and the god introduced into them all every kind of measure in every respect in which it was possible for each one to be in proportion and commensurable both with itself and with all the rest. For at first they were without any such proportion, save by mere chance (*tuchê*), nor was there anything deserving to be called by the names we now use – fire, water, and the rest.

In this case, the traces would be adumbrations, chance anticipations of, not something produced by, that of which they are traces. The use of the word 'trace' (*ichnos*) in this sense, as an adumbration or anticipation of what is to appear later, can be found in the Aristotelian *Historia animalium*:

> In children may be observed the traces (*ichnê*) and seeds of what will one day be settled habits, though psychologically a child hardly differs for the time being from an animal.[67]

Another possibility, which I think is far less likely, would be that the traces had been produced by elements (not Forms), these elements having existed earlier than the traces, sometime in the past. The word 'trace' can also have this sense, the sense of something left from a past era, a memory.[68]

6 The Place of the World

The analogies we have been following between political, architectural and cosmic models suggest that the demiurge will produce the world in a place, just as the legislator and architect will produce their city or building on a site, in a place. And so indeed does the demiurge bring order to a 'place'

---

[67] *Historia animalium* 8.1.588a27–588b1 (trans. A. Thompson). See also 588a19, 608b4.

[68] See Plutarch, *De Herod. malign.* 860a. This possibility might be elaborated as follows. In the *Critias* (see chapter 5, n. 55), obscure echoes (*akoai*) of ancient Athens survived catastrophe so as still to be heard in contemporary Athens. In cosmological terms, this could suggest that traces of an earlier world-order survived a cosmic catastrophe, to be ordered anew by the demiurge. Against this explanation, however, one can object that there is no suggestion in the *Timaeus* that the world *as a whole* has a history alternating between cycles of disorder and of order (of course cataclysms such as that which destroyed ancient Athens are said to have taken place).

(*chôra*), a disordered milieu to which he gives structure. The genealogical analogy which we followed in the previous chapter (section 6), the analogy between the *genesis* of the world (its mixed pedigree, divine intelligence and necessity) and the autochthonous origin of the ancient Athenians (Athena and Hephaistos, and the earth of Attica) also introduces the theme of the place of the world. The physical and metaphysical complexities of Plato's concept of the world's 'place' (*chôra*) are considerable and have stimulated much discussion.[69] Here, while not attempting in any way to deal with the *chôra* of the *Timaeus*, I would like simply to make some observations which we may derive from the comparisons that can be made between political, architectural and genealogical 'places' and the place of the world.

An architect will obviously seek a site for the projected building which is suitable, sufficiently large, well-situated and stable enough to serve as a good foundation (*hedra*)[70] for the building. The city-planner and legislator will also seek out the best area for the projected city. In the *Laws*, great attention is given to determining the characteristics of the best place (*chôra*) for a good city: it must be situated at a sufficient distance from the seashore (protecting it from the corrupting influence of external trade) and of a sufficient size for its defence from outside attack.[71] The earth of Attica is also given close attention in Critias' description of the origin of ancient Athens: Critias stresses the fertility and abundant nature that once characterized Attica, before erosion, denudation and depletion of the soil had set in.[72]

It is plausible then to suppose that Plato is thinking in an analogous way of the place in which the world is made. The terminology he uses points in this direction: not only the use of the terms *chôra* and *hedra*,[73] but also his references to this place as 'nurse' (*tithênê*), 'receptacle' (*hupodochê*) and 'mother',[74] images which could evoke the analogy with the earth from which the ancient Athenians were born as described, for example, in the *Republic* (414e) and in the *Menexenus*:

> They are children of the soil (*autochthonas*), dwelling and living in their own land. And the country (*chôra*) which brought them up is not like other countries, a stepmother to her children, but their own true mother; she bore

---

[69] See, for example, Miller (2003), chapter I; Broadie (2012), 198–237; Slatter (2012).
[70] See Hellmann (1992), 66.   [71] *Laws* 704c ff., 738cd.   [72] *Critias* 110d, 111d.
[73] *Timaeus* 52a8–b1.
[74] 49a6, 50b6, d2–3, 51a4–5, 88d6; Plato's use of the image of a receptive matrix (*ekmageion*, 50c2), on the other hand, seems to refer to technical production.

6 The Place of the World

them and nourished them (*threpsasês*) and received them (*hupodexamenês*) and in her bosom they now repose.[75]

However, there are important differences between the place of the world and the places of good cities and buildings. The place of the world is not a rich soil with a favourable climate, but is indeterminate, moving, chaotic. It is not a place chosen among various possible places. There can be nothing outside it which could threaten the world's absolute self-sufficiency (32c–34a): even the best possible body, or place, if it has neighbours, is not entirely independent. So the demiurge leaves nothing outside the world. He circumscribes it as a sphere which contains and controls all places. A strange 'place' for a world, itself a strange, indeed unique 'animal'.

---

[75] 237b5–c2, transl. B. Jowett; see *Republic* 414e2–4; see further Ruben (2016), 211, on the relation of *chôra* to the theme of autochthony.

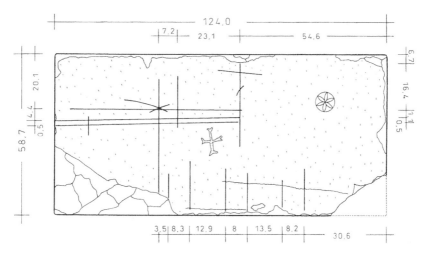

Figure 4 Architectural planning sketch from the temple of Athena at Priene (second half of the fourth century BC), published and discussed by W. Koenigs (see Chapter 3, n. 27).

CHAPTER 4

The Beauty of the World

In the *Timaeus* Plato describes the world as the 'most beautiful' (*kallistos*, 29a5) of generated things. Perhaps indeed his speech is the first systematic description of the beauty of the world. It is, at any rate, one of the most influential statements of the theme. The Stoics were deeply convinced by it[1] and later, in the third century AD, at a time when Gnostic movements were propagating contempt and hate for the world, Plotinus, interpreting the *Timaeus*, would write magnificent passages on the beauty and value of the world.[2]

But what does Plato mean by the 'beauty' of the world? What makes the world beautiful? In this chapter these questions will be approached first (1) by a brief discussion of the distinction Plato appears to make in the *Timaeus* between beauty and the good.[3] In one passage (*Timaeus* 87c) 'measure' seems to relate to this distinction. It will be useful then (2) to look at a section of another late work of Plato's, the *Philebus*, where the themes of beauty, goodness and measure may be compared in more detail. The theme of measure will then take us back (3) to the *Timaeus*, in order to examine the role played by measure, in particular mathematical measure, in constituting the beauty of the world. I would like to discuss in detail the way in which mathematical structures make for the beauty of soul and body in the living whole that is the world.[4] In examining these themes, we will be considering what, in the previous chapter, I have described as the 'detailed plans' the demiurge, as architect, used in realizing his model in the work of making the world.[5]

---

[1] See P. Hadot (1992), 185–8.

[2] Plotinus, *Enn.* 2.9.17; 5.8.8 and 13. A 'most beautiful world (*kallistos ... kosmos*)' is mentioned in a fragment of Heraclitus (fr. 124), in the version printed in DK. However, the source of the fragment, Theophrastus *Metaphysics* 15, 7a15, as edited by Laks and Most, dissociates *kallistos* and *kosmos*.

[3] The relation between beauty and the good in ancient philosophy and mathematics is discussed in a recent issue of *Classical Philology* 105 (2010), in which the contribution by Barney (2010) is most illuminating in relation to the theme of the present chapter. However, she is primarily concerned with other texts and contexts in Plato.

[4] Rachana Kamtekar has helped me with her detailed comments in thinking through issues raised in this chapter.

[5] See Figure 4, and Chapter 3, n. 27.

65

66   The Beauty of the World

I   A Distinction between Beauty and the Good

It is often the case that the 'beautiful' (*kalos*) and the 'good' (*agathos*), in ancient Greek texts, are closely related in meaning. 'Beautiful', we find in these texts, can refer to moral quality and is a word not yet affected by the separation of aesthetics from ethics characteristic of modern thought. The closeness of the beautiful and the good in ancient Greek discourse is said in a nutshell by the expression *kalos kagathos*, which designates an admirable person.[6] It thus seems prudent to be wary on the whole of separating beauty from the good when speaking of Greek philosophical texts. Yet in Plato's *Timaeus* the main speaker, Timaeus, does seem to make a distinction between the beautiful and the good, at least in some parts of his speech.[7] If he does indeed do this, we would need to know in what way the distinction is made and what the distinction means for the relation between beauty and the good.

A first passage where the distinction can be found is at the beginning of Timaeus' speech, where he raises the question as to which model it is that the demiurge would have used in making the world:

> We must go back to this question about the world: After which of the two models (*paradeigmata*) did [the world's] builder (*tektainomenos*) produce it – after that which is always in the same unchanging state, or after that which has come to be? If, now (*men*), this world is beautiful (*kalos*) , and (*te*) its maker is good (*agathos*), clearly he looked to the eternal; on the contrary supposition (which cannot be spoken without blasphemy), to that which has come to be. Everyone, then, must see that he looked to the eternal; for the world (*men*) is the most beautiful (*kallistos*) of generated things and (*d'*) he is the best (*aristos*) of causes. (28c5–29a6).

The Greek particles *men/te, men/de* express a contrast between the beauty of the world and the goodness of the demiurge. It is because the demiurge is good and wishes the good that he makes a world which is most beautiful.

The same contrast can be found a little later in the text:

> Desiring, then, that all things should be good and, so far as it might be, nothing imperfect, the god took over all that is visible – not at rest, but in discordant and unordered motion – and brought it from disorder into order, since he judged that order was in every way the better. Now it was

---

[6] See *Timaeus* 46e4, 88c6.
[7] Translators of the *Timaeus* do not always pay sufficient attention to this distinction, which consequently disappears in their translation; see for example Cornford's version of the two passages discussed in the next two paragraphs. In other places in the *Timaeus* (e.g. 68e2, 92c8), a clear distinction does not seem to be intended.

not, nor can it ever be, permitted for the best (*aristôi*) to produce anything but the most beautiful (*kalliston*). (30a2–7)

The goal of the demiurge is the good: he wishes to produce a world which is unified, harmonious, well-functioning, a 'felicitous god'.[8] In producing this world, by imposing order on disorder, he achieves this goal and the result is a world which is most beautiful. From this we can infer that the beauty of the world is what results when the good is realized in the world.

Before developing these ideas in more detail, we should note that the world is the most beautiful *of generated things*. The model of the world (the eternal paradigm) is *also* described as 'most beautiful', the most beautiful of *intelligible things* (30d2).[9] It thus seems that the question of the relation between the good and beauty concerns two levels: that of the model and that of the product made after the model. If the product, the world, is most beautiful because in it the good is achieved as far as possible, then in what sense is its model most beautiful? Perhaps, we might already suppose, in the sense that it is precisely the *model* of how the good can be realized. But these inferences will require further discussion later. At any rate, we can say for the moment that the beauty of the world is not described simply by saying that the world realizes the good intended by the demiurge: it does this by being modelled after the most beautiful intelligible model (28a6–b2, 30c5–d2). To this we should also add that it is not just (or simply) the model which makes the world beautiful: by being a living animal having intelligence, Timaeus also says, the world can be 'more beautiful', 'most beautiful' (30b2–6).

Bringing these aspects together, one might say, then, that the question of the relation between beauty and the good involves several factors: the relation between the good and the beauty of the intelligible paradigm or model; the realization of the good as the beauty of the world, by reason of the world's relation to its model and due to the ensouled and rational life of the world. But before pursuing these themes further in the *Timaeus*, it may be helpful to take account first of the treatment of the relation between the good and beauty in another text, in the *Philebus*.

2   The Residence of the Good

A distinction between the good and beauty appears towards the end of a discussion presented in the *Philebus* concerning the good, understood as that which can make human life happy (11b4–5, d4–6). The competing

---

[8] See Chapter 3, section. 4.
[9] Beauty also characterizes the political model developed by the legislator in the *Laws* (746b8).

68 The Beauty of the World

claims of pleasure and intelligence to be the good are considered and neither, by itself, seems to satisfy completely.[10] A long analysis is proposed, differentiating between sorts of pleasure and sorts of intelligence (and knowledge), with a view to making a selection and a mix of them that would come near to the good.

> Then here, one might say, we have at hand the ingredients, intelligence and pleasure, ready to be mixed, the materials in which, or out of which, we as builders (*dêmiourgois*) are to build something – that would not be a bad image.[11]

Since neither pleasure nor intelligence can claim to be, by itself, the complete good (61a1–2) and thus claim 'first prize', the question arises as to which of them may still obtain a 'second prize':

> We shall have to grasp the good, either precisely or at least in outline (*tupon*), if we are to know to what we must give, as we put it, the second prize. (61a4–5)

It is proposed, then, to look for *where* the good is, in the way that one might look for someone by finding out first where the person lives (*oikêsin*, 61a9–b2). The good would seem to 'reside' in a certain mixture of kinds of knowledge and pleasure. This mixture includes forms of knowledge and pleasures which are pure and true and accompany virtue. Other pleasures which bring folly, evil and irrationality are to be excluded from a mixture that is to be the 'most beautiful' and peaceful, if one wishes to see, in the mixture, what the good might be 'in man and in the universe' (63e7–64a3).

> To me it appears that in our present discussion we have produced what might be called an incorporeal ordered system (*cosmos tis asômatos*) for the beautiful control of a body which is ensouled. . . . We now stand already at the entrance (*prothurois*) of the residence of the good. (64b6–c3)

What makes a mixture valuable and good is 'the nature of measure (*metrou*) and symmetry (*summetrou*)' (64d9).

> So now we find that the power of the good has taken refuge in the nature of the beautiful. For measure and symmetry everywhere, I imagine, are beauty and virtue. (64e5–7)

Although the progression of this argument is somewhat allusive, it does suggest a distinction between the good and beauty, as if beauty were *where*

---

[10] See already *Republic* 505bd.

[11] 59d10–e3 (Hackforth trans., slightly modified). The image of the demiurge takes up a theme introduced earlier in the *Philebus* (27b1) of a demiurge who is a cosmic ruling intelligence (28c7) identified as Zeus (30d1–2).

3 Measure in the World 69

the good is found, where it 'resides' (or 'takes refuge').[12] Beauty itself seems to have to do with an order in which the principal factors which make the order valuable are measure and symmetry. This incorporeal order is described in the following pages, and we find that what is of primary importance or value in the mixture is measure, the measured and the appropriate (66a6–8). These are followed, in the order, by the 'symmetrical' (*summetron*), the beautiful, the complete (*teleon*) and sufficient (*hikanon*) and suchlike (66b1–2). After them come intelligence, forms of knowledge in soul and finally, in the last place, certain pleasures (66b6–c5).

The image used in these final pages of the *Philebus* of a residence and its entrance appears to concern domestic architecture rather than something on a more monumental scale such as the *propulaia* of a temple. Even so, it seems that analogies can be made with the cosmic construction of the *Timaeus*. The good, in the *Philebus*, is tracked down in its 'residence', which is approached by its entrance. The good takes refuge in the beautiful. The beautiful has to do with an order (*cosmos*), in which measure and symmetry appear to be crucial: they are responsible (*aitia*, 64d4) for giving the order its value. The order, in the mixture of ingredients, is constructed by the speakers in the dialogue, in particular by Socrates, as an order *for* the life of a soul in body, a life that may thereby be happy. The order itself is incorporeal, a *tupos*, a model for life, we might say, in a comparison with the *Timaeus*.

The analogies this suggests with the cosmic making of the *Timaeus* reinforce our impression that, in the *Timaeus*, the good is to be distinguished from beauty, that beauty is where the good is to be found, realized in the most beautiful world. The *Philebus* gives much emphasis to the importance of measure in producing an order where beauty appears. This brings us back to the *Timaeus*, to investigate the function which measure might have in the ordering of the world.

3 Measure in the World

A connection between the good, beauty and measure is suggested by Timaeus towards the end of his speech, when dealing with the relation between the human soul and body:

> All that is good is beautiful, and what is beautiful is not without measure; accordingly a living creature that is to possess these qualities must have symmetry. Symmetries of a trivial kind we readily perceive and compute; but the most important and decisive escape our reckoning. For health or

[12] I attempt later (section 4) to describe what it might mean for the good to 'reside' in beauty.

70   The Beauty of the World

> sickness, virtues or vices, the symmetry or lack of measure between soul and
> body themselves is more important than any other. (87c4–d3)

What is good is beautiful, and what is beautiful presupposes measure.[13]
'Symmetry' (*summetria*) here seems to be the opposite of 'without measure' (*ametria*). As concerning the relation between soul and body, the
one involves health and virtue, the other sickness and vice in body and
soul. But prior to the relation between soul and body in humans, there is
the symmetry constituted by the making of soul in general and of the
body of the universe. I would like therefore to go back to these more
cosmic 'symmetries', as they are described earlier in Timaeus' speech, in
order to identify in particular what measure or symmetry it is which can
make the soul and body of the world beautiful.[14]

(i)   The Making of Soul (Timaeus 35a–39e)

The demiurge of the world makes soul first (a)[15] by constituting (35a1 ff.)
what Cornford[16] describes as 'soul-stuff', a third kind of existence, made
up by mixing together 'being', 'identity' and 'difference', as these three
are found both in indivisible and in divisible being (two kinds of existence presumably corresponding to that which is eternal and that which is
changing and generated, as these are distinguished earlier, at 29a).
The mixing appears to be complete, although some force (35a8) is
required to join 'difference' to 'identity'! The 'soul-stuff' thus produced
seems to be conceived as a sort of two-dimensional strip or band: it must
have both length and breadth, since later it will be divided 'lengthways'
into further bands (36b7), but length seems to be its prominent
dimension.[17]

The demiurge then (b) divides this stuff (35b4 ff., lengthways, it seems)
by measuring off intervals in it (36a1, *diastêmata*). This is done by marking
off a portion (*moira*) of the whole (35b4–5), then by doubling and tripling
this portion, in alternating succession. Thus:

---

[13] Compare *Statesman* 284a8–b2.
[14] I cover in the following roughly the same ground as Vlastos (1975), chapters 2 and 3, but in search of different things.
[15] 35a1 suggests a contrast between (a) that 'out of which' (*ek tônde*) soul is put together and (b) the 'way' in which (*toiôide tropôi*) it is put together. With this we might compare (a) the mixing of knowledge and pleasure in the good life as described in the *Philebus*, and (b) the order given to this mix by measure (section 2).
[16] Cornford (1935), 67.
[17] One might even wonder if soul is three-dimensional, given that it is a sort of strip or band.

3 Measure in the World 71

the portion (1) doubled: 2; doubled: 4; doubled: 8;
the portion (1) tripled: 3; tripled: 9; tripled: 27;
which gives the series of intervals thus produced: 1, 2, 3, 4, 9, 8, 27.

The portion functions, I believe, as a measure,[18] which, by doubling and tripling in alternating succession, produces a series of determinate intervals (or lengths) which are in proportion to the measure (commensurable), as doubles and triples of it. These proportions yield 'geometrical' progressions (1, 2, 4, 8; and 1, 3, 9, 27), or 'geometrical equalities' (identical ratios in 1 : 2 = 2 : 4 = 4 : 8; and in 1 : 3 = 3 : 9 = 9 : 27), the progressions being produced by the successive and alternating operations of doubling and tripling the measure. The length of the first portion, used as measure, is not given (and perhaps not pertinent).

Once the succession of proportional intervals is marked out in the soul-stuff, thus *dividing* it, these intervals are then *united* (36a) by the insertion, in the intervals, of two other proportionalities, 'harmonic' and 'arithmetic' proportions, which give 'identical' (*tautôi*) and (quantitatively) 'equal' (*isôi*) relations (36a3–5).[19] The 'hemiolic' (2 : 3), 'epitritic' (3 : 4) and 'epogdoadic' (8 : 9) intervals thus produced are completed by a final interval: 256 : 243.

The summary I have attempted to give of Plato's text is intended to emphasize (I hope reasonably) certain points: that an essentially one- (verging on two-) dimensional being is structured by imposing determinate intervals which both divide it and unite it; these intervals are proportions (of a given measure of the being) which express identity in the form of different kinds of equality (identity of ratios in geometrical and harmonic equality, quantitative identity in arithmetic equality). The proportions are first generated by operations of doubling and tripling a measure, operations which can thus be considered as ways of making identity dimensional, at various degrees (doubling, then tripling): the intervals thus constituted, as equalities, are dimensional expressions of identity. The structure of soul-stuff thus consists of proportions (see 37a4), which give it identity expressed as different kinds of equality. Kinds of equality also mean kinds of inequality (equality of ratios in inequalities of quantities, and the reverse). Thus geometrical equality can also be described as an 'unequal

---

[18] See Del Forno (2005), 8, who provides a full and clear analysis of the mathematics of this section of the *Timaeus*, and Robins (1995), 380, 385–6.

[19] Plato seems to be making use of a theory of proportions formulated (if not invented) by his Pythagorean friend Archytas. See Archytas fr. 2 (Huffman [2005], 163–81). The three proportionalities might be expressed as follows (see Huffman [2005], 169): geometrical proportion is based on identity of ratios (e.g. 1 : 2 = 2 : 4, i.e., the ratio of 2); harmonic proportion is based on the identical fraction of the extremes (e.g. 6 : 8 = 8 : 12, i.e., the mean exceeds and is exceeded by the same fraction [1/3] of each of the extremes); arithmetic proportion is based on identity of quantity (e.g. 2 − 1 = 3 − 2, i.e., the same quantitative difference of 1).

72 The Beauty of the World

proportion' (*anisôi summetrôi, Laws* 744c).[20] Degrees of equality can be supposed to obtain in relation to their proximity to identity.

The mixing of ingredients making up soul-stuff serves to introduce the capacity in soul to know both intelligible and sensible beings (37a2–37c5), whereas the structuring of soul by a system of proportions seems to be designed to introduce the account of the movements of the heavens and their production of time. The demiurge splits the soul-stuff, once structured, lengthways into two bands (36b7), each band being bent into a circle, the outer circle being designated (*epephêmisen*) by the demiurge as that of the identical, the inner as that of the different (36c4–5). The outer circle, that of 'the identical and the similar' (36d1), is that of the invariant movement of the fixed stars. The inner circle, that of the different, is divided again into seven unequal circles (those of the sun, moon and planets), of which three correspond to the double, three to the triple interval,[21] three having a 'similar' speed, four a dissimilar speed, all moving in ratio (*logôi*, 36d6).

Without going into the astronomical details of this system, the way in which it articulates the distances and speeds of heavenly bodies, we can at least observe that it reflects a hierarchy of value in which the identical precedes the different and both express themselves in (in)equality: the double and triple, the similar and dissimilar. The structured, proportionate movements of the heavens mark out in turn the parts of time, the most evident of which are the divisions into day, month and year. Time expresses, imitates, in number (*kat' arithmon*) – which here must refer to proportions (see 38a7) – the unity of its eternal model, the intelligible paradigm (37d6, 39e1–2).[22]

At this point, it might be useful to take stock of what has been seen so far, as it might relate to the questions raised at the beginning of this chapter. If what produces the beauty of the world is the realization of the good in it, this realization is achieved through imitation of the most beautiful model, the intelligible paradigm, and through the presence of rational soul in the world (section 1). Now if time, as the proportionately structured movements of the heavens, is an imitation of the model, these proportions are first given to soul, when it is constituted by the demiurge. It follows from this, I propose, that the demiurge imitates the intelligible model in structuring

---

[20] Such proportions as the equal and the double are referred to as 'symmetries' in *Republic* 530a1; *Philebus* 25d11–e1. For 'symmetry' as commensurability, see *Theaetetus* 147d–148b.

[21] 36d2–3; six intervals between the seven circles.

[22] In speaking of the making of time, Timaeus seems to have the demiurge redouble his efforts to imitate the intelligible model (37c6–d1), even though it seems that time results from the structure of soul. Does Timaeus wish to remind us of the theme of the imitation of the intelligible model, which is not made explicit in the account of the demiurge's making of soul? Or is Timaeus, as in some other places (see the next section), a bit confusing in his way of presenting things?

3 Measure in the World 73

soul. Rational soul makes the world beautiful in that it is structured in proportions which make of the ordered heavenly movements which it carries out an imitation of the model.[23] The proportions, as different kinds of equality/inequality, are expressions of different degrees of identity/difference, at first in the quasi one-dimensional nature of soul and then in the two- (and three-) dimensional heavens.

(ii) The Making of the Elements (53c–56c)

If the world, as a whole, is the most beautiful of generated things, it is not uniformly beautiful or perfect. The heavens represent what is most luminous and most beautiful (*kalliston*) in the world (40a2–4), which also includes lower levels of existence, a hierarchy amusingly suggested in the conclusion of Timaeus' speech in the account of the fall of souls from their former, fiery, stellar lives to the depths of slithering, murky, aqueous indignity. These levels correspond to the different elements of which the body of the world is constituted. So, having described the making of the soul of the world, Timaeus also needs to account for the making of its body. Body is made up from the elements of fire, air, earth and water, and thus Timaeus offers an account of how these elements are produced.

However, Timaeus had already spoken of the elements (at 31b–32c), before dealing with the soul, thereby reversing the proper order of value which his discourse should have followed, which puts soul before the body.[24] There he had spoken of how fire and earth, required to make the world visible and tangible, were bound by the demiurge to each other by means of two intermediate elements, air and water, acting as the mean terms of a geometrical proportion.[25] Geometrical proportion was used to bind, to unite the elements, whereas, in the making of soul, as we have seen, this proportion serves to divide up soul-stuff. Geometrical proportion both divides and unites, through the equality, i.e., the identity of ratios that it yields. The link between equality, identity and unity was indicated then by Timaeus:

> And of all bonds the most beautiful (*kallistos*) is that which makes itself and the terms it connects a unity (*hen*) in the fullest sense; and it is of the nature of a [continued geometrical] proportion to produce this most beautifully. . . . For as the first term is to the middle, so is it itself to the last . . . so all [the terms of the proportion] come to be necessarily identical

---

[23] We remember (see section 2) that measure and proportion are essential to the good and beautiful in the *Philebus* (64c–66b).
[24] See Chapter 2, section 6.   [25] See Chapter 3, section 4.

74 The Beauty of the World

> (*ta auta*), and, in becoming identical (*ta auta*) to each other, they will all make a unity (*hen*). (31c2–32a7)

Timaeus then corrects the error in the order of his account by dealing with the production of soul (35a ff.), before returning again later (at 53c) to the elements, describing now in detail the way in which they were each made by the demiurge.

If the demiurge makes the soul-stuff, before structuring it, he does not make the stuff of the elements, which pre-exists in a chaotic, irrational, indeterminate *milieu* which includes 'traces' or pre-elements (52d–53b).[26] The demiurge does not make this stuff, but simply imposes rational order on it (e.g. 53b4–5). Timaeus approaches the constitution of the elements in two steps, discussing first (53c–54d) certain mathematical structures, and then (54d–56c) dealing with the production of the elements from these structures.

The discussion of mathematical structures concerns geometrical figures, in particular different kinds of triangles. In comparison with the one-dimensional, linear structures of the proportions used in ordering soul, geometrical figures are two-dimensional structures out of which three-dimensional bodies can be built. A possible explanation of Timaeus' concentration on triangles, in particular, would be that they are the simplest rectilinear figures (out of them squares and oblongs can be produced), with which bodies can be built; circles seem to be figures reserved for souls. Timaeus asserts (53c8–d2) that all triangles derive from triangles having one right angle and two acute angles, which triangles he distinguishes into two kinds: those with (two) equal sides and two half right angles (right-angled isosceles triangles, in Cornford's terminology); and those with unequal sides and two unequal angles (right-angled scalene triangles). He then says:

> This [geometrical shape] . . . we suppose to be the origin (*archê*) of fire and the other bodies. . . . But the causes (*archas*) of these from above (*anôthen*) god only knows and he of men who is the friend of god. (53d4–7)

We have already met this enigmatic passage.[27] Our present enquiry may allow us soon to shed some light on it.

Having raised the question as to what the four 'most beautiful', dissimilar bodies might be that can be changed into each other, Timaeus then returns to his triangles and tells us (54a1–2) that there is only one form (or nature) of the isosceles triangle, whereas there are unlimited sorts of scalene triangles, of which the 'most beautiful' is that which, when doubled, makes an equilateral triangle (54a6–7). It is precisely *because* it produces an equilateral triangle,

---

[26] See Chapter 3, section 5.   [27] See Chapter 3, section 4.

4 Some Further Reflexions and Conclusions

Timaeus suggests, that this scalene triangle is the most beautiful.[28] Its beauty seems to derive from the fact that it can, by doubling, constitute an equilateral triangle. (The doubling of the right-angled isosceles triangle produces a square.) The equilateral triangle is characterized by equality (of sides and angles) and the best scalene triangle achieves this beauty by doubling, thus turning its inequality (of sides and angles) into the equality of the equilateral triangle. Equality and doubling thus obtain here also, as in the structure of soul, but now in the two-dimensional proportions of plane figures.

Timaeus then constructs the bodies of the four elements from these 'numbers' (*arithmôn*, 54d4).

From isosceles triangles: a cube (4 x 6 isosceles triangles) = earth;
From scalene triangles:
a pyramid having equal and similar parts (2 x 3 x 4 scalenes) = fire;
an octahedron (2 x 3 x 8) = air;
and an icosahedron (2 x 3 x 20) = water.[29]

The section closes with the following summing up:

And the proportions (*analogiai*) of [the elements] concerning their multiplicity (*plêthê*), motions and other properties, everywhere god, as far as necessity allowed or gave consent, has exactly completed and harmonized in due proportion. (56c3–7)

4   Some Further Reflexions and Conclusions

For our purposes, we do not need, I think, to get involved further in Timaeus' elemental Legoland, or, rather, in the demiurge's detailed planning and production of things.[30] Perhaps enough indications have been collected from Plato's text to support the following inferences as regards the relations between the good, beauty and measure as they characterize the world.

I have proposed that what makes the world beautiful is the realization in it of the good. To be clearer about what this 'realization' is, it might be useful

---

[28] Harte (2002), 244–7, following Artmann and Schäfer (1993), prefers a somewhat different explanation of the beauty of these scalene triangles, referring to the continuous geometric proportions that the composition of solids from these triangles produces, geometrical proportion being (*Timaeus* 31c2, quoted earlier) the 'most beautiful' of bonds. The explanation is attractive, but is not precisely what Timaeus says in justifying his preference. This is not to say that considerations such as those offered by Harte are not also in the background of Timaeus' account.

[29] These geometrical bodies are elegantly illustrated in Vlastos (1975).

[30] In my account I have left out in particular the problem of the transformation of elements into each other, a process which the interchangeability of triangles is supposed to allow.

76 The Beauty of the World

to refer to an attempted definition of beauty that we find in another work, attributed to Plato, the *Greater Hippias*. There (295c–296e), Socrates suggests that the beauty of something (a horse, a ship, a law, etc.) be defined in terms of its functioning in a useful way in the sense that it is beneficial (*ôphelimos*). What is beautiful thus produces (*poioun*), it is the cause (*aition*) of the good (296e8–297a1). This corresponds, it might seem, to the relation of beauty and the good in the *Timaeus*, as described in this chapter, and might thus be considered an adequate definition of beauty. However, the definition fails in the *Greater Hippias* because beauty is described as producing the good in the particular sense of actually generating it, in the way, for example, that a father engenders a son (297bc). And so, given that causes are different from their effects, beauty is not good, nor the good beautiful, which seems to be a totally unacceptable consequence of the definition. The argument is so crude as to be suspect. One could also have thought (in a sort of Socratic *pensée d'escalier*) that beauty 'realizes' the good, not in the sense that it actually produces it, but in the sense that a complex whole, in achieving its good, its goal, becomes beautiful. Beauty does not create the good, but characterizes the world when the world attains the goal (the good) that the demiurge seeks to achieve for it.

Another way of conceiving of beauty as a realization of the good would be to describe beauty as the expression, the manifestation of the good.[31] Indeed Plotinus, in dealing with the question of the relation between beauty and the good, describes beauty as the intelligible expression of the good, the 'light' of the good, or as Marsilio Ficino translated Plotinus, the 'splendour' of the good.[32] This conception has the advantage of situating beauty, not as the cause (as in the *Greater Hippias*) of the good, but as its consequence. However, it also raises questions about what 'manifestation' might imply: is the manifestation something additional to what it manifests? Manifestation implies someone to whom it is manifest: who sees, and how do they see the beauty of the world? Such questions, for the modern reader, might point to the relativity of beauty to the beholder. However, the modern supposition that such relativity means that beauty is in the eye of the beholder, that it is a matter of personal, subjective taste, rather than an objective reality, would, I think, be rejected both by Plato and by Plotinus: from the differences in our perception of beauty it does not necessarily follow that beauty itself is something subjective and relative, but rather that our capacity to perceive beauty is varied. For

---

[31] This has been suggested to me by R. Kamtekar.

[32] Plotinus, *Enn.* 6.7.21 and 22. In Plotinus, however, the relation between the good (a transcendent, ineffable first cause of everything) and beauty (its first product, intelligible being) forms part of a metaphysical landscape very different from that of Plato.

4 Some Further Reflexions and Conclusions 77

Plotinus, to be able to perceive beauty, we must become ourselves beautiful.[33] For Plato, the beauty attained when the demiurge makes a good world is there, in the world. The world is beautiful in virtue of the fact that it is a world which functions well, in which the good is therefore present, not in virtue of the good becoming somehow 'manifest' (as if some additional property called 'beauty') in it. We are part of the world and we can observe and imitate this beauty, as far as we can. I return to this point at the end of this section.

The realization of the good is achieved in that (a) the demiurge orders the world in imitation of the most beautiful model, the intelligible paradigm. But what causes the world to be beautiful, we have also seen, is that (b) it is animated by rational soul. These two aspects in fact belong together, since the order of heavenly movements and of time, an imitation of the model, reflects the structure of rational soul, as the demiurge articulated soul when making it. From this I have inferred that the demiurge imitates the intelligible model in structuring soul, this imitation expressing itself in the heavenly movements carried out by soul.

The structure in question is one made up of proportions ('symmetries') which correspond to various kinds of equality/inequality, which in turn express identity/difference in a dimensional being. Identity, given dimension, becomes the equality between portions differentiated in that dimension. The account of the making of the elements, in which we reach the constitution of three-dimensional body, makes use of the same themes as those appearing in the structuring of soul: here also, equality, as a proportion constituting two- and three-dimensional objects (geometrical figures and bodies), is fundamental. It is produced by processes of multiplication (at first by doubling), which extend in a range going towards greater degrees of inequality. It thus appears that the demiurge uses the same principles in ordering the elements and body as those which he uses in ordering the soul. Much distinguishes soul from body (e.g., the demiurge makes soul-stuff, but not the stuff of bodies), yet the order which structures them is, in essence, the same: it is an order of proportions expressing equality/inequality and developing from one-dimensional being to three-dimensional body.[34]

I have proposed that equality is identity expressed in a dimension marked off by differentiated portions. The principle of equality, the *archê* mentioned in the second last passage cited earlier (53d4–7), would then appear to be identity, which should thus be added to our description of the intelligible

[33] *Enn.* 1.6.9.
[34] Robins (1995) stresses the importance of proportion in Plato's conception of the mathematical sciences.

model.[35] Identity, given dimensional expression in proportions of equality, would in turn be a requirement for realizing the goal of unity in a complex whole.[36] Wishing to realize the good in the universe, his goal, in particular its unity, the demiurge responds to the requirement of identity in his model by finding its nearest expression, in (one- to three-) dimensional being, in degrees and kinds of equality.[37] These structures of proportionality are the equivalent of what can be described as the detailed plans which the Greek architect, having chosen his model, elaborates in the course of actually carrying out his project.[38] More generally, we might conclude that mathematical structures are what serves to express and translate, in soul and body, the intelligible model.[39]

But perhaps such inferences are too audacious, since such things are known only by god and by the man 'who is the friend of god'! It may also be too audacious to suggest as well that what makes the intelligible model itself 'beautiful' is that it realizes, in its function *as paradigm* (as Platonic Form), the good. But such an inference could be made, in a comparison with the beauty of the world. The beauty of the world, the global beauty in which the good is realized, is achieved through the structuring of the world in terms of proportions (equalities) which express in particular, I propose, the requirement of identity in the intelligible model. As expressing this requirement, both geometrical proportion and the scalene triangles which produce equilateral triangles are 'most beautiful'. However, the model realizes the good, and thus is most beautiful, in a different sense: it is beautiful in the sense that it includes the principles and requirements permitting of the realization of the good in any complex whole and, first of all, in the world. The model must be beautiful in a different way from the way in which the world is beautiful, if we reject the Bardesanes view of the model as just another world.[40]

---

[35] To identity we should in all likelihood add difference, as part of the model, since difference is found with identity in the intelligible unchanging being which the model is and which provides the demiurge with ingredients for soul-stuff, and since the two bands into which this stuff is split are the circles of the identical and that of the different (section 2).

[36] See 31c2–32a6, quoted earlier.

[37] Equality is generated by doubling and (then) tripling an identical measure. Plato also seems to give geometrical equality priority in comparison with harmonic and arithmetic equality (31c2–4). Equality is first listed, followed by the double, among those factors which belong to limit in the *Philebus* 25a7–8.

[38] See Figure 4 and Chapter 3, section 3. The iterative mathematics of the demiurge's planning also evokes the iterative procedures of classical Greek architecture.

[39] As there is a distinction between the model the demiurge uses and the world which he organizes on the basis of the model, so might we distinguish between the good, as the goal which the demiurge has in view, and the good that is in fact realized in the world.

[40] See Chapter 3.

5 A Temple to Divine Wisdom

In organizing a good city in the *Laws*, distributing property in terms of geometrical equality, the lawgiver exhorts us with these words:

> Don't neglect what by nature is likeness, equality, identity and the concordant, either in number or in any faculty producing what is beautiful and good (*kalôn kagathôn*). (741a)

The citizens of a good city, and we as inhabitants of the world of the *Timaeus*, can observe these principles as expressed in the heavens and thus organize our lives so that they, too, will become beautiful and good. This is already hinted at in the *Timaeus* (47bc), but not developed:

> God invented and gave us sight in order that we might observe the circuits of intelligence in the heaven and profit by them for the revolutions of our own thought, which are akin to them, though ours be troubled and they are unperturbed; and that, by learning to know them and acquiring the power to compute them rightly according to nature, we might imitate the perfectly unerring revolutions of the god and reduce to settled order the wandering motions in ourselves.

How these hints might be developed, by having recourse to Plato's *Laws*, will be the theme of Chapters 6 and 7.

5 A Temple to Divine Wisdom[41]

In AD 532, Emperor Justinian began the construction of a church in Constantinople, to replace an earlier church on the site which had been burnt down in riots that had ravaged the city and had left many thousands dead. However, Hagia Sophia was to be much more than just a replacement: in its enormous scale, in the wealth of materials used and in the beauty of its design, it was to become immediately and to remain, in the Istanbul of today, an object of amazement and admiration. We might venture the idea that Justinian, a most Christian emperor, had built a Christian Parthenon for his New Rome. It was especially the interior of the church that amazed, an astonishing display of marble, mosaics, gold and silver, decorating a space structured with great elegance: in the heart of the building a square formed by four immense pillars, which support four semi-circular arches, themselves supporting, together with the pendentives linking the arches, the rim of a circular dome which curves up in radii converging at the summit in a central point.

---

[41] I summarize here O'Meara (2005), where the interested reader can find a more detailed discussion and references.

80   The Beauty of the World

Justinian's architects, Anthemius of Tralles and Isidorus of Miletus, were mathematicians and collaborated in their mathematical work with another, more prominent mathematician, Eutocius. Eutocius taught in the Platonic school in Alexandria, perhaps as the successor of Ammonius, himself a pupil of the great teacher and head of the Platonic school in Athens, Proclus. Ammonius had taught mathematics in Alexandria, as part of the curriculum of Platonic philosophy, as had Proclus in Athens, and we are fortunate to be able still to read Proclus' commentary on Euclid's *Elements*, a basic text of Platonic geometry, in his view. If we look at this commentary, we find that Proclus is less interested in the technicalities of geometry than in the way in which geometrical figures can be read as images of transcendent divine causes, as these causes produce reality. Thus the progression of geometrical figures, from the point to a line, circle, square and other rectilinear figures, images the progression of reality from a first cause, unique and absolute in its simplicity, to lower levels of reality of increasing multiplicity and complexity. This devolution of reality is structured by degrees in the interplay between unity, simplicity, identity, determinateness, on the one hand, and multi-plicity, complexity, difference, indeterminateness, on the other, an interplay in which the first set of factors is primary, being nearer the first cause, and the second set secondary, being a departure from this cause. These factors express themselves in modes appropriate to the various levels of reality, so that, for example, unity and identity express themselves as equality at a lower level, and their opposites express themselves as inequality. In the progression of geometrical figures, the line flowing out from the point introduces indefiniteness, which is limited by a drawing back of the line to form a circle around the point. The circle is the first, most perfect figure, expressing in its unity, simplicity (one line), definiteness, equality (of radii), the absolute unity and simplicity of the point. After circles come figures made of two lines (semicircles); figures made of three lines (triangles); quadrilateral figures (squares and oblongs) and figures with yet more lines. At each level in the progression, equality is prior in value to inequality. Thus equilateral triangles are prior to other triangles, and squares prior to other quadrilaterals, just as circles are prior to rectilinear figures. Following this logic, circular equilateral triangles (triangles made up of three equal concave circular lines) would be prior to rectilinear equilateral triangles. The stereometrical equivalents to such circular triangles are spherical triangles (triangles cut in a sphere), which were studied by Menelaus, a mathematician read by Proclus.

If now we come back to Hagia Sophia and enter the church, looking up to the summit of the great dome, we observe a progression of the dome from its summit to its circular rim, which leads down to semi-circular

5 *A Temple to Divine Wisdom* 81

Figure 5 Hagia Sophia, Istanbul. View of the central dome from below.

arches joined by spherical triangles (the pendentives), all resting on the square base formed by the four pillars. It is as if we see, in this architectural sequence, an image of sequence of the progression of reality from a transcendent divine cause, a progression which also invites us, as observers, up, in a movement of return of the mind's eye, to the first cause. Observers familiar with Proclus' metaphysical interpretation of geometry would, I think, have been able to interpret the meaning of the design of the building in which they were, and understand its beauty. And, in his interpretation of Euclid, Proclus himself had drawn the metaphysical lessons that he learnt from his long study of Plato's *Timaeus*. If Plato, in describing the making of the world in the *Timaeus*, could find inspiration in the procedures followed by architects, whose masterpiece on the Acropolis, the Parthenon, he could often see, so could the architects of Hagia Sophia be inspired in their design by the world described in the *Timaeus*, as interpreted by Proclus.

Interlude

Plato did not finish composing the feast of speeches of which the *Timaeus* and *Critias* are parts. Having spoken of the becoming of the world and of man, Timaeus completes his contribution to the feast and is followed by Critias, who undertakes to speak, as had been agreed, on ancient Athens as a good city which had shown its value in defeating the imperial power of Atlantis. However, Critias' speech does not go far: he tells of the rise of Atlantis and sets the stage for the conflict with ancient Athens, but there his speech stops.[1] And we do not have the contribution which Hermocrates was due to make and which probably concerned the war between Atlantis and ancient Athens. We do not learn much about how what had made ancient Athens a good city is related to what makes the world good according to Timaeus. Some indications of such a relation are given in the *Timaeus*,[2] but a detailed description of how this came about is missing.

Perhaps Plato did not get around to finishing the *Critias* and writing a *Hermocrates*, or perhaps he lost interest. At any rate, the last part of his life is filled with yet other literary projects, also conceived on a truly monumental scale, all of which, it seems, were left unfinished. He had planned a set of four dialogues, the *Theaeteus-Sophist-Statesman-Philosopher*, of which the fourth part does not appear to have been written.[3] And Plato was not able, it seems, to complete a final revision of his last work, the *Laws*, a massive text.[4] In these unfinished projects, in particular in the *Statesman* and in the *Laws*, Plato discusses what makes for a good city and suggests links between the good city and the structure of the

---

[1] Ruben (2016), 322–30, argues that Critias' speech is far from corresponding to a true realization in action of Socrates' good city. However, the early, abrupt stop to Critias' speech means that the matter must remain uncertain.

[2] See Chapter 4, section 4.

[3] See *Sophist* 217ab, *Statesman* 257a. Notwithstanding these programmatic passages, there has been some discussion as to whether Plato really intended to write the *Philosopher*; see Gill (2012).

[4] See Schöpsdau (1994), 136.

84 Interlude

world. It thus seems reasonable to look to these texts for what might serve as a substitute, to some degree, for what is missing from the *Timaeus-Critias* sequence of speeches. This is the object of the following chapters.

Of course, what will be found in the *Statesman* and in the *Laws* cannot be considered to be intended so as to fit perfectly into the sequence of the *Timaeus-Critias*. The *Statesman* and *Laws* belong to other projects and contexts. In particular, the *Laws* describes the model of a good city which is 'second best' in comparison with an ideal city such as that which is indicated in the *Timaeus*.[5] However, the *Statesman* and the *Laws* may reasonably be thought to go some way to giving an idea of the way in which Plato might have understood the relation between a good city, as exemplified in ancient Athens, and the ordered world in which it was born. At any rate, these texts give some insight into how Plato, in his later years, understood the relation between the structure of the world and that which can make a city good.

[5] See Chapter 3, section 2.

PART II

The City of the Statesman *and the* Laws

Figure 6 Athena defeating Encelados. An image such as this is likely to have been seen on Athena's *peplos*.

CHAPTER 5

The Statesman: *A New Robe for the Goddess?*

The sequence of four texts to which the *Statesman* belongs – *Theaetetus*, the *Sophist*, the *Statesman*, the *Philosopher* – has, as its dramatic date, the beginning of the legal proceedings which would lead to the trial of Socrates in 399 BC.[1] Socrates is thus considerably older than he was at the time of the feast of speeches of the *Timaeus-Critias*. The four texts are also dialogues, not formal speeches, dialogues between:

(I) Socrates and the young Theaetetus (then hardly more than a boy, *Theaetetus* 142c), a pupil of the mathematician Theodorus, in search of a definition of knowledge;

(II) the next day, between Theaetetus and a foreign guest (*xenos*) from Elea introduced by Theodorus (*Sophist* 216a), in search of a definition of the 'sophist';

(III) between the guest from Elea and another very young man, who takes over Theaetetus' role (*Statesman* 257c), Socrates' namesake (young Socrates), seeking to define the 'statesman'[2];

(IV) and, with a view to defining the 'philosopher', a dialogue between . . . ? We can only speculate about who might have been the main protagonists of the *Philosopher*.[3]

The guests from abroad had been named in the *Timaeus-Critias*. Here the guest from Elea is not named. He would have belonged to a later generation than that of Parmenides and that of Zeno who, in the *Parmenides*, had come from Elea for the Panathenaic festival when Socrates was a young man. It is curious that the later works of Plato

---

[1] *Theaetetus* 142c, 145c and especially 210d. On the trial of Socrates as the background to the series of four dialogues, see Miller (1980), 1–3.

[2] Miller (1980), 5, relates the young Socrates of the *Statesman* to a Socrates who seems to have been a member of the Academy, suggesting thereby (54–5) a resonance between the dramatic date of the *Statesman* (**T** 1) and the time, late in Plato's life, when it was written (**T** 2).

[3] See Gill (2013), 31, n. 7.

87

88 The *Statesman*: A New Robe for the Goddess?

introduce unnamed guests: here the guest from Elea, and, in the *Laws*, the guest from Athens. The guest from Elea appears to be associated with the philosophy for which Parmenides had made Elea famous.[4] But were Parmenideans still active in Elea, after the generation of Zeno?

If the *Statesman* has a different dramatic date and reflects a different, more informal conversational atmosphere than what we find in the *Timaeus-Critias*, it also seems, however, that the dialogue takes up themes inspired by the Panathenaic festival, a context which is so important to the *Timaeus-Critias*. In particular, comparisons have been made between the use of weaving and a woven cloth, as providing an illustration of political science in Plato's *Statesman*, and the robe (*peplos*) presented to the goddess at the Panathenaic festival.[5] In this chapter I would like to propose further reflections on this comparison. At first I will summarize information concerning Athena's *peplos*, the circumstances of its making, its iconography and the way in which it was presented to the Athenians and to the goddess at the Panathenaic festival. I will then come back to the *Statesman* in order to discuss the extent to which the cloth woven at the end of the dialogue may be seen as a *new* (or alternative) robe for the goddess. In what way might we say that what appears at first in the dialogue to be no more than an image of political science in general can develop so as to produce, at the end of the text, a fabric which may have a specific reference to the *peplos*? The image of political science given in the *Statesman* is, however, incomplete: I will argue that there is more to political science than what the guest from Elea suggests. What this might be, and how it is to be acquired, will be the subjects of the last sections of this chapter, in which I would also like to sketch the relations between political science and legislation, as these are indicated in the dialogue.

1 The *Peplos*

The climactic event of the Panathenaic festival was the great procession which followed the Panathenaic Way up to the Acropolis in order to present a new robe to the goddess Athena.[6] Work on the weaving of the

---

[4] On this, see Miller (1980), 13–14; Blondell (2002), 318–26.
[5] Scheid and Svenbro (1994), 31; Blondel (2005), 59.
[6] Cf., for example, Parke (1977), 38–41; Brulé (1987), 99–105 (with detailed evidence from inscriptions); Barber (1992), 103–17 (with illustrated examples of weaving techniques and of the *peplos*); Holtzmann (2003), 229–40; Parker (2005), 253–69; see Figure 1. There is some dissension among experts concerning various details of the making of the *peplos* and its presentation at the Panathenaea.

1 *The* Peplos

robe had begun nine months before, at the festival of the Chalkeia. At first the project of a robe was chosen by the *Boulê* (the Council), according to a report in the Aristotelian *Constitution of the Athenians*, but this decision was given later to another body, the *Dikastêrion*, due to favouritism shown by the Council. The Council decided on '*paradeigmata* and the *peplos*' (49, 3). The phrase is imprecise and the Greek text may need correction: as it stands, the text can be taken to mean that the Council chose projects (*paradeigmata*) for buildings *and* the *peplos*; as corrected, the text speaks of the Council choosing projects *for* the *peplos*.[7] The task of making the robe was extremely prestigious, it is clear, and a major, very expensive undertaking. It was begun by the *arrhephoroi*, the young girls in the service of Athena, and by the priestess of the goddess, and was carried out by young girls chosen from the Athenian elite,[8] who worked presumably under the supervision of older, experienced women.

When the temples in Athens were rebuilt and the Parthenon finished, the new statue of Athena made by Phidias for the Parthenon was so large (about 12 m. high), that it seems to have implied the making of an enormous robe. At least this is one possible explanation[9] for the practice that is found by the end of the fifth century of transporting the robe in the procession by hanging it on the mast of a ship moving on wheels up to the foot of the Acropolis.[10] This curious arrangement would have had the advantage of conveying a very considerable piece of weaving in such a way that it would be seen by all those who watched the procession as it crossed the city.

The manufacture of such an enormous cloth, presumably involving expensive materials (saffron, for example) and the highest standards of workmanship, must have necessitated the collaboration of a large number of skilled workers. Reports on the design embroidered on the robe – designs could vary – indicate that it depicted scenes from mythology connected with Athena, in particular her victory over the Giants, scenes such as could also be seen on the sculpted metopes of the Parthenon: Athena with chariot and horses, Zeus overcoming the

---

[7] The text is plausibly corrected by Blass to read: 'paradeigmata for the peplos' (cf. Rhodes [1981], 568). For *paradeigmata* as building projects, see Chapter 3, section 3.

[8] Cf. Brulé (1987), 99–105. [9] Cf. Parke (1977), 39.

[10] Barber (1992) reports a modern scholar's theory (accepted by Holtzmann [2003], 238, but questioned by Parker [2005], 269, n. 71) that *two peploi* were made, a smaller one (made by girls and women) and the large one (made by men) transported as a sail. It seems somewhat unlikely that the large *peplos* would have actually been draped on Phidias' chryselephantine statue of Athena, in the way that a far smaller *peplos* had served to clothe the earlier smaller wooden statue (*xoanon*) of the goddess.

90   The *Statesman*: A New Robe for the Goddess?

Titans with thunderbolts, Athena overcoming the Giant Encelados.[11] Perhaps we can imagine that the *peplos* was something similar (but on a far greater scale) to the sacred banners carried today in processions for the crowd to see at religious feasts in Italy, Spain or Switzerland, for example, banners showing the Virgin crushing the serpent, or St. George transfixing the dragon.

2   The *Paradeigma* of Weaving in the *Statesman*

Panathenaic themes can be traced in a number of Plato's later dialogues (and obviously not just in them).[12] In particular, the occasion of Parmenides' visit to Athens in the *Parmenides* was to see the Panathenaic festival.[13] At that time Socrates was young. Later in his life, when he was a mature man, he received visitors from abroad in the *Timaeus-Critias*, with whom he celebrated the goddess, as we have seen, on the occasion of her great festival. The dramatic setting of the sequence of four dialogues to which the *Statesman* belongs, as noted earlier, is still later, when Socrates faces the end of his life.[14] But here also we can find Panathenaic themes. The *Sophist* (246ac) introduces the theme of the victory of the gods over the giants,[15] a scene represented, as mentioned previously, on the Parthenon and in part on the *peplos*. But the *gigantomachia* of the *Sophist* is reformed: neither gods nor giants prevail; both groups find themselves criticized for their ontological limitations. And another Panathenaic motif may be present in the *Statesman*, if indeed the use made there of the example of weaving and of a woven cloth involves reference to Athena's robe. Let us look at this possibility more closely.

In the *Statesman* (274d1), we find a reference to Athena (the goddess is not named) as the divine donor, with her brother Hephaistos, of crafts to

---

[11] Euripides, *Hecuba*, 466–75, and scholia; Plato, *Euthyphro* 6c; and Figure 6. Plato stresses the variety of colours in Athena's *peplos* (*Euthyphro* 6c1–3). Having many colours (*poikilia*) is closely associated with weaving in Plato's *Republic* (373a6–7, 401a2; note 378c4: *poikilteon*). Children and women are said to be much impressed by a multi-coloured garment (557c7–8): Plato may be alluding here to Athena's *peplos*. The *Republic* also discusses the importance of woven images, as well as painted images and the products of other arts, for moral education (401a).

[12] Cf. Nagy (2002), 94–8, who discusses the *Parmenides* and the *Timaeus-Critias* – but not the *Sophist* and the *Statesman* – in this connection.

[13] The example given in the *Parmenides* (131bc) of a large cloth or sail (*histion*), which could cover many people, may allude to the *peplos* presented as a sail at the Panathenaea (section 1).

[14] Cf. *Theaetetus* 142c, 145c, 210d.

[15] See also *Republic* 378c, a passage which Burnyeat (1999), 258–9, relates to the *peplos* (see also earlier, n. 11).

2 *The* Paradeigma *of Weaving in the* Statesman   91

humans.[16] She is, in particular, the patroness of weaving, celebrated, for example, in the poetry of Leonidas of Tarentum.[17] Weaving itself enters the discussion in the *Statesman* a little later (279b), when, in the long search to define the 'statesman', the guest from Elea introduces weaving as a *paradeigma* that will be of help in the search. The paradigmatic method to be used here, itself illustrated by a *paradeigma* (277d–278e), involves using a simpler and more easily grasped object so as to discern relations in a more complex matter.[18] Here, weaving will serve to bring out what statesmanship ('political' or 'royal' science) is, as distinct from other expertises which also claim to 'care' for human communities. The *exemplum* of weaving is introduced as if weaving were something pretty unimportant in comparison with that which it is supposed to show, statesmanship (279ab). The modesty of weaving contrasts with the grandiose (and overblown) *paradeigmata* provided by the myth which had been told just before of the ages of Kronos and Zeus (277b). Weaving, we could infer (if we were ancient Greeks), is woman's work,[19] and pretty minor (*smikrotaton*) in comparison with statesmanship. But at least it is 'at hand' (*procheiron*), and will do.

Despite this modest beginning, the following discussion of the art of weaving becomes quite detailed and elaborate, so much so that the text has been read as a major source for our knowledge of the craft (and terminology) of ancient Greek weaving.[20] The guest from Elea describes various artisanal operations and skills which contribute to the production of woven woollen cloth: carding, spinning, etc. The detail of the whole analysis surprises, if one thinks of weaving as something relatively simple.

The analogy between weaving and statesmanship in the *Statesman* has already been extensively discussed by modern scholars, and it may suffice here to stress some of its major points. The guest from Elea brings out the 'architectonic' (i.e., architectural) function (as Aristotle calls this function[21]) of weaving: weaving is a skill which involves directing and using the

---

[16] Athena also appears with her brother Hephaistos in the *Critias* (109c). In not being named, is the goddess's importance understated in the *Statesman*? Perhaps not: the divine demiurge of the *Timaeus* is also not named.

[17] See later, n. 23.

[18] Goldschmidt (1947) remains a fundamental study of this method. This sense of *paradeigma*, as an illustrative *exemplum*, should be distinguished from *paradeigma* as project and *paradeigma* as an exemplar to be copied, as we find these in the *Timaeus* (see Chapter 3).

[19] Cf. El Murr (2002), 53–4.

[20] Cf. El Murr (2002), 70–3, who points out, however, that Plato himself coined much of the technical terminology found in the text.

[21] *Nicomachean Ethics* 1.1.1094a27; Aristotle is referring to the architectonic function of 'political science'.

92   The *Statesman*: A New Robe for the Goddess?

products of a series of other skills which are at its service. These subsidiary skills are to be distinguished from weaving in that they are skills involving the production of the materials and tools that will then be used in weaving. Thus weaving is defined more precisely, not as the set of all procedures that contribute to producing the components of cloth and the woven cloth itself, but as the skill which coordinates these procedures, which combines and unites these components, which binds together warp and woof so as to make the final product, cloth (283ab). So also is statesmanship ('political science') a directive science, which governs and uses the produce of all the subsidiary (political and educational) skills which vie with it in claiming to care for the community.

Weaving comes back again at the end of the *Statesman*, where the guest from Elea describes the statesman as 'weaving' the city, in the sense that he directs the skills which prepare and educate the citizens, whom he weaves together in their differences into a harmonious whole, binding them (309c–310b) both with immortal bonds (true opinions about the beautiful, the just and the good) and with mortal bonds (marriage).[22] The result is a harmonious city, a 'smooth and "fine-woven" (*euêtrion*) fabric, as they say'.[23]

As the concluding words of the dialogue put it:

> Then let us say that this marks the completion of the fabric which is the product of the art of statesmanship, the weaving together, with regular intertwining, of the disposition of brave and moderate people, when the royal expertise, bringing their life together in agreement and friendship and making it common between them, completing the most magnificent (*megaloprepestaton*) and best of all fabrics (*huphasma*) and covering all the other inhabitants of cities, both slave and free, holds them together with this twining and, so far as it belongs to a city to be happy, not falling short of this in any respect, rules and directs. (311bc, trans. Rowe, slightly modified)

From its humble beginnings, weaving thus leads to the striking 'image' (*eikôn*, 309b5), at the end of the text, of no ordinary piece of woven cloth, but of a magnificent, well-woven fabric: the harmonious city woven for all

[22] We might compare this work of the statesman with that of the demiurge who binds soul and body with immortal and mortal bonds in the *Timaeus* (36a7, 41b, 43a2–6). But the bonds of the *Timaeus* are those used by masons (see Chapter 3, section 4), whereas the bonds of the *Statesman* are those made in weaving.

[23] 310e10–311a1. An interesting (but later) occurrence of the word *euêtrios* is found in the poetry of Leonidas of Tarentum, where the term refers, however, to a weaving *instrument*, a shuttle (dedicated to Athena), not to a garment (*Anthologia Palatina* VI, 289).

its inhabitants by the statesman.[24] A lowly and ordinary craft has produced an impressive depiction of the work of art of true statesmanship. We might say that just as the many skills and expertises needed in the rebuilding of the temples on the Acropolis of Athens find an echo in Plato's description of the making of the good and beautiful universe of the *Timaeus*,[25] so too do the coordinated skills and expertises required in producing the *peplos* for the goddess find a new interpretation in the work of political science in the *Statesman*.

3 A New *Peplos* for the Goddess?

To what extent might we consider this fabric, woven by the states-man at the end of the dialogue, as representing, in some sense, a new *peplos* for Athena, a goddess who not only conferred crafts such as weaving on humans, but also founded Athens and in particular the best city that Athens once was (*Timaeus* 23d–24d)? The term *peplos* is not used in the *Statesman*: the only explicit occurrence of the term in Plato, as designating Athena's robe, is found in the *Euthyphro* (6c), which, however, has the same dramatic date as that of the *Statesman*.[26]

It has been suggested[27] that Plato's well-woven fabric may be inspired by the cloth woven in Aristophanes' *Lysistrata*, produced in 411 BC, which itself is a reversal of the scenes depicted on Athena's *peplos*: Lysistrata weaves a garment of peace (574–86), not the garment of war and victory that was the *peplos*.[28] These comparisons suggest in turn[29] that Plato's well-woven fabric may also be a response to the *peplos*, a rejection of the political vision implied by the *peplos* in favour of another vision, one of a city of virtue and of harmony. Just as Plato criticizes the poets in *Republic* Book II for their unworthy depictions of the gods and just as the *Timaeus* represents a god, the demiurge, who acts as a god *should* in making the cosmos, operating quite differently from the

---

[24] In the *Republic* (557c), Plato had compared the democratic constitution with a variegated garment, and he comes back to the comparison between a woven garment and the fabric of a city in the *Laws* (734c–735a).

[25] See Chapter 2, section 5.

[26] See above, nn. 11 and 15, for probable references to the *peplos* of Athena in the *Republic*.

[27] El Murr (2002), 57, 61–6; Blondell (2005), 57 (with references to earlier studies); denied by Scheid and Svenbro (1994), 31.

[28] In *Knights*, 565–94 (produced in 424) and in *Birds*, 827–31 (produced in 414), Aristophanes had already emphasized the belligerent character of the Athena of the *peplos*.

[29] See Blondell (2005), 59, 61.

94   The *Statesman*: A New Robe for the Goddess?

gods of the poets' cosmogonies,[30] so also is the representation of the political ideal in the fabric woven at the end of the *Statesman* a critical reversal of that which had been promoted on the *peplos* presented to Athena.

The fabric woven in the Platonic dialogue is in important respects different from Lysistrata's garment.[31] Lysistrata's vision of a Panhellenic peace does not adequately resolve the problem of the conflict of diverging interests and parties, nor explain on what basis such conflict might be resolved. Plato's statesman disposes of a science and of a control of subsidiary expertises which is designed to produce a city of virtuous citizens who live in harmony and attain the good. The fabric he weaves is thus quite different from that of Lysistrata, and both propose political visions different from that represented on the Panathenaic *peplos*.

4   The *Statesman*: A Text Woven for the Goddess?

One might consider furthermore the possibility, not only that Plato elaborates a new political ideal in the fabric of the concluding pages of the *Statesman*, but also that the text itself is a weaving with a view to producing this ideal and is thus, in a sense, like the new fabric it offers, a texture in honour of the goddess of what would be a good city. Proclus had suggested[32] that the *Timaeus* is, in a sense, a *peplos* woven by Plato. But perhaps we should say rather that the world built in Timaeus' speech is a temple constructed in honour of Zeus, and the good city woven in the *Statesman* a new robe for his daughter.

We should distinguish in this regard between the dialogue, as Plato's weaving, and the weaving conducted *in* the dialogue by the guest from Elea and his interlocutor, the young Socrates. We find indications in the text which point to the latter weaving.[33] At 267ab, the guest from Elea suggests 'stringing together' and 'weaving' (*suneirômen, sumplekein*) the results from the preceding discussion. At 286d, the dismissal of an appropriate 'length' (*mêkos*) for pleasure may allude to the length of flock produced by carding (see 282e). It has also been proposed[34] that the method of definition by division might be compared with the operation of carding: the separating

---

[30] See Chapter 2, section 4.
[31] For full and detailed discussion of this, see Lane (1998), 164–82; El Murr (2002), 61–6.
[32] Proclus, In *Timaeum* I, 134, 1–135, 15; cf. Hadot (1983), 282. On the comparison, common in antiquity and present in Plato (cf., for example, *Timaeus* 69a7–8), between weaving and composing a text, cf. Blondell (2002), 336–8; Blondell (2005), 50; Nagy (2002), 71–2.
[33] See already *Sophist* 268c5–6.   [34] Blondell (2005), 51, 56; see *Sophist* 226bd.

4 *The* Statesman: *A Text Woven for the Goddess?* 95

out of a 'pure' strand (in this case the statesman) from other (discarded) fibres and wool material (268c10). Pursuing this further, we can say that the practice of definition by dichotomous division ('carding'), leading at first to unsatisfactory results, is followed (and corrected) by the guest from Elea's mythological tale of the ages of Kronos and Zeus. This story takes account of the youth of the young Socrates, who appears to be still not far from childhood (268e). Mythological stories can also be part of the background to a weaving project: stories told (yarns!) as the context of what will be woven, perhaps designs or images (cartoons) of the stories to be woven.[35] After a return to the dichotomic method, the guest from Elea introduces a third method, the use of a *paradeigma* (illustrated by an example taken from children learning to read, 277e), that of weaving. Thus the guest from Elea weaves on with a new method, itself using the *paradeigma* of weaving. And this new method leads to the description of the magnificent fabric of the city produced by the statesman. We have seen that the term *paradeigma* has a variety of meanings in Plato, including not only the meaning of *exemplum*, the meaning first introduced in the comparison with weaving, but also other meanings such as that of a preliminary project (as earlier[36] in the text in the Aristotelian *Constitution of the Athenians*) or that of a model to be copied.[37] The *exemplum* of weaving thus becomes, as the woven fabric reaches completion at the end of Plato's text, a *project* illustrating what the work of political science might look like.

Weaving, earlier in the *Statesman*, had first entered the discussion, as we have seen, as a lowly skill, to be observed in the daily lives of women. We may, therefore, think that Plato did not have in mind in particular the grand and elaborate robe presented to Athena on her feast. However, by the time we reach the end of the dialogue, the woven garment has become 'the most magnificent and best of all fabrics', a fabric with which political art envelops (*ampischousa*, 311c4) all of the inhabitants of cities. No longer an ordinary woven cloth, this fabric woven by the statesman can only be compared, in its grandeur, quality and scope, with Athena's *peplos*. In Plato's dialogue, however, the iconography, the political message carried by the fabric has been changed.

---

[35] Iphigenia, in exile in Tauris, recalls the time when, in Argos, she wove mythical stories, including that of Athena and the Titans (Euripides, *Iphigenia in Tauris* 222–4; see also 814–17). The cosmological myth of the *Statesman* seems to visualize the world as some kind of spinning top (270a), an image that would appeal to a child, but which also evokes the cosmic spindle (for spinning) of the cosmological myth of Er of *Republic* Book X: a child's world filled with spinning, that of toys and that of the weaving women who look after the child.

[36] At note 7.   [37] See Chapter 3.

96   The *Statesman*: A New Robe for the Goddess?

Coming back to the dialogue as a woven cloth (itself presenting at the end a magnificent fabric), if we can say that the guest from Elea and the young Socrates weave, in the dialogue, then we can compare the young Socrates, in his youth in relation to his mentor, to the young girls who are tutored and coached by experienced women in weaving the *peplos*. However, the young Socrates is not an apprentice in the weaving that is statesmanship: he is introduced to the use of basic techniques that might be employed in order to produce a *definition* of the statesman. It is as if the *Statesman* is a propaedeutic, not to statesmanship in particular, but to dialectical skill.[38] The text is not simply, then, the weaving or the woven cloth of statesmanship. It is a series of preliminary exercises in philosophy, with a view to showing what this weaving might be like. But as such it may still in a sense be said to be a celebration of Athena, as patroness of the good state.

5   An Incomplete Definition of Political Science

The young Socrates enthusiastically endorses the image of the statesman produced by the guest from Elea in the concluding words of the dialogue: 'You have again most beautifully completed (*apetelesas*) for us, dear guest, the royal man, I mean the statesman' (311c7–8). But this sounds like the enthusiasm of an apprentice impressed by the work of a master.[39] We may wonder if the work really is finished.[40] For, in Plato, a craft such as weaving involves two aspects: knowledge of the structure to be produced; and the skill involved in handling the materials in which this structure is to be produced.[41] Thus, in the comparison of philosopher-kings with painters in the *Republic*,[42] the philosophers frequently look, in one direction, at the Forms (Justice, etc.) and, in the other direction, at what they want to produce in the citizens, mixing and blending the colours in the image that

---

[38] Cf. 257c, 285d, 286e–287a; Ferber (1995), 63–75. In seeking to define the statesman, who weaves the fabric of a good city, the guest from Elea compares this defining to sculpting an image (cf. 277a, 297e). He thus produces an image of the weaver-statesman. Athena was herself a weaver, as well as the warrior-goddess shown in her sculpted images, her statues on the Acropolis. In any case, such artistic representations are superseded by the delineation in *words* (*logôi*, 277c, cf. 286a6–7) of the statesman in the text.

[39] In this respect, it is not necessary to assign the last words of the dialogue to the older Socrates, still less to add more words to the Greek text so as to give the young Socrates something to say; on this question, see Rowe (1995), 245; Gill (2013), 28–31. Gill (2012), 201, suggests that Plato deliberately creates a puzzle as to which Socrates it is who is speaking at the end of the *Statesman*.

[40] Compare young Socrates' premature declaration at 277a1 that the work may be completed. Miller (1980), 110–12, suggests that the inquiry in the *Statesman* is incomplete, since it does not reveal the knowledge of beauty, justice and goodness which is the foundation of statesmanship.

[41] Karfík (2007), 130.   [42] 500e–501b, quoted in Chapter 3, section 2.

5 An Incomplete Definition of Political Science

they make. So also, in weaving a complex fabric such as the *peplos* of the goddess, the weaver not only needs skill in combining woollen strands but must also presumably be following a design, pattern or cartoon in doing this. Even the demiurge himself, in the *Timaeus*, needs a pattern to follow in his making of the world. It is true that political science is distinguished from productive crafts (such as weaving) in the *Statesman*: it does not belong to the sort of knowledge involved in producing objects, but is rather a 'directive' knowledge which coordinates and directs other skills (260c). However, the 'directive' skill with which it is compared is architecture (259e–260a), and architecture also uses patterns, *paradeigmata*, in carrying out its work.

If the philosopher-kings' knowledge of the *paradeigma*, the Forms of Justice, Moderation, etc., is discussed in the *Republic*, the skill required in the execution of their task, the 'mixing' and 'blending', is somewhat neglected there. On the other hand, the *Statesman* gives some attention to the executive aspect of political science, but appears to say nothing of the knowledge of the pattern to be followed in the 'weaving' of the fabric of a good city.[43] Weaving is not only the intertwining of warp and woof; it can also be the embroidery in various colours of an image, an iconography which follows a pattern as a model.[44] We can come in this way to the conclusion that the guest from Elea's delineation of political science in the *Statesman* is actually incomplete. Young Socrates' enthusiastic endorsement at the end is not the last word. The image made by the guest from Elea is unfinished.

What, then, might the pattern be which political science must know, if it is to carry out its executive tasks successfully and produce the best of cities? We could suppose that this is where the following text of the sequence, the *Philosopher*, might have been expected to shed some light: there is a knowledge which is higher than that of the 'statesman', that of the 'philosopher', which includes what the statesman needs to know as the pattern for his activity. This knowledge of the philosopher plausibly corresponds to what had been described as 'dialectic' just before the *Statesman*, in the *Sophist* (253ce). There, dialectic, the science of the philosopher (as opposed to the false claims of the sophist, 253c), is the ability to distinguish and coordinate what are there called 'major kinds': being, identity, difference, rest, motion.

---

[43] On the deficiencies of the 'architectonic' concept of political science, as presented in the *Statesman*, see Schofield (2006), 164–82.

[44] See above, n. 11.

98 The *Statesman*: A New Robe for the Goddess?

These major kinds appear to correspond, in part at least, to features of the intelligible *paradeigma* which the demiurge imitates in the *Timaeus*. But is this what the statesman must know, as well as having the executive skills appropriate for political ordering? Must the statesman be a god or 'friend of god', as Timaeus puts it (*Timaeus* 53d6–7)?[45]

A more accessible pattern, the ordered movements of the heavens, is suggested in some passages of the *Timaeus*,[46] and it might be thought that something similar is indicated in the cosmological myth that the guest from Elea tells the young Socrates in the *Statesman*. In this myth, the guest from Elea describes a 'world-order . . . which we imitate and follow for all time, now living and growing in this way, now in the way we did then' (274d). However, the imitation involved here is not that which could lead to the emergence of a good city, but that which actually links our biological rhythms (age to youth / youth to age) to the alternating cycles of the world, as it moves in one direction, in the age of Kronos, and then in the opposite direction, in the age of Zeus (273e5–274b1). This cosmological myth, in which Plato, once again, evokes (tongue in cheek) the Athenians born of the earth (271b), is told by the guest from Elea to the young Socrates, almost as a child's story (268de), in order to make the following points: since men, in the present cycle of the world, the age of Zeus, must take care of themselves and their lives (274d), they are not the herd of some god; the statesman, the possessor of political science, is not a god, and his care of the city is not adequately described as 'herding' (274e–275a).[47] The cosmological myth of the *Statesman*, I propose, is not equivalent, on its level of discourse, to the cosmological myth of the *Timaeus*: one is told by a master to his young apprentice; the other by a philosopher and statesman to his festive companions. And the myth told by the guest from Elea does not provide much help with seeing how the order of the world could provide a pattern for political science in its goal of producing a good city.

---

[45] Some scholars have seen in the mention of the 'greatest', 'most valuable', 'most beautiful' things, in the *Statesman* (285e–286a) a reference to the Forms (for a recent discussion, see Thein [2013]). But the mention is somewhat vague; perhaps matters are involved which, at the moment, are beyond the reach of the young Socrates.

[46] See Chapter 2, section 5.

[47] For analysis of the myth and its function in the *Statesman*, see El Murr (2014), 143–88. Lane (1998), 108–10, suggests that the universe, in the age of Zeus, is a model for humans in that they can imitate the autonomy (vis-à-vis god) shown by the universe (i.e., in that they do *not* depend on the order of the universe). One might also regard the age of Kronos as exemplifying a golden age, in some respects, and thus the goal of political science, happiness (see Karfík [2013], 123). Yet it is an age without political order and not, perhaps, for humans (El Murr [2014], 180–8).

6 Political Science and Legislation

The sequence of dialogues to which the *Statesman* belongs deals with knowledge (or science, *epistêmê*): what it might be (*Theaetetus*); what pseudo-knowledge is – that of the sophist – in comparison with the knowledge of the philosopher (*Sophist*); what political science may be (*Statesman*), as distinct from the knowledge of the philosopher. Those disposing of these sorts of knowledge (or pseudo-knowledge) are identified with them, such that the statesman (*politikos*) is identified with his political science: what makes him a 'statesman' is the possession of political science, whether or not he actually has responsibilities and is active. As a specialist of political science, he is a *politikos*, even if he has no opportunity to make use of this science (259b, 292e). Plato's statesman is thus very different from the modern 'politician': the modern politician acts, with or (more likely, perhaps) without the appropriate expertise; Plato's statesman has the expertise, whether or not he acts. The central issue for Plato is to describe a science, or specialist expertise, dealing with the good of the *polis*, comparable to other expertises such as that of the doctor.

In this regard, the sequence of dialogues takes up issues which had been explored before by Plato, in particular in the *Euthydemus* and the *Gorgias*. The *Euthydemus* introduces a 'political art (*technê*)' as dealing with the good of the city. It is identified as a 'royal (*basilikê*) art' in the sense that it 'rules' over other arts and expertises in making men wise, good and happy (291c, 292ce). In the *Statesman*, political science is also identified as 'royal' and as ruling over other expertises (such as expertise in military affairs, in judicial matters, in rhetoric). But the *Euthydemus* does not go much beyond conceiving of such a political art.[48] In the *Gorgias*, Socrates counters the pretentions of sophists and rhetors to 'rule' in the city. He describes their pretentions as counterfeits of a true 'political art' (464b–465c), which cares for the good of the soul, as a doctor and sports trainer care for the good of the body. 'Political art' includes a legislative function (comparable to the trainer's role in keeping the body fit and healthy) and a judicial function (comparable to the doctor who heals disorders in the body). This 'political art' evokes the knowledge of the good for humans that Socrates had declared himself as seeking in the *Apology*. But is this art then equivalent to philosophy? In the sequence of dialogues including the *Statesman*, it seems, as noted earlier, that Plato wishes

---

[48] See El Murr (2014), 13–16.

100   The *Statesman*: A New Robe for the Goddess?

to distinguish between philosophy ('dialectic') and political science.[49] He also rejects, as before in the *Gorgias*, the pretensions of the sophist, but he admits rhetoric, in a subordinate role, to the extent that it can be made use of by political science (*Statesman* 304d).

The relations between political science, legislation and jurisdiction, as sketched in the *Gorgias*, also appear to change in the *Statesman*, to the extent that legislation now seems to be considered, not as a (primary) part of political science, but as an expression of this science, whereas jurisdiction is no longer a (secondary) part of this science, but is relegated to the role of a subservient art. The guest from Elea strongly emphasizes the primacy of political science and political wisdom (*phronêsis*) in relation to legislation: political science is superior to law (294a, 297a). The sole criterion of what makes for a good city is the presence or absence of this science. But what, then, is the need for legislation?

The guest from Elea explains the matter as follows. He compares the statesman to a trainer of group sports, in Athens[50] and elsewhere (294d). The trainer must develop a programme for the group as a whole, rather than coaching each athlete on an individual basis. So also do laws apply generally to all citizens, irrespective of particulars, of differences in individuals and circumstances. Legislation is thus somewhat 'coarse' (*pachuterôs*, 295a), as is the trainer's programme (*pachuteron*, 294e), in its prescriptions, as compared to the finer approach that would be possible if the statesman were in a position to accompany each individual at every moment (294ad). It thus appears that legislation is not the foundation of a good state, but it is required as a (somewhat deficient) *means* for governing the state as a whole. It expresses in a rough and ready way the science of the statesman and it may be written or unwritten.

The guest from Elea then imagines that the statesman might go abroad. He will fix his laws as memoranda (*hupomnêmata*, 295c). On his return, he can change the laws, as circumstances change (295cd). However, in the absence of his expertise, the laws must remain unchanged. The situation reminds us of the story told about Solon,[51] who, having established his laws

---

[49] See the interesting discussions of this distinction in Lavecchia (2006), 145–6 and in El Murr (2009) and (2014), 66–73.

[50] Athletic competitions between groups were included, for example, in the greater Panathenaic festival. The guest from Elea mentions running and wrestling. In the *Parmenides*, the elderly Parmenides suggests that Socrates, then in his youth, needs philosophical training and agrees, reluctantly, to go through exercises with the young Aristotle, for Socrates, to whom Zeno joins himself (135d, 136de), thus forming a small group.

[51] Herodotus I, 29–30; Aristotle, *Ath. Pol.* 11,1; Plutarch, *Life of Solon*, 25, 5–6.

6 Political Science and Legislation   101

in Athens, to prevent the Athenians changing them, left for ten years to travel to Egypt (where, according to the *Timaeus*, he heard the story of Atlantis), Cyprus and Sardis in Asia Minor.[52]

It seems, then, that legislation can express political science, as a ruling ('royal'), directive science, in a rough, general way. Laws can be changed to the extent that political science requires this. But in the absence of the statesman, they must remain unchanged. However, if legislation were *not* to be the expression of political science, if no such science were available, how then could legislation be made? What would make it good? Legislation appears to be part of the 'weaving' aspect of political science, its directive (or prescriptive) function: how does it relate to what might be the model inspiring this science? What if no such model is known?

The *Statesman* does not provide very much help with these questions and what we are told is somewhat obscure. If the only true or correct political constitution is that based on political science and if it includes a written legislation expressing this science, then, the guest from Elea suggests, it might be that other cities may make use (*chrômenas*) of this legislation, although not themselves disposing of political science (297d). But we are not told how such cities could have access to the legislative expression of political science. Plato also mentions legislation not based on political science, but deriving from decisions taken by an assembly (*ekklêsia*) of non-experts, people not having the necessary and appropriate expertise in political science (298cd).[53] Such legislation is incorrectly founded. Its deficiency may possibly be mitigated in the case, mentioned by Plato (300b), where much experience (*peira*) and some advisors may be involved. Yet here also, legislation is bereft of the requisite foundation in science.

The guest from Elea speaks of constitutions other than that based on political science as 'imitating' it in the following passage:

> This is the constitution which alone we must say is correct ... and all the others we are talking about we must say not to be genuine (*gnêsias*), and not really to be constitutions at all, but to have imitated (*memimêmenas*) this

---

[52] Solon's laws were inscribed on wooden pivoting panels, *axones* or *kurbeis*, fragments of which could apparently still be seen in Plutarch's time (see preceding note). There is a reference to the inscription of laws on *kurbeis* in the *Statesman* (298d), in connection, however, with absurd (inexpert) legislation. Broadie (2012), 165, suggests that in the *Timaeus*, Solon visited Egypt *before* undertaking his legislative reforms; however, the text does not actually say this, indicating merely that Solon had to return to Athens from his travels to deal with factional strife (21c6–d1).

[53] The anti-democratic implications of this are clear: Plato believes that there can only be a few experts, if any at all, in political science, just as is the case for other expertises such as medicine (292e–293a, 297bc, 300e).

102   The *Statesman*: A New Robe for the Goddess?

one – those we say are 'well-governed' (*eunomous*) for the better, whereas the others have imitated it for the worse. (293e)

But what could this imitation, for the better or for the worse, possibly be?

The guest from Elea returns to this idea a little later (297c) and gives some clues as to what he might mean. (i) Imitation for the worse appears to take place when action is undertaken, outside or against (*para*) the established laws, by an individual or a multitude not possessing political science (300de). This is 'imitation' in the sense that the statesman can also set aside the laws he has established; it is bad imitation in the sense that the individual or multitude in question does not have the science justifying this action. Correspondingly, (ii) imitation for the better obtains when people, not having the necessary science, never act outside the established laws (301a). It thus appears that the imitation involved is quite restricted in scope[54]: it does not appear to entail that a legislation based on political science be actually known to cities and copied by them (without being understood) in their own legislation. In the absence of science, cities can imitate true legislation, for the better, by sticking to their established laws; they imitate for the worse in giving themselves, illegitimately, the right to supersede legislation. It is perhaps in this restricted sense that we may read the guest from Elea's statement about people who 'come together and write things down, chasing after the traces (*ichnê*) of the truest constitution'.[55]

7 World/City/Home: the *Timaeus*, the *Statesman* and the *Philebus*

Before moving to the *Laws*, where there will be more scope for dealing with the questions raised in the preceding section, it might be appropriate to pause by attempting a brief correlation between the three dialogues which have been discussed in particular thus far, the *Timaeus*, the *Philebus* and the *Statesman*. Perhaps one might relate the *Timaeus*, the *Philebus* and the *Statesman* to each other in the following way. The *Philebus* concerns an order (*cosmos*) to be brought to our (human) lives (64b), just as the demiurge, in the *Timaeus*, brings order to the world. In dealing with this order, the speakers of the *Philebus* track down the good in its residence

---

[54] I follow here the detailed analysis provided by Rowe (1995), 232, with further discussion by Rowe, in Rowe and Schofield (2000), 245–9, and by El Murr (2014), 235–57.

[55] 301e. We are reminded of the 'traces' of the four elements in the *Timaeus* (see Chapter 3, section 5). What these political 'traces' might be is unclear. Might there be a connection, in part at least, with the obscure 'rumours' of ancient Athens that still survived in Athens according to the *Critias* (109e2; see Chapter 1, n. 17)? Compare the memories of the reign of Kronos surviving in the reign of Zeus, in the myth of the *Statesman* (271ab).

7 *World/City/Home: The* Timaeus, Statesman *and the* Philebus   103

(*oikêsis*, 61a9), finding that it has taken refuge, as beauty (64e), in the entrance (*prothurois*, 64c). The word *prothuron* is a term belonging to domestic architecture,[56] its equivalent in monumental architecture being the *propulaia* of a temple. As, then, the good of the city resides in the temple of its god (or goddess) and its beauty in the *propulaia* (the *propulaia* of Mnesicles on the Acropolis were built at the time of the finishing of the Parthenon), so also may it reside in the domestic 'home' (*oikos*) of human lives, as indeed it also resides in the *cosmos*, which, however, being all-encompassing, needs no entrance. So might we link the *Philebus*, the *Statesman* and *Timaeus*, as dealing with the good and the beautiful in human life, at home, in the city and in the world.

---

[56] Cf. Hellmann (1992), 349; El Murr (2010), 374–6.

Figure 7 The law code at Gortyn, Crete.

CHAPTER 6

The Legislators of the Laws

Plato's *Statesman* introduces important ideas on the subject of what would constitute a city which is good. Such a city must be founded on 'political science' if it is to be good. This science, which directs, 'rules', other social and political competences, finds expression in legislation of which other cities might make use, thus becoming good in their turn as adopting a legislation based on political science. However, Plato leaves a number of questions open in the *Statesman*, as noted in the previous chapter. Legislation is an expression of and a means used by political science in order to achieve its ends. But how, one wonders, is political science to be acquired? And what is the actual content of political science and the relation of this content to the legislation which the statesman, who possesses political science, develops? Might the knowledge which is political science include a 'model' that inspires political science in legislating? If there is such a model, how would it relate to the Forms or, perhaps, to a world-order such as that of the beautiful and good world of the *Timaeus*? What relation might there be between knowledge of what makes the world-order good, as this order is described in the *Timaeus*, and the science and legislation which would establish a good city such as ancient Athens? Other cities may make use (*chrômenas*) of good legislation based on political science, according to the *Statesman* (297d). But how are they to do this? How do they gain access to this legislation? And if no such access is available, how could there be any legislation that might be, to some degree, good?

More help can be found with these questions if we turn to Plato's last major project, the *Laws*. In this chapter and in the next, I would like to propose a reading of the *Laws* which takes up these questions. In proceeding like this, I must, of course, leave aside many other subjects Plato covered in this vast work. In the *Laws*, we find many statesmen, many legislators and legislations of various sorts. In this chapter I will consider two groups of legislators: the three interlocutors of the dialogue, who develop a legislative code in their discussion (*logôi*, 702e); and the legislators who are part of the

106   The Legislators of the *Laws*

legislative code thus developed. In the next chapter, I will examine the
political order that the three interlocutors elaborate in their legislation,
with the purpose of discerning the founding principles that might underlie
this order, the knowledge presupposed by this order. But first it will be useful
to consider the *mise en scène* of the text.

1 On the Road to Mount Ida

Three elderly gentlemen, Cleinias from Knossos, Megillos from Sparta and
an unnamed guest from Athena's city (626d), set out together in mid-
summer, in Crete, on a walk from Knossos to the cave on Mount Ida where
Zeus is said to have provided Minos, his son, with the legislation Minos
gave to the Cretan cities (624ab). In the course of their walk, the three men
discuss political structures and legislation. Under the impulsion of the
Athenian guest, they discuss what makes for good or bad constitutions and
laws, reaching criticisms of features of the institutions of each of the cities
which they represent (Knossos, Sparta and Athens) and developing the
legislative and institutional contours of what would be a good city. As it
happens, Cleinias has been designated (with nine others) by his city to
elaborate laws for the founding of a new colony in Crete (702cd). And so he
hopes that he may be able to make use (*chrêsaimên*) of the legislation he and
his interlocutors develop, during their walk, in his own task of founding
a future colony (702d, 722a).

 This scenario, for Plato's readers, is somewhat startling and baffling.
(One can imagine some of Plato's students mumbling: 'What on earth is
the old man up to now?') We are far from the familiar haunts of Socrates
in, or at most a little outside Athens. Socrates, old or young, is not there,
perhaps precisely because he must stay in Athens. But who, then, is this
unnamed guest from Athens? Why Crete? And when is this discussion in
Crete supposed to be happening?

 There does not seem to be any clear indication of the dramatic date
(**T** 1) of the dialogue. However, the Athenian guest would appear to refer
to events which took place near the time when Plato would have been
working on the text.[1] In other words, the dramatic date (**T** 1) may be quite
close to the date of composition (**T** 2). Socrates would then have long
been dead, as Parmenides was in the *Statesman*. However, the evidence is
not decisive: Plato is not above anachronisms and some hints can also be

---

[1] See 638b, which appears to refer to events that took place in 364 and 352 (Schöpsdau [1994], 209).

2 The Three Interlocutor-Legislators
107

found in the text pointing to an earlier dramatic date, perhaps a generation or more earlier.[2]

Who is the Athenian guest? Not Socrates, surely.[3] Plato himself, perhaps?[4] Plato seems to make gentle fun, in the text, of his three interlocutors, who play at legislation, an old man's game (685a, 712b, 769a). Is he making fun of himself? He would then be creating a distance between himself and the image of himself given by the Athenian guest. The guest from Athens is unnamed, as is the guest from Elea in the *Sophist* and the *Statesman*. If the guest from Elea is in some sense a philosophical avatar of Parmenides, would then the guest from Athens be an avatar of the Athenian legislator who could rival the mythical legislators of the Cretans (Minos) and Spartans (Lycurgos), i.e., Plato's ancestor, Solon, whose travels abroad feature in the *Timaeus* and perhaps in the *Statesman*?[5] Being an unnamed guest would then have a comparable function, in the *Sophist-Statesman* and in the *Laws*. But why Crete?

Perhaps the effect of distantiation can be achieved not just in time – the distance between **T** 1 and **T** 2 – but also in space and in culture. Crete, in both respects, is far from Athens (753a). In the *Laws* it appears as if Crete is quite cut off from the world shared by the Athenian and the Spartan (Cleinias does not appear to know Homer very well, 680c), an archaic place which, in its archaism, could serve as the sort of mythical place where a good city might possibly be founded, as ancient Athens, in the *Timaeus*, was founded in an archaic age.[6]

2   The Three Interlocutor-Legislators

The most immediate attraction of Crete, in the *Laws*, seems to be the story of the communication by Zeus on Mount Ida of legislation to Minos of Knossos. Zeus, in any case, had a special relation with Crete, where he was born and raised. And in instructing there his son Minos in legislation, he also gave Crete a special importance with respect to the divine origins of human laws. In going together on the path to Mount Ida, the three interlocutors are

---

[2] Megillos may correspond to a Spartan active in 410–17 and 396; see Nails (2002), 197–8; Piérart (2008), 531–2 (**T** 1 of 404–394). On anachronisms in Plato, see Erler (2007), 80.

[3] As Aristotle seems to think (*Politics* 2.6), because, it appears, it is Socrates who offers theories in the *Republic*, with which Aristotle compares those of the *Laws*. But Socrates notoriously did not travel (Plato, *Crito* 52b).

[4] For the similarities between the Athenian guest and Plato, see Schöpsdau (1994), 106–7.

[5] See Rowe (2007), 257; Chapter 5, section 6.

[6] See Morrow (1960), 17–18, on the archaic aspect of Crete. I am indebted to Irmgard Männlein-Robert for her help with this point.

in effect following in the footsteps of Minos, and the legislation they develop as they walk can be seen as placed under the protection and inspiration of Zeus (see 968b). Furthermore, Cleinias must think about the colony that is to be established in Crete and he hopes to be able to make use of the conversation with Megillos and the Athenian guest in his own planning of the colony. The legislation for a good city developed by the three interlocutors is thus somewhere on the way between the divinely revealed legislation of Minos and the project for a new colony that will subsequently occupy Cleinias.

If Crete and Cleinias can claim one divinely revealed legislation, that revealed by Zeus, Sparta and Megillos can claim another, that supposedly revealed by Zeus's son Apollo to the legislator of the Spartans, Lycurgos. The Athenian guest does not refer to Zeus' daughter, Athena, as the divine source of Athenian law, even if he himself is associated with the goddess (626d). Solon, the Athenian legislator, is not said to be divinely inspired, but he does not seem to be considered, in the *Laws*, inferior as a legislator to Minos and Lycurgos. Notwithstanding this (it seems graduated) divine authority of Cretan, Spartan and Athenian legislation, the three interlocutors subject the laws of their cities to criticism. The Cretan and the Spartan submit with good grace to the fundamental critique of their constitutions which is developed by the Athenian guest in Books I–III – theirs are cities organized for war which foster merely a narrow, military form of courage – just as the Athenian criticizes the excessive democracy of his own city. However, this critique does not necessarily touch the divine legislators: Minos and Lycurgos are not to be charged with the narrowness found in the Cretan and Spartan political systems (630d), and the excessive democracy of Athens represents a degradation that took place after the Persian wars (701ac). But what of the three interlocutors themselves? How do *they* develop legislation, as they follow the path taken by Minos?

It must be said that it is the Athenian guest who leads the way in the discussion. The Cretan and Spartan graciously follow him, in a spirit of hospitality and mutual esteem, even if his comments could easily have offended their citizen pride. The Athenian appears to be learned and competent in many fields, in mathematics, astronomy, cosmology, education, history.[7] Cleinias and Megillos can also contribute information and comments, but on the whole they are willing to follow the Athenian's lead, as far as they can. The fundamental point that the Athenian makes, in criticizing various constitutions and legislations, is that they are orderings aimed at

---

[7] Schöpsdau (1994), 106–7.

2 The Three Interlocutor-Legislators

achieving improper goals. The Cretan and Spartan states are organized with war and military courage as their goal. But the Athenian argues against this and for another goal for legislation: the common good, which, as we have seen, includes peace, freedom, intelligence and all four cardinal virtues, wisdom, moderation, justice and courage (in a wider sense).[8] Not only can this determination of the good, as the goal of legislation, serve as a basis for criticism of political structures which promote other goals, or a narrow and partial conception of this goal; it can also be used as a basis for developing a structuring of society, a legislative code, which will be the means for realizing the good of the members of this society. Thus the Athenian guest elaborates a legislative code for a good state in Books V–XII of the *Laws*, a code which, as I have pointed out,[9] is a 'paradigm' (in the sense of project) that can be used, in adapted form, in the founding of a city such as the one Cleinias is envisaging.[10] The Athenian claims that the model should be elaborated completely, before the move is made to founding a particular state.[11] And indeed the model he develops is extremely extensive and detailed.

In the next chapter, I would like to look more closely at the Athenian's legislative paradigm, with a view to describing the knowledge it involves. This knowledge can be considered part of the political science possessed by the Athenian guest, a science which allows him to legislate, in conversation with Cleinias and Megillos. We can already say that his political science includes a proper grasp of the good, as this concerns humans living together in society. It is this knowledge of the good, together with knowledge of other matters yet to be described (in the next chapter), which inspires good legislation taking the form of a paradigm. Even if

---

[8] See Chapter 3, section 2. Although the Athenian insists that one should promote the common good of the whole of the state (*sumpasês tês poleôs*), and not the interests of one segment of society, as opposed to those of another (715ab), this good appears to apply unequally, for example, to foreign residents and slaves; on this see Morrow (1976), in particular 43–4.

[9] See Chapter 3, section 2.

[10] As well as the term *paradeigma* (discussed earlier, Chapter 3, section 2), a related term, *hupographê*, is used in the *Laws* by the Athenian for the plan he proposes (737d7; see 734e6, 803a [boat-building] and *Republic* 504d6–7, 548d), a term which can also designate an architect's project, for example in an inscription from Priene in which the second-century BC architect Hermogenes dedicated the project of a temple he had contracted to build to *Agathê Tuchê* (see Hellmann [1992], 318; Koenigs [2012], 146). A further term used in the *Laws* is *perigraphê* (770b8, 876d7). *Paradeigma* also occurs in the *Laws* as used in the sense of exemplar (876e); see Chapter 3, section 3. In his *De anima*, Aristotle proposes a general sketch (413a9–10: *tupôi . . . hupogegraphthô*) of soul, to be specified later with respect to the different psychic functions, whereas in the *Nicomachean Ethics*, he provides an outline (*perigegraphthô*) of the good life for humans, which will be 'filled in' (*anagrapsai*) later (1098a20–22): the reference seems to be to painters who colour in a sketch; see Aristotle, *Generation of Animals* 2.6. 743b20–25: painters make sketches (*hupograpsantes*) which they fill in with colours; Plato, *Republic* 501ab (quoted previously, p. 43), *Statesman* 277bc, Männlein-Robert (2010), 122.

[11] See 746bd quoted earlier, Chapter 3, section 2.

110   The Legislators of the *Laws*

they walk in the footsteps of Minos, on his way to being instructed by
Zeus, the three interlocutors of the *Laws* develop *themselves* their legislative code for a good city.[12] Or rather the Athenian guest, who disposes of
wide scientific competences, develops this code in collaboration with
other elderly, experienced men. This code, as a paradigm, might then
be made use of, adapted, adjusted in various ways by Cleinias and his
fellow Cretans as they set about founding a colony in Crete which will
receive, in this way, good legislation by which it may live.

The *Laws* thus throws some light on matters which remain obscure in
the *Statesman*: how the statesman may develop legislation as an expression of his science; and how states may acquire and make use of good
legislation, even if they do not themselves originate it. These points,
however, will need to be refined as we move to the legislative code of the
Laws and examine the function of statesmen and legislators as described
in this code.

3   The Legislators in the Legislative Code of the *Laws*

The constitutional and legislative paradigm developed by the three interlocutors of the *Laws* includes, as its top magistrates, two groups which
overlap: the 'Guardians of the Laws' and the 'Nocturnal Council'.
The Guardians (or 'saviours') of the Laws are the most important executive
magistrates and include thirty-seven elected citizens of mature age (752de).
One of their primary functions is precisely that of protecting the laws. This
may be taken as corresponding to the requirement formulated in the
Statesman that legislation not be changed, particularly when the political
science which would justify this change is absent.[13] However, although this
'guarding of the law' is certainly important, it does not seem to exclude the
possibility of legislating. Ten of the Guardians of the Laws are members of
the Nocturnal Council, which has legislative functions. Furthermore,
a legislator, such as the three interlocutors of the *Laws*, who hands over
legislation to those who will guard his laws is aware of his limitations and of
the need, with the passage of time, for adjustments, corrections and improvements in his legislation: the Guardian of the Law (*nomophulax*) will then
also need to be a legislator (*nomothetês*, 769d–770a). The original legislator will try to effectuate this extension of the competence of the

---

[12] The sense in which the legislation of the three interlocutors, if not directly revealed by a god, can still
be considered divinely inspired will be considered in Chapter 7, section 6.

[13] In the *Laws* (656e) the Athenian guest refers in admiration to Egyptian educational laws that have
remained unchanged for 10,000 years!

3 The Legislators in the Legislative Code of the Laws   111

Guardian of the Law by instructing him, in a speech which the Athenian imagines, which reminds him precisely of the proper goal of legislation (770b–771a). Just as this goal is that in relation to which good legislation is developed in the first place, as a means of realizing the goal, so too is it in relation to this same goal that Guardians of the Laws will be able to legislate in making changes in the law, adjusting and improving it as time and need require.

The legislative function is most clearly assigned, in the constitutional paradigm of the *Laws*, to the 'Nocturnal Council', which is described in the last Book (XII) of the *Laws*. This is a body made up (961a) of the ten most senior Guardians of the Laws; the most distinguished citizens[14]; citizens who have been chosen as having the appropriate qualifications for going abroad, observing other political systems, reporting back to the Council regarding that which they have observed which might be advantageously adopted in the state's legislation. It is interesting that even in a good state, intellectual isolationism is to be avoided: there is something to be learnt from other states, where 'divine men' may also be found,[15] and a good state is always perfectible (951bc).

The primary function of the Nocturnal Council is that of guarding, protecting the state (961c ff.). What this means is constant attention to and knowledge of the good of the state (962a ff.), the goal (*skopos*) which the statesman, as a ruler, should clearly grasp. It is in relation to this goal that the ways in which (*tropos*) this goal may be achieved – be they laws, or people – will be considered. Thus, just as legislation, in the *Statesman*, is a means for achieving the political goal, the good, so here, in the *Laws*, the Nocturnal Council examines and adjusts legislation in constant reference to the goal of the state. It is an adequate knowledge of this goal which will justify a legislative practice which evolves, changing with time, with the changing of things, with new information and ideas brought by observations, at home and abroad, and by further scientific research. Through the Nocturnal Council, the paradigmatic state of the *Laws* will possess the political science[16] which will make of legislation, not something that is absolute in

---

[14] Referred to as priests at 951d, where the present and former ministers for education are also included in the Council and each member of the Council is to be accompanied by a carefully chosen younger man who is to receive an advanced scientific training, in particular as regards legislation: a sort of apprentice legislator (951e–952a).

[15] This seems to be a reference to figures comparable to Minos and Epimenides (another Cretan, and friend of Athens, mentioned at 642d). See *Phaedrus* 258c1–5.

[16] The Guardian of the Law is described as a 'legislating statesman' (*politikôi nomothetounti*) at 959e. Earlier in the *Laws*, being a proper 'statesman' has to do with having the proper political goal (628d), as compared with 'so-called statesmen' (693a). 'Political art' is mentioned at 650b, 875a.

112   The Legislators of the *Laws*

itself and unchangeable, but a means, a political instrument, to be constantly modulated and improved.[17] The essential knowledge involved is that of the proper goal. In stressing this, the Athenian guest takes up again, at the end of the *Laws* (961de), the critique of erroneous goals with which his discussion with Cleinias and Megillos had begun in Book I.

As well as having attained knowledge of the good of the state (his goal), such that he can explain it and show how good laws and actions relate to it (963a–966a), the legislator must also know about the gods, as far as it is possible for humans. In this connection, the Athenian refers (966c) to the argument developed earlier, in Book X, which sought to show that the gods exist, that they exercise providence and that they are good. This argument will be considered in Chapter 7 (section 6), in the context of a discussion of the cosmology of the *Laws*. It will suffice here to indicate that the argument had been developed as a means for persuading 'atheists', i.e., those who deny the existence of the gods or their providence or who affirm other gods, to abandon their beliefs. Here, at the end of Book XII, the Athenian stresses two claims that lead one to being persuaded about the gods (966de): first, that 'soul is what is most prior and divine of all the things whose movement, acquiring becoming, produces eternally flowing existence'[18]; and second, that intellect rules the movements of the heavenly bodies and of all in the universe that it has ordered. These two claims, which summarize the argument concerning the gods in Book X, but which also could be taken as expressing the essence of the cosmology of the *Timaeus*, show that the legislator must be competent in cosmology and astronomy. Far from being a source of atheism, as had been supposed to be the case for some philosophers, astronomy fosters belief in the gods and their ordering of the universe (967ac). And this, in turn, as will be seen in Chapter 7, is of importance to the life of a good state.

The Athenian then repeats the two fundamental claims:

> First, that soul is the most prior of all those things which have taken part in becoming, and that it is immortal and rules over all bodies; and second (a doctrine we've expounded often enough before), that the leader[19] of beings is reason in the heavens (967d).

To this knowledge which the legislator should possess the Athenian guest adds a mention of (unspecified) studies prior and necessary to astronomical

---

[17] See also 744a. On the Nocturnal Council's function in modifying law, see Bobonich (2002), 391, 408.

[18] For this translation, see Schöpsdau (2011), 596–7.

[19] I follow Diès' conjecture here; see Schöpsdau (2011), 600.

knowledge, and a comprehension 'of what is common in these in respect to the Muse' (967e). The references here are somewhat vague, but perhaps what is involved is the mathematical knowledge needed for astronomy,[20] and a musical and/or poetical intelligence relating to mathematical and astronomical truths. The legislator will then use this knowledge fittingly (*sunarmottontôs*) with respect to ethical and legislative practices, and will be in a position to provide, where possible, an explanation of these.

The Athenian guest has thus provided a sketch of the scientific competences required of the future legislators of the paradigm state he is outlining with his two companions. However, he refuses to go into further detail, at the moment, as regards the specifics of the curriculum which will be followed in the scientific education of the members of the Nocturnal Council.[21] A fuller account of this curriculum, if it is to be understood, presupposes, it appears, the scientific competence that is to be acquired (968de). The Athenian guest undoubtedly possesses this competence, but it is likely that his two companions do not. However, the Athenian expresses willingness to explain his views on a scientific curriculum, if the three companions go further and take the risk of engaging themselves in the founding of a state (968e–969d). It is with their willingness to take this risk – a toss of the dice (968e) – that the *Laws* ends, precisely at the point of transition from the elaboration of a political paradigm to the founding of an actual state. The end of the text points to a new beginning, left unwritten, yet to emerge in the mythical landscape of Crete.

4   Echoes of another Festival?

The three elderly gentlemen make their way towards Zeus' cave on Mount Ida. They are far from the noise and turmoil of Athens and its festivals. However, there are suggestions of the presence of an Athenian festival in the life of the paradigm which they elaborate. The festival is not the context of their discussion, but seems to be part of their description of the paradigm. Early in the discussion, the question of the pleasure of drinking arises: the Spartan Megillos expresses his condemnation of the drunken revellers he saw at festivals of Dionysus organized by the Athenians and in Tarentum, where the whole city was inebriated (637b). The Athenian attempts to show that drinking parties can have

---

[20] See 818c.

[21] One is reminded of the curriculum of studies to be followed by future philosopher-kings, as had been described in the *Republic* Books VI–VII. The pseudo-Platonic *Epinomis* (traditionally attributed to a pupil of Plato) seems to be intended to present this scientific curriculum in more detail.

114   The Legislators of the *Laws*

an educational function and he refers again in this connection to the
festival of Dionysus (650a). At this festival there was also dancing and
singing, whose educational importance is emphasised by the Athenian
(653d) and will be discussed in more detail in the next chapter. Dancing
and singing choruses performed as part of the competitions between
tragedies and between comedies which were organized during the City
(or Great) Dionysia in Athens.[22] The Athenian refers critically (701a) to
the 'theatocracy' that had evolved in democratic Athens, where catering
to subjective arbitrary pleasures, rather than seeking moral edification,
had come to dominate. Through a rigorous control of the productions of
the poets, the legislators of the paradigm state shape these public performances so that the state thereby will be made into the 'truest drama'
(*tragôdia*), an 'imitation of the most beautiful and best life' (817b).[23]
It thus looks as if Plato wishes to include the Dionysia in the life of his
paradigm state in the *Laws*, reforming the festival so as to take advantage
of its powerful educational and political potential in shaping a good
society.[24] Dionysus is reformed in the *Laws*, as Zeus is in the *Timaeus*
and Athena is in the *Statesman*. Comparing Plato's reformed Panathenaic
and Dionysian festivals, we can visualize the Panathenaic festival of the
Timaeus and the *Statesman* as bringing us high up on the Acropolis,
towards the divine rationality (Zeus) which structures the movements of
the heavens and the political science (Athena) which makes use of this
rationality in organizing a good city, whereas the Dionysia of the *Laws*
brings us back to the foot of the Acropolis, to the theatre of life shared
together by the citizens of the good city in a life-long educational framework to be described in the next chapter.[25]

   Both the Panathenaic festival and the Dionysia have a curious link with
the Academy. The Panathenaic torch-race which brought fire to the altar of
Athena on the Acropolis started at the altar of Eros in the Academy. And
a statue of Dionysus was temporarily lodged in a shrine at the Academy
before being brought in procession to the sanctuary on the south flank of the
Acropolis for the beginning of the festival of the Dionysia.[26]

---

[22] On this festival, see Pickard-Cambridge (1988); Monoson (2000), 88–110, reviews more recent
studies. Plato's *Symposium* presents a feast in honour of Agathon, winner with his tragedy in the City
Dionysia, a feast which ends in general inebriation. On the relation between the *Symposium* and the
Dionysia, see most recently Riegel (2015).
[23] On this passage, see the discussion in Laks (2010); Prauscello (2014), 119–28.
[24] The Dionysiac theme in the *Laws* is explored in detail by Panno (2007), part I.
[25] El Murr (2014), 221–3, detects the presence of something like a satyr-play (satyr-plays followed the
trilogies of tragedies at the Dionysia) in the *Statesman* 291a–303d.
[26] See Parke (1977), 45, 126–7.

5 Concluding Remarks

The *Laws* provides us with an example of a situation described in the *Statesman*, but which seems otherwise somewhat obscure, the situation of states acquiring and making use of good legislation which they themselves have not developed. In the *Laws*, such a situation would be that of the founding of a new colony, such as that envisaged by Cleinias, which will receive its legislation in the form of a model from competent legislators such as Solon or the Athenian guest. However, it appears from the *Laws* that it will not suffice that a new colony merely receives legislation and guards it by keeping it unchanged: there will need to be a continuous process of examination of legislation in relation to the political goal, modifying and improving it. This process will require of those responsible for guarding and improving the laws a legislative competence, a grasp of political science adequate to the task.

The three interlocutors of the *Laws* themselves develop a legislative code and the structure of a good state in their discussion. I have argued that this code and structure constitute a 'paradigm', to be used and adapted in founding a city such as the one Cleinias is planning. The paradigm gives the institutional contours of a good city, as well as its laws, and, in this context, outlines the competences required of magistrates who not only guard the laws but may also change them. These competences include, in the first place, a clear and complete knowledge of the good, as the goal of human life in a political community. But the Athenian guest also adds other competences, in particular in cosmology, astronomy, mathematics and, it seems, the domain of the Muses. The indications he gives on these matters are somewhat vague, but it seems such competences are required in the legislative work, to which they contribute in some way.

In the next chapter, I will attempt to describe the cosmological, astronomical and musical background to the political structures sketched in the paradigm developed by the Athenian guest. This will allow us to see in more detail what the Athenian guest might have in mind as regards the knowledge which the legislators are to acquire in his paradigm state, thus providing a fuller picture of the scope and content of political science. In this connection, it will be possible to make use of the cosmology of the *Timaeus* and to show in more detail how this cosmology can be the context in which a good state may be planned, how a good and beautiful world may be the context for a good life for humans.

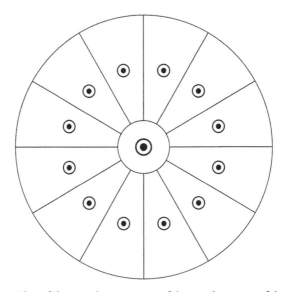

Figure 8 Plan of the spatial organization of the paradigm state of the *Laws*.

CHAPTER 7

The Order of the City of the Laws *and Its Model*

The three legislating interlocutors of the *Laws* develop a project, a paradigm of a good state, to be used, with adjustments, adaptations and comprises, in the founding of an actual state, in the present instance the new colony in Crete to be founded by Cleinias and his fellow Cretans.[1] We can suppose that the three old men of the dialogue – actually, in effect, the Athenian guest – in elaborating their paradigm in the form of a political structure and legislative code, do this on the basis of knowledge. In the *Statesman*, as we have seen, legislation is the expression of knowledge, of political science. The legislating Guardians of the Laws who feature *in* the paradigm proposed in the *Laws* must also dispose of the science required when changes or improvements in law become desirable. Just as we can ask about the science which the legislators featuring in the paradigm city of the *Laws* are required to have (see Chapter 6, section 3), so might we also ask about the science which the designers of the paradigm, the Athenian guest and his two companions, use in elaborating it. And we can suppose that it must be essentially the same knowledge which is possessed, both by the legislating interlocutors of the *Laws* and by the legislators who are part of the interlocutors' paradigm. In this chapter, I would like to attempt to describe this knowledge in more detail, to the extent that it can be discerned in the organization of the paradigm state of the *Laws*.

Not only must the legislators of a state to be founded know the good, the goal which they seek to achieve in their political planning; they must also have a model, comparable to the model to which the world-maker, the demiurge, looks when making the world. Such a model, which I have described as a set of functional requirements in the *Timaeus*, is made visible to some extent, I will show, by the order of the universe. Thus the order of the paradigm state of the *Laws* is inspired by the functional requirements which are also expressed in the order of a good and beautiful universe such

---

[1] See Chapter 3, section 2.

117

118   The Order of the City of the Laws and Its Model

as that described in the *Timaeus*. Citizens of such a state, or rather of an actual state founded according to this political paradigm, will live a life comparable to some extent to that which the ancient Athenians are supposed to have lived in the *Timaeus*. How this could work may become clearer through closer analysis of the paradigm state of the *Laws*.

In examining the structure of the paradigm state of the *Laws*, I will first sketch the spatial and temporal organization of the state, with reference in particular to the function of religion in the life of the citizens.[2] Their life is filled with religious festivals in which they join – dancing, singing, watching, listening – which serve to maintain and strengthen the moral and political education and life of the state. I will introduce some comparisons between the principles on which this life of religious festivity is organized and the order of the cosmos as described in the *Timaeus*, with the purpose of showing that the same functional principles are found in both, rendered visible in the movements of the heavens and assimilated by the citizens of the paradigm state in their daily lives. As these principles make the cosmos beautiful, in making it good, a 'happy god', so also do they allow the citizens of the paradigm state to live good lives, lives of beauty and happiness.

1   The Name of the Paradigm State

The paradigm state the three old men elaborate in their discussion on the way to Mount Ida is sometimes named 'Magnesia' in modern studies.[3] However, this is not strictly speaking correct. The paradigm, as a political project, does not, as yet, have a name: it will acquire a name when it is realized (as far as possible) in the founding of a specific state in a particular place from which a name might be derived. The Athenian guest asks:

> Well, now, how should we describe our future state? I don't mean just its name: I'm not asking what it's called now, nor what it ought to be called in the future. This might well be suggested by some detail of the actual foundation or by some spot: perhaps a river or spring or some local gods will give the new state their own style and title. (704a)

---

[2] I will not discuss the elaborate system of magistrates and officials, the methods by which they are chosen (by election and lot), for which detailed descriptions can be found in Morrow (1960), chapter 5; Piérart (2008). Nor will I discuss the theme of persuasion vs. compulsion in the *Laws*, as this has been examined in more recent studies (see, for example, Bobonich [2002], 97–106).

[3] The name 'Magnesia' is not mentioned in the *Laws*, contrary to what Moore (2012), 7, asserts; Plato refers to the city of the 'Magnesians'. For a survey of the relevant passages, see Piérart (2008), 7–9.

2 The Spatial Organization of the Paradigm State 119

The distinction between the nameless paradigm and a (partial) realization of it in a particular state, in a particular place, with a name, is made clear by the Athenian at the end of the work, when the paradigm has been elaborated and his Cretan colleague must now turn to founding a colony in Crete:

> So I bid you, Cleinias, take the business in hand: establish the state of the Magnesians (or whatever other name God adopts for it), and if you're successful you'll win enormous fame. (969a)

The state of the Magnesians (Magnesia) is the particular state that Cleinias may found in Crete, not the paradigm he and his colleagues have traced in words in the preceding discussion. This paradigm could also inspire the founding of other states, in other places, which would have correspondingly different names.[4]

2 The Spatial Organization of the Paradigm State

Even if the description of the paradigm state in the *Laws* appears to be very extensive and detailed, it is not always complete, or always clear. However, we can begin with some of its general structural features, in particular with its structure in space and the distribution of its citizens in this structure.[5]

The land of the state must have, as far as possible, the form of a circle, in the centre of which will be placed the Acropolis.[6] There must be sufficient land to make the population economically self-sufficient, in a life characterized by fairly modest needs. The population should itself be sufficiently large so as to be in a position to defend itself and assist its allies, and sufficiently small so as to assure the unity of the state (737d). The number of 5,040 households is suggested, on the grounds that this number can be divided by many factors and so is very useful for administrative purposes in making various distributions of goods and functions (737d–738a, 740d, 746d). Although a figure is not given by Plato, scholars calculate that this

---

[4] See the remarks made by Laks, in Rowe and Schofield (2000), 202–3. The link between the paradigm state and the colony Cleinias intends to found means that in some places we find an anticipatory mention of the Magnesians in the discussion of the paradigm (see 848d, 860e, 919d, 946b). On the origin of the name 'Magnesian', see Piérart (2008), 9–12, who, however, does not adequately distinguish the paradigm state developed in the *Laws* from the colony to be founded in Crete by Cleinias.

[5] For an overview, see Morrow (1960); Stalley (1983); Schöpsdau (1994), I, 107ff.; Bobonich (2002), chapter 5; Piérart (2008).

[6] 745b; see Figure 8; Piérart (2008), 17ff. (who provides a plan, 22).

120   The Order of the City of the Laws and Its Model

must mean a population of about 20,000 to 30,000 citizens, reaching 50,000, or even more, if foreigners and slaves are included.[7]

The land is and must remain the property of the state. It cannot be sold, but is distributed among the 5,040 households and then passed on in the family or newly distributed by the state (740ae). If the land is distributed equally, a very limited inequality is allowed with regard to the distribution of mobile goods. The latter are distributed between four property classes so as to take account of differences between the merits of the citizens, a distribution made according to the principle of geometrical equality: each receives in proportion to what is due.[8] Extremes of wealth and poverty are excluded (744d). There will then be a general, if differentiated, equality as regards possessions among the citizens. Each household will have two homes, one in the centre of the state, one in the country. The households will be grouped in twelve tribes, each of which will inhabit one of the twelve regions into which the land will be divided (745b). Each region will have its own centre, a village which will be like a smaller version of the city at the centre of the state.[9] The twelve tribes are themselves subdivided further into 'demes', which, however, are not explained with sufficient clarity and detail.[10]

3 The Spatio-temporal Organization of Religion

The life of the citizens of the paradigm state is filled and very deeply marked by the religious institutions which are put in place in the state.[11] This can be seen if we consider both the spatial and the temporal organization of religion in the state. The land belongs entirely to the state, but it is also entirely sacred (741c1–2): it belongs to the gods, to the goddess of the hearth (Hestia) and to other divinities. Each of the twelve regions and tribes is consecrated to a god and stands under that god's protection. The twelve regional/tribal gods might seem to correspond, very roughly, to the traditional twelve Olympian gods of the Greeks. But they are not named, as the paradigm state is not named: probably these regional gods would receive names in the founding of a specific state, where local religious

---

[7] On this, see, for example, Brisson and Pradeau (2006), vol. I, 429–33. The *Symposium* (175e) speaks of more than 30,000 attending the City Dionysia, when Agathon's tragedy was performed.

[8] 744bc; on geometrical equality see also 757ae, where the political value of geometrical equality is emphasized as a principle of justice. See Chapter 3, section 4.

[9] See Piérart (2008), 19ff.

[10] See Morrow (1960), 123–5, who refers to the Cleisthenic organization of the Athenians into ten tribes.

[11] See Reverdin (1945); Panno (2007), chapter 4.

3 The Spatio-temporal Organization of Religion

conditions would be respected and local gods included.[12] The Acropolis, at the centre of the land, will contain three temples, the temples of Hestia, Zeus and Athena (745b). All around, spread throughout the land, one will find many more temples and sacred precincts dedicated, not only to the main gods, but also to many subordinate local gods, demons and heroes. In each of the twelve regional villages, one will find, as in the Acropolis, temples of the three main gods, together with the temple of the regional god (848d).

Filled in this way with sacred places, the land is made sacred. The religious organization corresponds to the spatial and political structure of the land: a centre surrounded by twelve regions and tribes. The order of the gods is made manifest by the distribution of temples and sacred precincts: the god of each region resides in the regional centre, accompanied by the three main divinities which also reside at the centre of the state. This organization of religious space, where a differentiated multiplicity is brought to unity, mirrors, we could say, the way in which land and population are distributed in the state. A citizen of the state could also think that the spatial organization of the state reflects the order of the gods.

Just as space, the land of the state, is sacred, so is time in the life of the state made sacred. The gods are celebrated unceasingly. Religious feasts take place every day, throughout the entire cycle of the year (828b). In this way, the population remains in continuous contact with the gods. Unity and multiplicity are brought together in the religious calendar, as they are in religious space. For each region and tribe there will be two religious celebrations every month: one in honour of each one of the twelve regional gods, one in honour of one of the gods of each of the demes of the tribe (771d, 828c). In this way, throughout the year, each tribe will celebrate all of the tribal gods, as well as the gods of each deme. Thus the various segments of the population find their place in the religious calendar, which also unites them. There will be, in addition, many other religious celebrations, in the country, in the villages, at the centre, as well as participation in the great religious festivals of the Greeks (950e–951a). A precise religious calendar is not fixed in the *Laws*.[13] This would rather be the task to be undertaken when founding a particular state, in a particular place, where local religious beliefs would need to be integrated (see 738bd). If we are surprised at the ubiquity and frequency of religious celebrations in the

---

[12] 747e, 771d; Morrow (1960), 434ff. The twelve regional gods do not include Zeus and Athena, as we will see in a moment; Pluto is named at 828d. See Schöpsdau (2003), 342.
[13] The need to fix a religious calendar is mentioned at 799a, 809d.

122   The Order of the City of the Laws and Its Model

paradigm state of the *Laws*, Plato's Athenian contemporaries would have been less impressed: they were familiar with a very rich and full religious calendar, spread throughout the year, occupying much of their time, culminating in great festivals such as the two great festivals of Athens, the Panathenaea, when Timaeus, Socrates and their friends offered appropriate hymns to the goddess, and the City Dionysia.[14]

In short, we can say that the life of the citizens of the paradigm state of the *Laws* is organized, in space and in time, so as to be in continuous contact with the gods. The gods are celebrated everywhere and ceaselessly. The citizens are organized so as to carry out these celebrations, dancing, singing, offering sacrifice, praying. These activities – not working, or making money – seem to be what is most important in community life.[15]

4 Cosmic Order and the Organization of the State

In considering the way in which the paradigm state of the *Laws* is organized, in the disposition of land, tribes, villages and centre, in the spatio-temporal arrangement of religious life, we can observe correspondences between this organization and the order of the universe as described in the *Timaeus*. An argument is developed in Book X of the *Laws* so as to establish two principles: that soul is the original cause of movement in the universe; and that rational and virtuous soul causes the cyclical movements of the heavens.[16] This conception of the universe is fundamentally consistent, with respect to the two principles, with that which Timaeus developed in the *Timaeus*. The argument of *Laws* Book X, as I will suggest later (section 6), is closely related to the policy to be followed by the legislators in the paradigm state and does not go into the architectural details involved in the rational planning of the universe – the project to be used, the realization of this project by means of mathematical structures – as described in the *Timaeus*. However, it is these details which reveal the correspondences between cosmic order and the organization of the paradigm state and which will help explain the reasons for these correspondences. Having recourse here to the more elaborate cosmology of the *Timaeus* might also be supported by the reminder that this cosmology is presented in the *Timaeus* as the first

---

[14] See Chapter 6, section 4. Isocrates, in his *Panegyricus* (46), describes Athens as being, for its visitors, a perpetual festival (*panêguris*).
[15] For the exclusion of private religion, see *Laws* 909d–910d.   [16] See Chapter 6, section 3.

4 Cosmic Order and the Organization of the State   123

part, the setting, of the story of a good state, ancient Athens, whose goodness appears to relate to the beauty and goodness of the cosmos.[17]

The following structural correspondences between the cosmic order of the *Timaeus* and the organization of the paradigm state of the *Laws* might be noted[18]:

1. The cosmos is a god; the land of the state is sacred (*Laws* 741c1–2).
2. The cosmos is of spherical shape, the shape of perfection, completion and self-sufficiency[19]; the land of the state is circular in shape and is complete, self-sufficient and, like the cosmos, in fear of no external danger.
3. A soul animates the cosmos. Both soul and the four basic elements constituting bodies are structured by means of mathematical proportions. Geometrical proportion, in particular, is an important unifying and differentiating order. This proportion also unifies and differentiates the inhabitants of the state.[20]
4. The moon, sun, the five planets and the fixed stars are spherical, like the cosmos (*Timaeus* 40a), and move in circles around the earth, as the villages of the state encircle the centre and Acropolis.
5. In their 'dance' (*choreia, Timaeus* 40c3–4) around the earth, the celestial bodies structure cosmic time. Moon, sun and the fixed stars mark out the lunar month, day and night, and the year of twelve months. (The other celestial bodies, the planets, also mark out temporal periods, which are known, however, only to specialists, astronomers.[21]) Similarly, the population, space and time of the paradigm state are organized in twelve tribes,[22] regions, and months, the tribes having twelve gods surrounding the Acropolis and its gods.

---

[17] See Chapter 2, section 1. It is argued, for example by Mohr (1985), chapter 11, that the cosmology of *Laws* X introduces some doctrines at odds with those of the cosmology of the *Timaeus*. However, the rhetorical purpose and philosophical limits of the argument of *Laws* X need to be noticed (see Görgemanns (1960), chapter IV.2): it is an example of the sort of speech (see 888a) to be given to citizens who may cast doubt on the fundamental values of the paradigm state (see section 6). See also Vlastos (1939); Kahn (2013), 214–19.

[18] See Chapters 3 and 4, for more details on the cosmic order, which I summarize here. Some of the following correspondences are noted by Pradeau (1998), 176, who adds others which seem to me less pertinent.

[19] *Timaeus* 33b–34b; see *Laws* 898ab.

[20] See above, p. 120. The comparison between soul and state, which is so prominent in the *Republic*, reappears in the *Laws* (689ab).

[21] *Timaeus* 39cd; see *Laws* 818a, 966e: what is involved is greater periods of time, where the planets are involved, such as the 'Great Year' mentioned here in the *Timaeus*; see de Callataÿ (1996). Plato also describes the dance of the heavens as the painted frieze of the heavens (above, Chapter 3, n. 57) and as its moving embroidery (*Republic* 529c7, *Timaeus* 39d2).

[22] The correspondence between the division of the population and the celestial order is pointed out in *Laws* 771b.

124   The Order of the City of the Laws and Its Model

It thus looks as if the paradigm state of the *Laws* reflects the organization of the cosmos.[23] However, the correspondence between them need not be absolute. The world Timaeus elaborates in the *Timaeus* is the best possible world, a truly perfect world, absolutely self-sufficient, living in unity and peace. The celestial bodies are the highest level in the differentiated perfection of the world. However, the paradigm state can only represent a relative perfection: it can claim only relative self-sufficiency and is designed for humans, with their weaknesses (853c–854a). Furthermore, when the paradigm state will be made use of in founding a particular state, such as the colony to be founded by Cleinias, various adjustments and compromises will need to be made in view of given conditions: the varying contours and quality of the land, the differing origins, character and education of the future inhabitants.

In examining the mathematical structures used by the demiurge of the *Timaeus* in ordering the universe (see Chapter 4), I have suggested that these structures serve to realize, in the 'place' of the world, the functional requirements (Forms) included in the model, or paradigm, used by the demiurge, requirements which must be satisfied if the goal which is sought, the good, is to be achieved. Thus the spherical shape of the universe achieves unity in that this shape realizes the functional requirements of similarity, self-sufficiency, completion.[24] The same requirements are realized in the sphericity of the celestial bodies, in their circular paths, and, partially, in humans who are spheres – heads! – carried by limbs (*Timaeus* 44de). The geometrical proportions which structure soul and the four elements, I have argued, realize, through 'equality', the requirement of 'identity', which makes for unity.[25] Time is marked out by the movements of the heavens, which consist primarily of the movement of the fixed stars, which corresponds to 'identity'. From this movement and from that corresponding to 'difference' are constituted the movements of the other celestial bodies, moon, sun and planets.[26] However, 'identity' is what is primarily achieved. Thus time, as a differentiated expression of identity, represents an image of unity (*Timaeus* 37d6–7). In general, then, it would appear that these mathematical structures allow for satisfying the requirements of identity, self-sufficiency, completion, and thus for achieving the goal sought by the demiurge when bringing the good into the universe.

We could say the same, I propose, with regard to the mathematical organization of the paradigm state of the *Laws*: the structure fulfils the

[23] Reverdin (1945), 63.   [24] *Timaeus* 33b6, d2, 34b2; see Chapter 3, section 4.
[25] *Timaeus* 32c1–4; see Chapter 4, section 3.   [26] *Timaeus* 36d, 38c–39c; see Chapter 4, section 3.

5 Religion as Ethical and Political Education

same requirements and thus contributes to achieving a comparable goal. An indication of this is found in the words of the Athenian guest, spoken in the context of a discussion of the mathematical distribution of land and mobile possessions among the members of the paradigm state:

> My dear sirs, do not fail to honour, in accord with nature, similarity, equality, the identical and consonant, both with regard to number and with regard to all that which can produce what is beautiful and good. In particular, your first task now is to keep the said number as long as you live; you must respect the upper limits of the total property which you originally distributed as being reasonable. (741ab)

It would seem that the legislator – both the legislator who designs a paradigm state and the legislator who will use it – must have knowledge of the same functional requirements as those which constitute the paradigm of the world the demiurge uses. One can infer from this that political science must include this knowledge, as well as the other competences already noted earlier (Chapter 6, section 3). In this case, knowledge of the Forms (as the functional requirements of the *Timaeus*) would be presupposed by the legislation of the *Laws*, as it seems to be required, but not covered, by the description of political science in the *Statesman*.[27] Political science (and the legislation in which it finds expression) may include, but is not identical with, astronomy: this science must also know the principles which provide the model for making a good and beautiful world, itself using these same principles in making a good city.

5 Religion as Ethical and Political Education

Everybody in the paradigm state – man and child, the free and slaves, male and female – takes part in the religious festivities, in the sacred dances and songs which constantly take place (665c).[28] Performed within the framework of a spatial and temporal order which corresponds, in its mathematical structure, to the order of the movements of the heavens, these celebrations allow the participants to assimilate the functional laws which find expression in the movements of the heavens. And so the life of the state, like the life of the world, can be made beautiful and good.

---

[27] Chapter 5, section 5.

[28] See Peponi (2013), which includes essays discussing various aspects of the cultural programme of the city of the *Laws*, including especially choral singing and dancing; Belfiore (2006), 204–11; and especially Prauscello (2014), part II, a very detailed and interesting discussion of choral dancing in the *Laws* in relation to its Greek cultural background.

126   The Order of the City of the Laws and Its Model

However, this general correspondence need not mean, as we have seen, that the detailed organization of the religious celebrations in the state must be derived directly from the model provided by the choreography of the astral gods. In this regard, it might be of interest to look in more detail at the way in which the religious life of the paradigm state is organized.

It emerges fairly early in the *Laws* that the Athenian guest understands religious festivals as part of the moral education of the members of the state:

> Education, then, is a matter of correctly disciplined feelings of pleasure and pain. But in the course of a man's life the effect wears off, and in many respects it is lost altogether. The gods, however, took pity on the human race, born to suffer as it was, and gave it relief in the form of religious festivals to serve as periods of rest from its labours. They gave us the Muses, with Apollo their leader, and Dionysus; by having these gods to share their holidays, men were to be set straight again, and thanks to them, we find refreshment in the celebration of these festivals. (653cd)

The Athenian guest conceives of the education of the young as a matter of associating pleasure and pain with moral values, with virtues and vices, in such a way that, through its association with pleasure, virtue will be acquired. With adulthood, this moral education may wear off and even be lost. Religious festivals help to remedy this, restoring and strengthening a moral education which, in adults, may have been weakened. Religious festivals are thus a form of 'continuing education' in virtue, so to speak, constantly refreshing, restoring, strengthening the moral character of the inhabitants.[29] The children, while being educated, already take part in the festivals and so are prepared for, and begin, a lifelong participation in festivities which prolongs their early education. I will note here some aspects of the conception of education developed in the *Laws*, as concerning children and religious celebrations which involve the whole population. Many curious details of this educational plan must, of course, be left aside.

The *Laws* introduces a scheme for universal public compulsory education (perhaps the first ever), administered by the most important of the magistrates of the state (765d), the minister of education, and by his subordinates. Education involves the training both of body (*gumnastikê*)

---

[29] We should distinguish this use of festivals from what motivates pleasure-seekers (*Republic* 421b2–4) or avid festival-goers in pursuit of beautiful sights or choral performances, but of no more (475de). Socrates had himself gone to the Piraeus to take part (pray) in the festival for Bendis, observing the processions and tempted to stay to see a novel horse race (327a–328a).

5 Religion as Ethical and Political Education 127

and of soul (*mousikê*) (795d). It begins very early: the Athenian guest introduces the idea of a pre-natal physical education (*gumnastikê*) of the embryo in the womb. Cleinias, the Cretan provincial, is astonished at this idea (789a), as if hearing the latest flaky idea coming from America! But the Athenian persists: he suggests that the body of the embryo will benefit from a constant gentle rocking movement by the mother when she takes walks, and, after birth, by the mother and nurses when cradling and carrying the infant.[30] The mother and nurses not only rock the infant; they also sing to it. Thus they also make use of *mousikê*, the education of the soul (790e). Today, a pregnant woman might play Mozart to her womb.

As the child grows, its education in soul and body continues. *Gumnastikê* will include dancing (*orchêsis*) and wrestling (795e1): it promotes the 'virtue' of the body, whereas *mousikê* educates the soul in virtue, in particular through the voice (673a). What is involved is bringing order (*taxis*), through dancing and singing, to the chaotic movements and cries of the young. Two aspects of this order are distinguished: *rhuthmos* and *harmonia*.[31] *Rhuthmos* appears to be diachronic, an ordering of movements in a temporal sequence, whereas *harmonia* is synchronic and has to do with an order of simultaneous consonant intervals, for example the proportions that are the octave, the 'hemiolic' (the fifth) and the 'epitritic' (the fourth).[32] If *rhuthmos* characterizes the rational order of bodily movements in a temporal sequence, it is found again in *mousikê*, which also makes use of *harmonia*.[33] If dance can achieve good rhythm (*euruthmos*) in movement (795e6), music will achieve both good rhythm and harmoniousness (*euarmostos*) in song (655a6; see *Republic* 522a). Some mathematical knowledge seems to be required in designing this rational order (747a3–4).

The beauty (*to kalon*) of such an order structuring dancing and singing is to be judged solely by the extent to which it embodies or represents virtue (655b). Dancing and singing choruses should imitate virtuous characters in action.[34] They will sing the praises of demons, heroes and the deceased who have

---

[30] 789b–790e; Pelosi (2010), 15–20. The Athenian refers to the rocking of a boat (790c9–d1). Gülgönen (2011) relates this rocking (pendular) movement to the circular movement of the heavens (see 898a8–b3), suggesting an assimilation of the infant's movements to those of the heavens.

[31] 653e3–654a5; 665a; see Schöpsdau (1994), 262–3; Panno (2007), 146–50.   [32] See earlier, p. 71.

[33] The speech about *mousikê* which Socrates gives in the *Republic* (403c5), supposedly inspired by the Greek musician Damon, falls into two parts: on *harmonia* (398c1–399e9), and on *rhuthmos* (399e9–403c5).

[34] 655d, 798e; see Pelosi (2010), 52–65, and Gülgönen (2011), who discusses the use of various kinds of dance as showing various virtues, in particular courage (war-dances) and moderation (dances of peace). Lucian's dialogue *On Dancing* gives many examples of characters, actions and stories being displayed in dancing.

128   The Order of the City of the Laws and Its Model

distinguished themselves by their virtuous lives, in addition to singing hymns to the gods who will also represent moral goodness (801ae). All participants in these performances will take pleasure in and assimilate this imitation, to the extent that they have acquired the habit of associating pleasure with virtue (656b). The legislator will see to it (by persuasion or compulsion) that poets use rhythm and harmony to embody and teach virtue (659de, 660a, 661c). In other words, the goal to be achieved through bringing order to dancing and singing is virtue, assimilated both by those who act and those who watch and hear. If appropriate choreographies and songs are found, they are to be fixed in law. No new-fangled or modish innovations not conforming to the criterion of virtue will be allowed. The Athenian refers in admiration to the Egyptians, who have displayed their dancing styles and music in their temples, keeping them unchanged for 10,000 years (656d, 798e–799a). But he claims that Athens, too, once had a good codification of music (700bd), when it lived under the rule of law (700a).

Besides taking part in a chorus, diligently singing virtue to the whole state (664c), children will also receive an education in mathematics,[35] in astronomy, in instrument playing (the lyre), and in literature (809bd). The written works to be studied may be in verse or prose, but they must be composed so as to conform to the moral objectives of education. The Athenian proposes a model (*paradeigma*, 811bc) of such a work to which the legislator can look in determining appropriate readings for the young. The model is none other than the discussion which the Athenian and his companions have been having on their way to Mount Ida: *his* discourse is a model![36] The laws of the state, if they are good, can also be edificatory literature, to be read by every citizen (858d–859a). The Athenian suggests that these laws be provided with preambles, 'preludes'(*prooimia*),[37] which persuade the citizens to accept the law (723a), and himself composes such preambles, which show the need for laws by pointing to the priority, in moral value, of the soul and of virtue in leading a good life.[38] In other words, the rationale of laws derives from the goal in relation to which the state is organized.

---

[35] 747b; see also 820a–822c, where the young should learn the relation between the commensurable and the incommensurable, together with some astronomical knowledge.

[36] 811ce; the Athenian refers elsewhere (858e) to the writings of other legislators, Solon (also a poet) and Lycurgos. See the interesting suggestions made by Capra (2014), 170–3, on the relation Plato may have seen between his dialogues and the literature of a good state of the future.

[37] The Athenian plays on the word *nomos* as meaning both a song ('nome') and law (722de, 799e): laws are also, so to speak, songs.

[38] 726a–734e. These preambles are discussed, for example, by Görgemanns (1960), Bobonich (2002), 97–119, and Laks (2005), 115–63.

6 The Gods of the Laws

The child is trained in body and soul in rehearsing and performing at religious events as part of the children's chorus, the chorus of the Muses. On becoming a young adult, he or she will then join another chorus (for those under thirty), which will cultivate and propagate the same values, a chorus dedicated to Apollo (leader of the Muses, *mousêgetês*). A third chorus, for the thirty to sixty-year-olds, will be dedicated to Dionysus.[39] This last group will also dance and sing, bringing with its seniority considerable authority to its moral mission. However, these elders may be reluctant, even ashamed, to sing in public: to soften them up and rejuvenate them, the Athenian suggests recourse to the gift of Dionysus, wine![40] Finally, there are those who are even older, who can no longer give such singing performances (not even, it appears, with the help of wine): they will tell stories (*muthologous*) about virtuous characters.[41]

Within the mathematical structures of the state reflecting those of the heavens, the religious life of the population is filled with dancing and singing which also involve mathematical order. The dancing and singing is then a sort of embodied mathematics. The dances and songs, as representations of virtue, are consecrated to the gods: they celebrate and invoke the gods, who accompany them. We need, then, to look more closely at these gods: Who are they? How do they relate to the structure of the universe?

6 The Gods of the *Laws*

The *Timaeus* distinguishes between the astral gods and the gods of traditional Greek religion, the Olympians, who feature in the poets' theogonies. The status of the latter gods remains unclear in the *Timaeus*; they appear to be somewhat marginal to Timaeus' story.[42] The same distinction is made in the *Laws* (930e9–931a3), where we find both astral gods (821bc) and the gods whose temples are on the Acropolis and those who are assigned to each of the twelve tribes. It is these central and tribal gods who seem to

---

[39] These groupings of the population are reminiscent of the grouping of the population in the festive procession represented on the Parthenon's frieze (which includes a group modern scholars describe as the 'handsome old men'). See also Prauscello (2014), 154–60.

[40] 665a–666c. The interest taken in the educational use of wine and of dancing may be connected with the festival of the Dionysia which seems to be part of the background to the political project of the *Laws* (see Chapter 6, section 4).

[41] 664d2–4. The Athenian guest, himself an old man, describes his discourse as *muthologia*, as compared to Cleinias' founding of a colony (752a). Perhaps Timaeus' discourse in the *Timaeus* is also such a story.

[42] See earlier, p. 31. Timaeus' offhand attitude to the poets' theogonies may be compared to that of the Athenian guest in the *Laws* (886cd). See also *Epinomis* 984d2–4.

130 The Order of the City of the Laws and Its Model

correspond, to some degree, to the traditional gods of the Greeks. The three central gods – Hestia, Zeus and Athena – are named; however, the twelve tribal gods are not.[43] Why three central gods? Why these three? The Athenian guest seems to be thinking of his paradigm state as applicable in the founding of a state somewhere in the Greek world. We might explain his choice of these three Greek gods as the central gods to the extent that they correspond to the (h)earth-place where the state is to be established (Hestia); the sky where rational order can be observed (Zeus); and the political science which realizes this rational order in the organization of the state in a place (Athena). But what of the other unnamed tribal gods? Could this be simply a matter of leaving blank spaces in the scheme of the paradigm state, to be filled by the particular deities associated with the specific place where a particular state might be founded?[44] Whatever they are, these deities will probably have to be reformed, as Zeus and Athena were reformed in the *Timaeus* and the *Statesman*, so as to be morally exemplary objects of religious celebration.

These issues concerning the central and tribal gods of the paradigm state should be distinguished, I think, from the question of the existence of god, as this question arises in *Laws* Book X, where an argument is developed proving that god exists. The context of the argument in Book X is very different from that, for example, of a medieval theologian who seeks to refute 'the fool who said in his heart: there is no god' (*Psalms* 13: 1), or that of a modern professor of the philosophy of religion analyzing syllogisms on the subject. In *Laws* Book X, the problem is a political one: how to deal with people in the state whose views on the nature of the universe contradict the fundamental principles on which the state is based and which determine its objectives and laws: the priority of soul, of virtue and of reason. These people deny that gods exist; or deny that gods care for mankind; or say that gods can easily be influenced by us by means of sacrifices and prayers (885b). The Athenian relates such views to a materialistic conception of the universe which desacralizes the stars (886d), saying they are just earth and stones, incapable of caring for human affairs (886d6–e2). The four elements arise by nature and chance (*tuchê*), not by reason of a god or rational skill *(technê)*. From these inanimate bodies arise other bodies, earth and the heavenly bodies, moving by chance (*tuchê*), and everything else in the universe (889bc). This view of the universe, which is the reverse of the account presented in the *Timaeus*, is related by the Athenian to a denial that there is a natural justice (889e8), to the

---

[43] See earlier, p. 120. [44] Ibid.

6 The Gods of the Laws

affirmation that what is most just is what is conquered by force (890a4), thus inspiring a policy directed at war, the defeat of others (890a8–9).[45]

In Book X of the *Laws*, the Athenian provides a speech setting forth arguments designed to persuade citizens of the paradigm state who would entertain such conceptions to think otherwise: to accept that the world is produced by soul guided by reason (893b–898e). By accepting this teaching, these people also accept the goals which inspire the paradigm state and which are the basis of its laws. If they do not accept this teaching, they represent a serious *political* danger and must be silenced or removed. The arguments constitute a prelude to the law on impiety, to be read by all citizens and available to be studied by all, including the less bright.[46]

The speech the Athenian proposes argues for the existence of god, that god's goodness, incorruptibility and care for human affairs by showing that the world is produced by soul guided by reason: the god in question is soul acting rationally in moving the world. There is no mention in the argument of the traditional gods of the Greeks. How seriously, then, should we take the central and tribal gods of the paradigm state?[47] I would like to mention in this connection two possible answers.

In his attempt to restore pagan religion in the fourth century AD, Emperor Julian organized the religions of his empire somewhat along the lines of the religion of the *Laws*: he combined a group of central divinities with a wide range of subordinate divinities corresponding to the beliefs of different nations, cultures and places.[48] These local divinities were recognized – for example the god of the Jews – within the specific area and nation to which they corresponded, but had no exclusive universal claim, being subordinated to a group of primary (Greek) gods. It seems likely that Julian accepted the multiplicity of these local divinities, if not the excessive claims made for them by their worshippers. Could Plato have accepted, in a similar way, the many deities which populated the different areas of the Greek world, seeking only to bring some order to the conceptions people have of them?

A more radical answer can be found later, in the tenth century, in al-Farabi.[49] The philosopher, who had some knowledge (perhaps indirectly) of

---

[45] On this argument and on Plato's response to it, see Neschke-Hentschke (1995), 140–52. Compare the argument in *Philebus* 28d–30e. At 709ab the Athenian refers already to a politics determined and dominated by chance (*tuchê*). Earlier, the Athenian had criticized the Spartan and Cretan constitutions as being directed at making war (see Chapter 3, section 2).

[46] 890d–891a, as pointed out to me by Chris Bobonich.

[47] The question as to Plato's attitude to the traditional gods of the Greeks is raised by Morrow (1960), 444, but he is careful to avoid settling for a cut-and-dried answer. Lefka (2013) provides a survey of Plato's references in the dialogues to the traditional gods of the Greeks.

[48] See O'Meara (2003), 120–3, and *Laws* 713cd.   [49] See O'Meara (2003), 194.

132   The Order of the City of the Laws and Its Model

Plato's *Laws*, sees religion as an image of philosophy. People who do not have the capacity and education for reasoning as philosophers may be given images of philosophical truths in the form of stories appealing to their imagination. This is important in the life of a good state. Run by philosophers, this state will make use of rhetoricians in order to communicate the philosophical truths on which the state is founded, in the form of the images of religion, to the population. *Any* religion may be used for this purpose, as long as the stories it tells are metaphysically correct, expressing basic philosophical truths. Applied to Plato, this approach would indicate that the traditional gods of the paradigm state, the central and tribal gods, exist as stories told to the citizens so as to inculcate and preserve the philosophical claims on which the state is based. These claims are understood by the responsible magistrates, by the members of the Nocturnal Council, who have the appropriate scientific training, who guide (and censor) the poets when they write hymns or other works about the gods, and supervise the teachers and the chorus-masters in their educational work.

The three interlocutors of the *Laws*, as they legislate on their walk to Mount Ida, seem to be divinely inspired (811c8–9). What god inspires them? Not Zeus, it seems, who instructed the Cretan Minos in the cave on Mount Ida, nor Apollo, who inspired the legislator of Sparta, Lycurgos.[50] Such legislators were themselves divine and legislated for children of the gods, whereas the three interlocutors are humans and legislate for humans (853c). The interlocutors, in particular the Athenian, legislate in discussing with each other. The divine inspiration is perhaps that which fills the universe[51] and which should fill the paradigm state: the rationality which makes the universe good and beautiful, the knowledge of this rationality which legislators should have.

> Where the ruler of a state is not a god but a mortal, people have no escape from evils and toil. The lesson is that we should make every effort to imitate the life men are said to have led under Kronus; we should run our public and our private life, our homes and our cities, in obedience to what there is of immortality in us, and calling the dispositions (*dianomê*) of reason 'law' (*nomos*).[52]

The god in us, the immortal, is reason, which expresses itself in law.[53]

---

[50] It is perhaps significant that if Zeus and Apollo inspire the Cretan and Spartan states, represented by Cleinias and Megillos, Athena is not mentioned as inspiring Athenian legislation. But it is the Athenian guest who does most of the legislative work in the *Laws*.

[51] The Athenian alludes (899b8) to Thales' saying that 'all is full of gods' in connection with the role of soul (or souls) in causing heavenly movements and time.

[52] 713e4–714a2, discussed by Neschke-Hentschke (1995), 156. See Nightingale (1993), 282–4.

[53] Compare Mayhew (2011), 324.

7 Astro-choreography

The heavens sing a harmony of the spheres[54]: astro-nomes! They also dance as a chorus in a passage in the *Timaeus* (40c3), as we have seen.[55] The swirling choruses of religious festivals in the paradigm state find their equivalent in the circling movements of the heavens.[56] As the choruses may evoke the heavenly spheres, so might these spheres, in their movements, evoke choruses. Plato's image of the dance of the heavens is discussed by Proclus in the fifth century AD, in his commentary on the passage of the *Timaeus*,[57] and elaborated in great detail by the Byzantine Platonist philosopher of the eleventh century, Michael Psellos, in the little encyclopaedia (the *De omnifaria doctrina*) which he dedicated to his imperial pupil, Michael VII.[58] I offer here a translation of this extraordinary text, as a final note to our comparison between the festivals of the paradigm state and that of the heavens:

> We will not force the account as regards those [women] who dance in a chorus. For that which they do – turning one way and then in the other way, singing first and then singing in response, both standing and moving together, bending away and turning back, advancing and retreating – this is an image of the heavenly movement and of the variegated dancing of the wandering (*planêtôn*) and fixed stars in the heavens. Thus moving together from the right, they image the movement of the fixed stars; but moving back from the left they mark the track of the wandering stars. And standing, they interpret the heavenly bodies which seem to stand fast, whereas in singing and counter-singing they clarify the ineffable meaning of counter-movements [in the heavens]. She who sings first cries out the first tune of the fixed stars, in relation to which the remaining tunes of the moving spheres are led. Advancing forward and then retreating, they trace the progressions and retrogressions of the stars. And brought together to the same point, they hint at the much-mentioned 'conjunctions' [of the stars], whereas being separated and bending back in many-facetted sorts of figures, they point to thousands of different celestial figures made from distances or conjunctions.

---

[54] See *Republic* 530d–531a; 616c–617d; *Timaeus* 35b–36d; 37ab; 38c–39d.

[55] Above, p. 123. See also *Epinomis* 982e. On astral choruses, see Kurke (2013), 140–6; Belfiore (2006), 204–5 (on the *Phaedrus*). J. Miller (1986) provides a wide survey of the theme in ancient literature.

[56] 'To be like the heavenly bodies ... Hayy prescribed himself circular motion of various kinds ... at times he would spin around in circles ... spinning around faster and faster ... ' (Ibn Tufayl, *Hayy ibn Yaqzan*, 166, trans. Goodman 146–7).

[57] Proclus, *In Timaeum* III, 145, 12–151, 9. See J. Miller (1986), 414–75.

[58] Psellos, *De omnifaria doctrina*, chapter 200. Proclus explains in particular the astronomical theory of the passage in Plato's *Timaeus*, whereas Psellos, who appears to be making use of Proclus' commentary, elaborates the choreographic image. Most of the technical terms Psellos uses are astronomical.

And when they weave their fingers with each other, they explicate the shared life of the moving heavenly lights and the one and common tie through which the parts (of the heavens) are constituted as living together in the whole. And now, when they strike together the earth, they reveal all the emanations which come to us from above. But when they change foot and with one foot jump over the earth, they interpret what in some places is unrelated and unbound to the things here below. And such a chorus dance, as a whole, is a most consonant exegesis of the heavenly circlings.

Epilogue

As an end of the explorations undertaken in this book, it might be useful to bring together some of the results that have emerged. Although the texts which Plato wrote towards the end of his life reflect a variety of projects and contexts, it does seem possible to compare them on the subject of the relation between cosmology and political philosophy, the relation between Plato's concept of the goodness and beauty of the world and his ideas as to what it is that would go towards making a political community where humans can lead good lives together. The series of speeches to which the *Timaeus* belongs invites us to think about this relation. If the political side of the relation is suggested, but not developed, in the cosmology of the *Timaeus*, the cosmological side of the relation, if detectable in the background, is not elaborated in the political philosophy of the *Statesman* and of the *Laws*. However, the presence of fundamental ideas underlying both the cosmology and the political philosophy of Plato's later works allows us to develop the relation between these two fields in more detail.

One of these fundamental ideas, I believe, is the distinction between the good conceived as the goal to be achieved in organizing a complex whole and the general functional principles which, in their application, allow for the realization of this goal. The goal (*skopos*) to be achieved (1) is a unity of the whole such that each part of it functions well and prospers, as part of the whole. The goal is not the war of one part with another, the success of one part at the cost of another, but a peace and harmony enjoyed by all. The set of functional principles (*paradeigma*) to be used (2) in order to achieve this goal – I have proposed calling these principles functional requirements or laws – concerns the structure to be established in a whole of parts: a structure, or order, making the attainment of the goal possible. At a maximum level of generality, spanning both the universe and political communities, these functional requirements include identity, difference, justice, completion, perpetuity. These structural laws are unchanging, I have proposed, in the sense that if ever any complex of

136   Epilogue

parts is to achieve the goal described previously (1), then it can achieve this by means of the structure which these laws establish.

Plato distinguished furthermore between the goal (1), the structural laws (2) and the actual production (3) of a particular whole of parts (a universe, a political community) according to the goal and the structural laws. The actual production of a whole of parts will have to take account of and accommodate various constraints which are given, which come with the place and the factors (pre-elements, people who will be the citizens) to be ordered when a whole is to be made. This seems to involve some limitations or adjustments in the application of the structural laws.

Furthermore, Plato appears to be inspired by the procedures which skilled artisans and experts follow, in particular those which architects use, when he distinguishes between the general structural laws – the project (*paradeigma*) which sets out general specifications – and the detailed planning (4) required in the realization of the project. This detailed planning in the cosmology of the *Timaeus* takes the form of mathematical structures which express functional principles in a way appropriate to the complex to be produced (geometrical equality expresses in the cosmos the principle of identity, which in politics expresses itself as justice). The detailed planning on the level of politics will concern specific political structures and laws which the founders of a future state such as the Cretan Cleinias will need to develop, while using the general paradigm of a state presented in the *Laws*.

Timaeus tells a tale of the making of a good and beautiful world. Is this an account of what, we suppose, *must* have happened, given what we know, if the universe in which we now live is to have come about? The tale would then be a fiction, in the way that any modern account of the origin of the universe is a fiction. Does Plato really believe that our universe is the best and more beautiful of all possible worlds? Or does Timaeus imagine what the best of universes *might* be like, if ever there were one, so that ancient Athens, in a mythical past, might find a suitable home? This seems to go too far. The universe of the *Timaeus* is not perfect throughout: it has its darker and irrational dimension. What concerns Timaeus most is to bring out the rationality which makes of the universe a place where the good is present, where beauty shines. Timaeus' concept of rationality, that of technical expertise, in particular that of the architect, is both a critique and substitute for the cosmogonic tales of the poets so full of irrationality and immorality. Timaeus' demiurge replaces the poets' Zeus, knowledge replaces brute force and lust. The *Laws* similarly dismiss cosmologies

Epilogue 137

which, while rejecting the traditional gods, replace them with the irrationality of chance.

The reform of Zeus represented in the figure of Timaeus' demiurge is part of a feast of speeches which functions as a critique of the Panathenaic festival surrounding it. Ancient Athens, which showed its virtue in conquering Atlantis, is not the Athens which celebrates, while Timaeus and his friends speak, the city's founding goddess, daughter of Zeus, Athena. The good city which Athena once founded is not that which now celebrates her. The belligerent goddess represented on the *peplos* carried and displayed in the Panathenaic procession is also reformed, I have suggested, in Plato's *Statesman*, where the statesman weaves a robe of peace and harmony. Like Zeus, Athena is reformed. The good city she once founded relates in some way to the good and beautiful world organized by the demiurge, but the *Timaeus* does not reveal much about how this is so.

The rational order of the world, its goodness, is based on knowledge, the knowledge of the goal and of the functional principles required for realizing this goal. The demiurge, in possession of this knowledge, is also able to calculate, to plan in detail, in realizing the project. We might therefore expect that the organization of a good political community will derive from a corresponding knowledge. But what is this knowledge? How does it relate to the knowledge which gives the world its rational order?

The *Statesman*, in describing political science, deals with the knowledge that would make a state good. However, the description, I have suggested, is far from complete. We learn a certain amount about political science as a directive (architectonic) skill organizing subordinate political competences – what I would describe as the detail planning and management involved in the realization of a project (4) – but little about the goal (1) and project (2) which must also be included in this knowledge. The *Statesman* presents legislation as the (somewhat deficient) expression of political science. We can suppose that legislation enters into the detailed planning which the possessor of political science will need to do in organizing a state which is to be good. But how can states be good, if political science is absent? The *Statesman* suggests that such states can make use of the legislation of a good state, but it is not clear how they can have access to this.

The *Laws* proposes a model legislation, to be used, with appropriate adjustments, by people, such as Cleinias, who set about founding a city. The *paradeigma* which is developed by the *Laws* appears to be much more detailed and specific than that which I have suggested is the model used by

138 Epilogue

the world's demiurge. It is, however, a 'second-best' model,[1] and its detail does not dispense the future founder of a city from the planning involved in realizing it. The future city will also need people who will reflect continuously on the adaptation and adjustment of legislation: they will need political science, in particular knowledge of the goal (1) against which any legislation or legislative change is to be measured. These guardians of the laws must also be competent in astronomy and mathematics. Astronomical knowledge also seems to underlie, in part at least, the paradigm state (the model) developed in the *Laws*. The life of its citizens, in space and in time, is ordered in a way which corresponds to the order of the heavens. However, it does not appear to be the case that their lives simply copy the visible movements of the stars, i.e., that these heavenly movements are exclusively the direct model on which the good state is based.[2] Rather, both the order of the heavens and the order of the state reflect the same functional principles. A visible expression of these principles can be seen (and admired) in the heavens and a political expression of these same principles (for example, in the distribution of property) can also be planned. I would like to suggest, therefore, that political science must include knowledge of the goal (1) and of the functional principles of a structure allowing for the achievement of the goal (2), as well as the executive competence required in realizing a good state ([3] and [4]). The functional principles (2) are those which the demiurge also knows in ordering the world. It thus looks as if political science includes knowledge of the Forms (as these functional principles), which is required for the design of a political paradigm such as that proposed in the *Laws* and for legislative changes in a state which has been founded following this paradigm.

Moving through the agora up to the foot of the Acropolis, the Panathenaic procession celebrated the goddess with the best that Greek art and expertise could offer: the magnificent weaving of the *peplos*, carried up through the Propylaia towards the Parthenon, where the beauty achieved by the architects, sculptors, painters, metalworkers and potters could be admired. These sights, I have suggested, inspired Plato in his description of the beauty of the world, a rational structure where the good can reside, an encircling astronomical frieze which can astonish us as we look up, as we carry a beautifully woven texture of life showing how humans can live well together. The Panathenaic festival was also

---

[1] The best model would perhaps be simpler and include fewer laws, greater unity being achieved, for example, by the requirement that all be shared in common (*Laws* 739ce, quoted earlier, p 45).

[2] Stalley's criticism (1983), 29, of Plato for making the good state depend directly on the order of the visible heavens seems therefore not to be justified.

Epilogue

a tremendous display of physical achievements in sport and of excellence in poetry and music. Another Athenian festival, the Dionysia, also displayed wonders, of dance, of song, of tragedy and comedy. The Dionysia, I have suggested, is reformed in the paradigm state of the *Laws*: dancing, singing, drinking, the theatre of the state are reformed so as to function as educational processes inculcating the same moral values as those woven by the laws. The life of the state is a festival, celebrated in the sight of another festival, that of the heavens.

***

While exploring the fascinations of Plato's work, we might feel that the world he constructed and the city he designed are pure fantasies, things already far removed, in time (**T 1**) and in place, from the time and place of his first readers, in the Athens of the mid-fourth century BC (**T 2**). I have suggested that the creation of a distance (between **T 1** and **T 2**) can have the effect of provoking the reader to think again about the present (**T 2**). The things Plato describes are too remote to be considered as directly applicable to the present, but they can provoke thought about the present and about what is fundamentally wrong with it. At a far greater distance from the scene of Plato's dialogues than Plato's readers, we (at **T 3**) may still, however, be provoked in this way. We also live in an Atlantis, the latest of a long series of powers organized for the purpose of making money and war, filled with murder within and constant killing on its edges. Plato's bright stars, showing the beauty of a rational, harmonious order, do not fill our sky. Our nights – if we see anything through the haze of pollution – are patrolled by other lights, miradors tracking our movements. Science serves globalized greed. We are heading, inexorably it seems, in the direction of the destruction of nature. The Parthenon has been desecrated, blown up and plundered; a concrete chaos covers the tired earth of Attica. We are confronted furthermore with the perspectives offered by violent, fanatical theocracies which threaten to destroy liberty and philosophy in the name of some self-appointed divine mission.

Reading Plato, we might find ideas which can be of use in the criticism of these political ideologies.[3] Much in him seems inappropriate or unacceptable. Plato's mythical world is not ours, his ideal city, tailored to the scale of a Greek *polis*, cannot be ours. But he can provoke us to think critically about the objectives and values which are currently imposed and to propose those

---

[3] For further discussion, see, for example, Lane (2012), on ecological concerns, and Lutz (2012), 180–2, on the critique that Platonic 'political rationalism' can offer with respect to proponents of divine law.

140 Epilogue

which should guide the human community, if we are to live in some sort of peace and justice. He can provoke us to think about the general principles which need to be used in pursuing these objectives and about the way in which our life can relate to the world of nature. This is the task, Plato would tell us, not of economics, nor of science, but of philosophy.

Bibliography

Ancient Authors

Anthologia Palatina. The Greek Anthology, trans. W. Paton, Cambridge, MA, and London 1916–18.

DK = H. Diels and W. Kranz, *Die Fragmente der Vorsokratiker*, Berlin 1952.

Diogenes Laertius, *Vitae philosophorum*, ed. M. Markovich, Stuttgart 1999.

Gregory of Nyssa, *In Christi resurrectione Or. III*, in: J.-P. Migne, *Patrologia graeca*, vol. 46, Paris 1858.

Ibn Tufayl, *Hayy ibn Yaqzan*, trans. L. Goodman, Chicago 2003.

Olympiodorus, *Commentary on the First Alcibiades of Plato*, ed. L. G. Westerink, Amsterdam 1982.

Philo of Alexandria, *De opificio mundi*, ed. R. Arnaldez, Paris 1961.

De Vita Mosis, I–II, ed. R. Arnaldez, C. Mondésert et al., Paris 1967.

Pindar, *Nemean Odes, Isthmean Odes, Fragments*, trans. W. Race, Cambridge, MA, and London 1997.

Plato, *Opera*, ed. J. Burnet, Oxford 1900.

Opera, ed. E. A. Duke, W. F. Hicken et al., vol. I, Oxford 1995.

Plotinus, *Enneads*, ed. P. Henry and H.-R. Schwyzer, Oxford 1964–82.

Plutarch, *Life of Solon*, in: *Plutarch's Lives*, trans. B. Perrin, vol. I, Cambridge, MA, and London 1914.

Life of Pericles, in: *Plutarch's Lives*, trans. B. Perrin, vol. III, Cambridge, MA, and London 1916.

An vitiositas ad infelicitatem sufficiat, in: *Plutarch's Moralia*, vol. VI, trans. W. Helmbold, Cambridge, MA, and London 1939.

De Herodoti malignitate, in: *Plutarch's Moralia*, vol. XI, trans. L. Pearson and F. Sandbach, Cambridge, MA, and London, 1965.

Porphyry, *Fragments*, ed. A. Smith, Stuttgart 1993.

Proclus, *In Platonis Timaeum*, ed. E. Diehl, Leipzig 1903.

Psellus, *De omnifaria doctrina*, ed. L. G. Westerink, Nijmegen 1948.

Theophrastus, *Metaphysics*, ed. A. Laks and G. Most, Paris 1993.

142   *Bibliography*

Modern Studies

Annas, J. (2010), 'Virtue and Law in Plato', in: Bobonich (2010), 71–91.

Artman, B. and L. Schäfer (1993), 'On Plato's "Fairest Triangles"(*Timaeus* 54a)', *Historia Mathematica* 20, 255–64.

Bader, F. (1965), *Les Composés grecs du type de Demiourgos*, Paris.

Balansard, A. (2001), Technè *dans les* Dialogues *de Platon*, Sankt Augustin.

Baltes, M. (1999), *Dianoêmata. Kleine Schriften zu Platon und zum Platonismus*, Stuttgart.

Barber, E. (1992), 'The Peplos of Athena', in: J. Neils (ed.), *Goddess and Polis*, Hanover, NH, 103–17.

Barney, R. (2008), 'The Carpenter and the Good', in: Cairns, Herrmann, Penner (2008), 293–319.

(2010), 'Notes on Plato on the *Kalon* and the Good', *Classical Philology* 105, 363–77.

Belfiore, E. (2006), 'Dancing with the Gods: The Myth of the Chariot in Plato's *Phaedrus*', *American Journal of Philology* 127, 185–217.

Betegh, G. (2003), 'Cosmological Ethics in the *Timaeus* and Early Stoicism', *Oxford Studies in Ancient Philosophy* 24, 273–302.

Black, J. (2000), *The Four Elements in Plato's Timaeus*, Lewiston, NY.

Blondell, R. (2002), *The Play of Character in Plato's Dialogues*, Cambridge.

(2005), 'From Fleece to Fabric: Weaving Culture in Plato's *Statesman*', *Oxford Studies in Ancient Philosophy* 28, 23–75.

Bobonich, C. (2002), *Plato's Utopia Recast*, Oxford.

(2010) ed., *Plato's Laws. A Critical Guide*, Cambridge.

Boys-Stones, G. and J. Haubold (2010) eds., *Plato and Hesiod*, Oxford.

Brisson, L. (1998), *Le Même et l'autre dans la structure ontologique du Timée de Platon*, third ed., Sankt Augustin.

(2005), 'Ethics and Politics in Plato's *Laws*', *Oxford Studies in Ancient Philosophy*, 28, 93–121.

Brisson, L. and J.-F. Pradeau (2006), *Platon Les Lois*, Paris.

Broadie, S. (2007). 'Why No Platonistic Ideas of Artefacts?', in: D. Scott (ed.). *Maieusis. Essays on Ancient Philosophy in Honour of Myles Burnyeat*, Oxford, 232–53.

(2012), *Nature and Divinity in Plato's Timaeus*, Cambridge.

Brulé, P. (1987), *La fille d'Athènes*, Paris.

Burnyeat, M. (1995), 'Eikos mythos', *Rhizai* 2, 143–65.

(1999), 'Culture and Society in Plato's Republic', *The Tanner Lectures on Human Values* 20, 215–324.

(2000), 'Plato on Why Mathematics Is Good for the Soul', in: T. Smiley (ed.), *Mathematics and Necessity. Essays in the History of Philosophy = Proceedings of the British Academy* 103, 1–81.

Cairns, D., F.-G. Herrmann, T. Penner (2008) eds., *Pursuing the Good. Ethics and Metaphysics in Plato's Republic*, Edinburgh.

Bibliography

Calvo, T. and L. Brisson (1997) eds., *Interpreting the Timaeus-Critias*, Sankt Augustin.

Capra, A. (2010), 'Plato's Hesiod and the Will of Zeus: Philosophical Rhapsody in the *Timaeus* and *Critias*', in: Boys-Stones and Haubold (2010), 200–18.

(2014), *Plato's Four Muses. The Phaedrus and the Poetics of Philosophy*, Washington, DC.

Carone, G. (2005), *Plato's Cosmology and Its Ethical Dimensions*, Cambridge.

Castelletti, C. (2006), *Porfirio sullo Stige*, Milan.

Clay, D. (1988), 'Reading the *Republic*', in: C. Griswold (ed.), *Platonic Writings, Platonic Readings*, New York, 19–33.

(1997), 'The Plan of Plato's *Critias*', in: Calvo and Brisson (1997), 49–54.

Cohen, D. (1993), 'Law, Autonomy, and Political Community in Plato's *Laws*', *Classical Philology* 88, 301–17.

Cornelli, G. and F. Lisi (2010) eds., *Plato and the City*, Sankt Augustin.

Cornford, F. (1935), *Plato's Cosmology. The Timaeus of Plato*, Cambridge.

Coulton, J. J. (1977), *Greek Architects at Work*, London.

De Callataÿ, G. (1996), *Annus Platonicus. A Study of World Cycles in Greek, Latin and Arabic Sources*, Louvain.

Del Forno, D. (2005), 'La struttura numerica dell'anima del mondo (Timeo 35 B 4 – 36 B 6)', *Elenchos* 26, 5–32.

Diès, A. (1960), *Platon Le Politique*, Paris.

Dixsaut, M. (1991), *Platon Phédon*, Paris.

Dover, K. (1980), *Plato. Symposium*, Cambridge.

Ebert, T. (1991), 'Von der Weltursache zum Weltbaumeister. Bemerkungen zu einem Argumentationsfehler im platonischen *Timaios*', *Antike und Abendland* 37, 43–54.

El Murr, D. (2002), 'La *symplokê politikê*: le paradigme du tissage dans le *Politique* de Platon, ou les raisons d'un paradigme "arbitraire"', *Kairos* 19 (*Platon*), 49–95.

(2009), 'Politics and Dialectic in Plato's *Statesman*', in: *Proceedings of the Boston Area Colloquium in Ancient Philosophy*, 25, G. Gurtler and W. Wians eds., 109–35.

(2010), 'Socrate aux portes du Bien: l'occasion manquée du *Philèbe* (61a–65a)', in: A. Brancacci, D. El Murr and D. Taormina (eds.), *Aglaia. Autour de Platon. Mélanges offerts à Monique Dixsaut*, Paris, 373–86.

(2014), *Savoir et gouverner. Essai sur la science politique platonicienne*, Paris.

England, E. (1921), *The Laws of Plato*, Manchester (repr. New York 1976).

Erler, M. (1997), 'Ideal und Geschichte. Die Rahmengespräche des *Timaios* und *Kritias* und Aristoteles' *Poetik*', in: Calvo and Brisson (1997), 83–98.

(2007), *Platon* (*Die Philosophie der Antike*, ed. H. Flashar, vol. 2/2), Basel.

Ferber, R. (1995), 'Für eine propädeutische Lektüre des *Politikos*', in: Rowe (1995a), 63–75.

(2007), *Warum hat Platon die 'ungeschriebene Lehre' nicht geschrieben?* Sankt Augustin.

Bibliography

Ferrari, F. (2003), 'Causa paradigmatica e causa efficiente: il ruolo delle Idee nel *Timeo*', in: Natali and Maso (2003), 83–96.

——— (2010), 'Der entmythologisierte Demiurg', in: Koch, Männlein-Robert, Weidtmann (2010), 62–81.

Festugière, A. J. (1966), *Proclus. Commentaire sur le Timée*, Paris.

Frede, D. (1996), 'The Philosophical Economy of Plato's Psychology: Rationality and Common Concepts in the *Timaeus*', in: M. Frede and G. Striker (eds.), *Rationality in Greek Thought*, Oxford, 29–58.

Garvey, T. (2008), 'Plato's Atlantis Story: A Prose Hymn to Athena', *Greek, Roman, and Byzantine Studies* 48, 381–92.

Görgemanns, H. (1960), *Beiträge zur Interpretation von Platons Nomoi*, Munich.

Gill, M. L. (2012), *Philosophus. Plato's Missing Dialogue*, Oxford.

——— (2013), 'Plato's *Statesman* and Missing *Philosopher*', in: Havlíček, Jirsa, Thein (2013), 27–39.

Goldschmidt, V. (1947), *Le Paradigme dans la dialectique platonicienne*, Paris.

Gülgönen, S. (2011), 'L'éducation musicale dans les *Lois*', *Journal of Ancient Philosophy* 5 (www.filosofiaantiga.com).

Hadot, P. (1983), 'Physique et poésie dans le *Timée* de Platon', *Revue de Théologie et de Philosophie* 113, 113–33 = P. Hadot, *Etudes de philosophie ancienne*, Paris 1998, 277–305.

——— (1992), *La Citadelle intérieure. Introduction aux Pensées de Marc Aurèle*, Paris.

Harte, V. (2002), *Plato on Parts and Wholes: The Metaphysics of Structure*, Oxford.

——— (2010), 'The Receptacle and the Primary Bodies: Something from Nothing?', in: Mohr and Sattler (2010), 131–40.

Haselberger, L. (1980), 'Werkzeichnungen am Jüngeren Didymeion. Vorbericht', *Istanbuler Mitteilungen* (Deutsches Archäologisches Institut, Abteilung Istanbul) 30, 191–215.

——— (1983), 'Bericht über die Arbeit am Jüngeren Apollontempel von Didyma', *Istanbuler Mitteilungen* 33, 90–123.

Havlíček, A., J. Jirsa and K. Thein (2013) eds., *Plato's Statesman*, Prague.

Havlíček, A. and F. Karfík (1998) eds., *The Republic and the Laws of Plato*, Prague.

Hellmann, M.-C. (1992), *Recherches sur le vocabulaire de l'architecture grecque d'après les inscriptions de Délos*, Athens.

——— (1999), *Choix d'inscriptions architecturales grecques, traduites et commentées*, Lyon.

Hentschke, A. (1971), *Politik und Philosophie bei Platon und Aristoteles. Die Stellung der 'Nomoi' im platonischen Gesamtwerk und die politische Theorie des Aristoteles*, Frankfurt.

Holtzmann, B. (2003), *L'Acropole d'Athènes. Monuments, cultes et histoire du sanctuaire d'Athèna Polias*, Paris.

Huffman, C. (1993), *Philolaus of Croton*, Cambridge.

——— (2005), *Archytas of Tarentum*, Cambridge.

Johansen, T. (2004), *Plato's Natural Philosophy. A Study of the Timaeus-Critias*, Cambridge.

Bibliography

Johnson, W. (1998), 'Dramatic Frame and Philosophic Idea in Plato', *American Journal of Philology* 119, 577–98.

Kahn C. (2013), *Plato and the Post-Socratic Dialogue. The Return to the Philosophy of Nature*, Cambridge.

Käppel, L. (1999), 'Die Paradegma-Inschrift im Tunnel des Eupalinos auf Samos', *Antike und Abendland* 45, 75–100.

Karfík, F. (2004), *Die Beseelung des Kosmos. Untersuchungen zur Kosmologie, Seelenlehre und Theologie in Platons Phaidon und Timaios*, Leipzig.

(2007), 'Que fait et qui est le démiurge dans le *Timée?*', in: *Études platoniciennes IV. Les Puissances de l'âme selon Platon*, ed. A. Macé, Paris, 129–50.

(2013), 'The World of Human Politics. The Conditions of Political Rule in Plato's *Politicus*', in: Havlíček, Jirsa, Thein (2013), 118–33.

Kato, S. (1995), 'The Role of *Paradeigma* in the *Statesman*', in: Rowe (1995a), 162–72.

Kleve, K. (1987), 'Did Socrates Exist?' *Grazer Beiträge: Zeitschrift für die klassische Altertumswissenschaft* 14, 123–37.

Koch, D., I. Männlein-Robert and N. Weidtmann (2010) eds., *Platon und das Göttliche*, Tübingen.

(2012) eds., *Platon und die Mousiké*. Tübingen.

Koenigs, W. (1983a), 'Pytheos – eine mythische Figur in der antiken Baugeschichte', in: *Bauplanung und Bautheorie der Antike. Diskussionen zur archäologischen Bauforschung* 4, 89–94.

(1983b), 'Der Athenatempel von Priene. Bericht über die 1977–1982 durchgeführten Untersuchungen', *Istanbuler Mitteilungen* 33, 134–75.

(2012), 'Syngraphai. Politischer Ablauf von Bauprojekten in der griechischen Antike', in: U. Kiessler (ed.), *Architektur im Museum 1977–2012* (Festschrift W. Nerdinger), Munich, 145–9.

(2015), *Der Athenatempel von Priene*, Wiesbaden.

Kurke, L. (2013), 'Imagining Chorality: Wonder, Plato's Puppets, and Moving Statues', in: Peponi (2013), 123–70.

Laks, A. (1990), 'Legislation and Demiurgy. On the Relationship between Plato's *Republic* and *Laws*', *Classical Antiquity* 9, 209–29.

(2005), *Médiation et coercition. Pour une lecture des Lois de Platon*, Villeneuve d'Ascq.

(2010), 'Plato's "Truest Tragedy": *Laws* Book 7, 817a–d', in: Bobonich (2010), 217–31.

Lane, M. (1998), *Method and Politics in Plato's Statesman*, Cambridge.

(2012), *Eco-republic. What the Ancients Can Teach Us about Ethics, Virtue, and Sustainable Living*, Princeton.

Lavecchia, S. (2006), *Una via che conduce al divino. La "Homoiosis theo" nella filosofia di Platone*, Milan.

Ledger, G. (1989). *Recounting Plato: A Computer Analysis of Plato's Style*, Oxford.

Lefka, A. (2013), *"Tout est plein de dieux". Les divinités traditionnelles dans l'œuvre de Platon*, Paris.

Lisi, F. (1985), *Einheit und Vielheit des platonischen Nomosbegriffes*, Königstein/Ts.

(2001) ed., *Plato's* Laws *and Its Historical Significance*, Sankt Augustin.

146 *Bibliography*

Lloyd-Jones, H. (1971), *The Justice of Zeus*, Berkeley and Los Angeles, CA.

Loraux, N. (1990), *Les enfants d'Athéna*, Paris.

Lutz, M. (2012), *Divine Law and Political Philosophy in Plato's Laws*, DeKalb, IL.

Männlein-Robert, I. (2010), 'Umrisse des Göttlichen. Zur Typologie des idealen Gottes in Platons *Politeia* II', in: Koch, Männlein-Robert, Weidtmann (2010), 112–38.

Mayhew, R. (2011), '"God or some Human": On the Source of Law in Plato's *Laws*', *Ancient Philosophy* 31, 311–25.

Menn, S. (1995), *Plato on God as Nous*, Carbondale, IL.

Miller, D. (2003), *The Third Kind in Plato's* Timaeus, Göttingen.

Miller, J. (1986), *Measures of Wisdom: The Cosmic Dance in Classical and Christian Antiquity*, Toronto.

Miller, M. (1980), *The Philosopher in Plato's* Statesman, The Hague.

Mohr, R. (1985), *The Platonic Cosmology*, Leiden.

Mohr, R. and B. Sattler (2010) eds., *One Book, the Whole Universe. Plato's* Timaeus *Today*, Las Vegas.

Monoson, S. (2000), *Plato's Democratic Entanglements*, Princeton.

Moore, K. (2012), *Plato, Politics and a Practical Utopia*, London.

Morrow, G. (1954), 'The Demiurge in Politics: The *Timaeus* and the *Laws*', in: *Proceedings and Addresses of the American Philosophical Association* 27, 5–23.

(1960), *Plato's Cretan City*, Princeton.

(1976), *Plato's Law of Slavery in Its Relation to Greek Law*, New York.

Mouze, L. (2005), *Le législateur et le poète. Une interprétation des Lois de Platon*, Villeneuve d'Ascq.

Nagy, G. (2002), *Plato's Rhapsody and Homer's Music: The Poetics of the Panathenaic Festival in Classical Athens*, Washington, DC.

Nails, D. (2002), *The People of Plato: A Prosopography of Plato and other Socratics*, Indianapolis, IN.

Napolitano Valditara, L. (2007), ed., *La sapienza di Timeo*, Milan.

Natali, C. and S. Maso (2003) eds., *Plato Physicus. Cosmologia e antropologia nel Timeo*, Amsterdam.

Neils, J. (2001), *The Parthenon Frieze*, Cambridge.

Neschke-Hentschke, A. (1995), *Platonisme politique et théorie du droit naturel*, vol. I, Louvain-Paris.

Nesselrath, H.-G. (2006), *Platon Kritias. Übersetzung und Kommentar*, Göttingen.

Nightingale, A. (1993), 'Writing/Reading a Sacred Text: A Literary Interpretation of Plato's *Laws*', *Classical Philology* 88, 279–300.

Notomi, N. (2010), 'The Nature and Possibility of the Best City: Plato's *Republic* in Its Historical Contexts', in: Cornelli and Lisi (2010), 113–23.

O'Meara, D. (2003), *Platonopolis. Political Philosophy in Late Antiquity*, Oxford.

(2005), 'Geometry and the Divine in Proclus', in: T. Koetsier and L. Bergmans (eds.), *Mathematics and the Divine: A Historical Study*, Amsterdam, 133–45.

(2016), 'The Poet as Demiurge in Plato', in: H.-C. Günther (ed.), *Political Poetry across the Centuries*, Leiden, 3–14.

Bibliography

Osborne, C. (1996), 'Space, Time, Shape, and Direction: Creative Discourse in the *Timaeus*', in: C. Gill and M. McCabe (eds.), *Form and Argument in Late Plato*, Oxford, 179–211.

Palagia, O. (1993), *The Pediments of the Parthenon*, Leiden.

Panno, G. (2007), *Dionisiaco e alterità nelle Leggi di Platone. Ordine del corpo e automovimento dell'anima nella città-tragedia*, Milan.

Parke, H. W. (1977), *Festivals of the Athenians*, London.

Parker, R. (2005), *Polytheism and Society at Athens*, Oxford.

Pelosi, F. (2010), *Plato on Music, Soul and Body*, Cambridge.

Pender, E. (2007), 'Poetic Allusion in Plato's *Timaeus* and *Phaedrus*', *Göttinger Forum für Altertumswissenschaft* 10, 21–57.

  (2010), 'Chaos Corrected: Hesiod in Plato's Creation Myth', in: Boys-Stones and Haubold (2010), 219–45.

Penner, T. (2006), 'The Forms in the *Republic*', in: G. Santas (ed.), *The Blackwell Guide to Plato's Republic*, Oxford, 234–62.

Peponi, A.-E. (2013) ed., *Performance and Culture in Plato's Laws*, Cambridge.

Perl, E. (1999), 'The Presence of the Paradigm: Immanence and Transcendence in Plato's Theory of Forms', *Revue of Metaphysics* 53, 339–62.

Pernot, L. (2007), 'Hymne en vers ou hymne en prose? L'usage de la prose dans l'hymnographie grecque', in: Y. Lehmann (ed.), *L'hymne antique et son public*, Turnhout, 169–88.

Pickard-Cambridge, A. (1988), *The Dramatic Festivals of Athens*, 2nd ed., Oxford.

Piérart, M. (2008), *Platon et la cité grecque. Théorie et réalité dans la constitution des Lois*, 2nd ed., Paris.

Pradeau, J.-F. (1997), *Le Monde de la Politique. Sur le récit atlante de Platon, Timée (17–27) et Critias*, Sankt Augustin.

  (1998), 'L'Exégète ennuyé. Une introduction à la lecture des *Lois* de Platon', in: Havlíček and Karfík (1998), 154–81.

Prauscello, L. (2014), *Performing Citizenship in Plato's Laws*, Cambridge.

Regali, M. (2010), 'Hesiod in the *Timaeus*: The Demiurge Addresses the Gods', in: Boys-Stones and Haubold (2010), 259–75.

  (2012), *Il Poeta e il demiurgo. Teoria e prassi della produzione letteraria nel Timeo e nel Crizia*, Sankt Augustin.

Reverdin, O. (1945), *La religion de la cité platonicienne*, Paris.

Rhodes, P. (1981), *A Commentary on the Aristotelian Athenaion Politeia*, Oxford.

Ricken, F. (2008), *Platon Politikos. Übersetzung und Kommentar*, Göttingen.

Riegel, N. (2015), 'The City Dionysia and the Structure of Plato's Symposium', *Ancient Philosophy* 35, 259–86.

Ritter, C. (1910), *Neue Untersuchungen über Platon*, Tübingen.

Robins, I. (1995), 'Mathematics and the Conversion of the Mind. *Republic* vii 522c1–531e3', *Ancient Philosophy* 15, 359–91.

Rowe, C. (1995a) ed., *Reading the* Statesman, Sankt Augustin.

  (1995b), *Plato:* Statesman, Warminster.

  (2007), *Plato and the Art of Philosophical Writing*, Cambridge.

  (2013), 'The Statesman and the Best City', in: Havlíček, Jirsa, Thein (2013), 40–50.

148 *Bibliography*

Rowe, C. and M. Schofield (2000) eds., *The Cambridge History of Greek and Roman Political Thought*, Cambridge.

Ruben, T. (2016), *Le Discours comme image. Énonciation, récit et connaissance dans le Timée-Critias de Platon*, Paris.

Rudolph, E. (1996) ed., *Polis und Kosmos. Naturphilosophie und politische Philosophie bei Platon*, Darmstadt.

Runia, D. (2001), *Philo of Alexandria. On the Creation of the Cosmos according to Moses*, Leiden.

Saunders, T. (1970), *Plato* The Laws, Harmondsworth.

Schäfer. L. (2005), *Das Paradeigma am Himmel. Platon über Natur und Staat.* Freiburg.

Scheid, J. and J. Svenbro (1994), *Le Métier de Zeus. Mythe du tissage et du tissu dans le monde gréco-romain*, Paris.

Schmitt Pantel, P. (1992), *La Cité au banquet*, Rome.

Schöpsdau, K. (1991), 'Der Staatsentwurf der Nomoi zwischen Ideal und Wirklichkeit. Zu Plato leg.739a1–e7 und 745e7–746d2', *Rheinisches Museum für Philologie* 134, 136–52.

　(1994), *Platon Nomoi (Gesetze) Buch I–III*, Göttingen.

　(2003), *Platon Nomoi (Gesetze) Buch IV–VII*, Göttingen.

　(2011), *Platon Nomoi (Gesetze) Buch VIII–XII*, Göttingen.

Schofield, M. (2006), *Plato. Political Philosophy*, Oxford.

Schuhl, P.-M. (^{2}1952), *Platon et l'art de son temps (arts plastiques)*, Paris.

Scolnikov, S. and L. Brisson (2003), eds., *Plato's Laws. From Theory into Practice*, Sankt Augustin.

Sedley, D. (2007), *Creationism and Its Critics in Antiquity*, Berkeley and Los Angeles, CA.

Senseney, J. (2011), *The Art of Building in the Classical World*, Cambridge.

Slatter, B. (2012), 'A Likely Account of Necessity: Plato's Receptacle as a Physical and Metaphysical Foundation for Space', *Journal of the History of Philosophy*, 50, 159–95.

Slaveva-Griffin, S. (2005), '"A Feast of Speeches". Form and Content in Plato's Timaeus', *Hermes* 133, 312–27.

Stalley, R. (1983), *An Introduction to Plato's Laws*, Oxford.

Snell, B. (1980), *Die Entdeckung des Geistes*, 5th ed., Göttingen.

Taylor, A. E. (1928), *A Commentary on Plato's Timaeus*, Oxford.

　(1929), *Plato. Timaeus and Critias* (trans.), London.

Thein, K. (2013), '"The Greatest and Most Valuable Things": On *Statesman* 285d9–286a7', in: Havlíček, Jirsa, Thein (2013), 162–77.

Tigerstedt, E. (1977), *Interpreting Plato*, Stockholm.

Vidal-Naquet, P. (1981), *Le Chasseur noir*, Paris.

　(2005), *L'Atlantide. Petite histoire d'un mythe platonicien*, Paris.

Vlastos, G. (1939), 'Disorderly Motion in Plato's *Timaeus*', in: G. Vlastos, *Studies in Greek Philosophy*, vol. II, Princeton 1995, 247–64.

　(1975), *Plato's Universe*, Oxford.

Index locorum

ARISTOPHANES
  Lysistrata
    574–86, 93
ARISTOTLE
  Constitution of the Athenians
    49.3, 89
  De anima
    1.2. 404b19–21, 53
  Historia animalium
    8.1.588a27–588b1, 61

HERACLITUS
  fr. 32, 28

OLYMPIODORUS
  In Alcibiadem
    2, 155–65, 1

PHILO
  De opificio mundi
    17–19, 48
    24–5, 48
PLATO
  Apology
    31d–32a, 21
  Critias
    106a3–4, 38
    106a4, 30
    108b3–5, 34
    108c, 20
    109c6–d2, 39
    109d–110b, 19
    109e2, 102
    110bc, 19
    110d, 62
    111d, 62
    113c, 22
    119c–120d, 22
    120e–121b, 22
  Euthydemus
    291c, 99
    292ce, 99

Euthyphro
  6c, 90, 93
Gorgias
  464b–465c, 99
  507e6–508a, 56
Greater Hippias
  295c–296e, 76
  296e8–297a1, 76
  297bc, 76
Laws
  624ab, 106
  626ab, 45
  626d, 9, 44, 106, 108
  628c, 45
  628d, 111
  630d, 108
  637b, 113
  638b, 106
  640b–641a, 16
  650a, 114
  650b, 111
  653cd, 126
  653d, 114
  653e3–654a5, 127
  655a6, 127
  655b, 127
  655d, 127
  656b, 128
  656d, 128
  656e, 110
  659de, 128
  660a, 128
  661c, 128
  664c, 128
  664d2–4, 129
  665c, 125
  665a, 127
  665a–666c, 129
  673a, 127
  680c, 107
  685a, 107
  688a, 45

Index locorum

PLATO (cont.)
692ab, 45
693a, 111
693bc, 45
693c, 45
700a, 128
700bd, 128
701ac, 108
701d, 45
702cd, 106
702d, 106
702e, 105
704a, 118
704c ff., 62
705e, 45
709ab, 131
710a, 114
712b, 107
713cd, 131
713e4–714a2, 132
715ab, 109
715ac, 45
716ce, 53
722a, 106
722de, 128
723a, 128
726a–734e, 128
734c–735a, 93
734e6, 109
737d, 119
737d7, 109
737d–738a, 119
738bd, 121
738cd, 62
739ce, 45, 47, 138
740ae, 120
740d, 119
741a, 79
741ab, 125
741c1–2, 120, 123
744c, 72
744a, 112
744d, 120
745b, 120, 121
745e–746d, 46
746b8, 67
746bc, 9
746d, 119
747a3–4, 127
747b, 128
752a, 129
752de, 110
753a, 107
757ad, 56
757ae, 120

765d, 126
769a, 107
769d–770a, 110
770b–771a, 111
770b8, 109
771b, 123
771d, 121
789a, 127
789b–790e, 127
790e, 127
795d, 127
795e1, 127
795e6, 127
798e, 127
798e–799a, 128
799e, 128
801ae, 128
801cd, 57
803a, 109
809bd, 128
811bc, 128
811be, 57
811c8–9, 132
811ce, 128
817b, 114
818a, 123
820a–822c, 128
821bc, 129
828c, 121
828b, 121
848d, 119, 121
853c, 132
853c–854a, 124
858d–859a, 128
858e, 128
860e, 119
875a, 111
876d7, 109
876e, 109
885b, 130
886cd, 129
886d, 130
886d6–e2, 130
889bc, 130
889e8, 130
890a4, 131
890a8–9, 131
890d–891a, 131
893b–898e, 131
898ab, 123
899b8, 132
919d, 119
930e9–931a3, 129
946b, 119
950e–951a, 121

Index locorum

951bc, 111
959e, 111
961c ff., 111
961a, 111
961de, 112
962a ff., 111
962a, 45
962b, 45
963a–966a, 112
966c, 112
966de, 112
966e, 123
967ac, 112
967d, 112
967e, 113
968b, 108
968de, 113
968e, 113
968e–969d, 113
969a, 119

Menexenus
237a6, 39
237b5–c2, 62

Parmenides
131bc, 90
135d, 100
136de, 100

Phaedo
66c5–7, 45

Philebus
11b4–5, 67
11d4–6, 67
25a7–8, 78
25d11–e1, 72
27b1, 28, 68
28c7, 68
28d–30e, 131
30cd, 28
30d1–2, 68
59d10–e3, 68
61a1–2, 68
61a4–5, 68
61a9, 103
61a9–b2, 68
63e7–64a3, 68
64b, 102
64b6–c3, 68
64c, 103
64c–66b, 73
64d4, 69
64d9, 68
64e, 103
64e5–7, 68
66a6–8, 69
66b1–2, 69

66b2, 56
66b6–c5, 69

Protagoras
319b, 49
326c7–8, 57

Republic
327a–328a, 126
373a6–7, 90
373de, 45
378bc, 32
378c, 90
378c4, 90
379c, 33
379b, 33
380c7, 57
380d2–3, 34
380d5–6, 34
390e, 34
398c1–399e9, 127
399e9–403c5, 127
401a, 90
401a2, 90
403c5, 127
414e, 62
414e2–4, 63
421b2–4, 126
433b4, 44
443b1–2, 44
443d–444b, 44
472c4–d7, 44
472cd, 47
475de, 126
500e2–501b7, 43
501ab, 109
504d6–7, 109
511bc, 9
522a, 127
529c7, 123
530a1, 72
530a4–6, 29
548d, 109
557c, 93
557c7–8, 90
583b2–3, 33
592b2–3, 21
592b4, 46
596b, 59
596ce, 59

Sophist
216a, 87
217ab, 83
226bd, 94
246ab, 32
246ac, 90
253c, 97

Index locorum

PLATO (cont.)
253ce, 97
268c5–6, 94
Statesman
257a, 83
257c, 87, 96
259b, 99
259e–260a, 97
260a7, 57
260c, 97
267ab, 94
268c10, 95
268de, 98
268e, 95
271ab, 102
271b, 98
273e5–274b1, 98
274d, 98
274d1, 90
274e–275a, 98
277a, 96
277a1, 96
277b, 91
277bc, 109
277c, 96
277d–278e, 91
277e, 95
279ab, 91
279b, 91
280d, 54
282e, 94
283ab, 92
284a8–b2, 70
285d, 96
285e–286a, 98
286a6–7, 96
286d, 94
286e–287a, 96
292e, 99
292e–293a, 101
293e, 101
294a, 100
294ad, 100
294d, 100
294e, 100
295cd, 100
295a, 100
295c, 100
297a, 100
297bc, 101
297c, 102
297d, 101, 105
297e, 96
298cd, 101
300b, 101

300de, 102
300e, 101
301a, 102
304d, 100
309b5, 92
309c–310b, 92
310e10–311a1, 92
311bc, 92
311c4, 95
311c7–8, 96
Theaetetus
142c, 87
145c, 87
147d–148b, 72
210d, 87
Timaeus
17a, 14
17a4, 14
17b, 15
17b5, 15
17c, 15
17c–19a, 16, 17
18bd, 46
19a8, 16
19c, 17
19d1–2, 20
19d–20b, 20
20a, 21
20a2, 35
20b6, 15
20bc, 15
20d, 15
20d2, 15
20d3, 15
20e6–21a3, 16
21a, 13
21c6–d1, 101
21d, 6
21e, 19
23b, 6
23d–24d, 93
23d5–e2, 19
23e4–5, 19
24a–d, 19
24b7–c7, 37
24bc, 27
24c4–d6, 19
25c4, 17
26c6, 17
26d6, 15
26e3, 13
27cd, 28
27a, 21
27d6, 58
28a, 59

Index locorum

28a4–5, 58
28a6, 28
28a6–b2, 41, 67
28b7, 38
28c2–4, 51
28c3, 27
28c3–5, 29
28c5–29a6, 66
28e5–29a6, 41
28e6, 35
29cd, 29
29a3, 51
29a4, 29
29a5, 65
29a6, 51
29d5–6, 34
29d7–30a2, 51
29e–30a, 30
30a2–7, 66
30b, 30, 51
30b2–6, 67
30c2–3, 51
30c4–31a1, 51
30c5–d2, 67
30d2, 67
31b–32c, 52, 73
31c2–32a7, 73
31c2–4, 78
32c–34a, 63
32c2, 51
32c2–3, 30
33a1, 51
33a7, 51
33ad, 56
33b–34b, 123
34b10–35a1, 38
34b4–9, 51
34b8, 51
35a ff., 74
35a1, 70
35a1 ff., 70
35a–39e, 70
35a8, 70
35b4 ff., 70
35b4–5, 70
36a, 71
36a1, 70
36b7, 70, 72
36c4–5, 72
36d1, 72
36d2–3, 72
36d6, 72
37a2–37c5, 72
37a4, 71
37c6–d1, 30, 72

37d, 56
37d6, 72
37d6–7, 124
38c–39d, 30
38a7, 72
38c3, 30
39cd, 123
39d2, 123
39e1–2, 72
39e7–40a2, 52
40a, 123
40a2–4, 73
40c3, 133
40c3–4, 123
40d4, 31
40d–41a, 28
40d6–41a2, 31
41a1, 33
41a4, 31, 34
41a7–b7, 31
42d6, 31
42e5–6, 34
42e5–8, 31
42e7–43a5, 54
43a4, 57
44d3–6, 54
44de, 124
46c8, 51
46e6, 57
47bc, 79
47e3–48a7, 39
48b, 53
48d4–e1, 33
48e–49b, 59
49a6, 62
49b7–e7, 60
50b4–6, 60
50b6, 62
50be, 60
50c2, 62
50c5, 59
50c6, 51, 60
50d2–3, 39, 62
51a2, 59
51a4–5, 62
51b6, 60
51b7–c1, 53
52a8–b1, 62
52d–53b, 74
53c, 74
53c–54d, 74
53c–56c, 73
53a2 ff., 60
53a7–b5, 60
53b, 53

Index locorum

PLATO (cont.)
- 53b2, 59
- 53b4–5, 74
- 53c4 ff., 60
- 53c8–d2, 74
- 53d4–7, 53, 74, 77
- 53d6–7, 98
- 54a1–2, 74
- 54a6–7, 74
- 54d4, 75
- 54d–56c, 74
- 55c6, 58
- 55d7, 30
- 56c3–7, 75
- 68e7–69a5, 37
- 69b2–c1, 61
- 71e–72b, 37
- 87c, 65
- 87c–89c, 37
- 87c4–d3, 69
- 88d6, 62
- 90cd, 27
- 90d1–7, 37
- 91d–92c, 54
- 92c6–9, 36
- 92c8, 51

PSELLOS
De omnifaria doctrina
- 200, 133

General Index

Academy, 4, 6, 7, 87, 114
Acropolis, 13, 19, 27, 82, 88, 89, 93, 96, 103, 114, 119, 121, 123, 129
agathos, 66, 79
aim (*skopos*), 45
Al-Farabi, 131
animal, 30, 42, 51, 52, 53, 55, 56, 63, 67
animal genera, 52, 53, 54, 55
Apollo, 1, 49, 108, 126, 129, 132
apprentice, 96, 98
architect, 35, 48, 49, 50, 54, 57, 58, 61, 62, 65, 78, 80, 82, 109
architecture, 49, 50, 57, 58, 61, 62, 69, 78, 82, 91, 97, 103, 122
astronomy, 72, 108, 112, 113, 115, 125, 128, 133
atheist, 112
Athena, 9, 13, 16, 18, 19, 20, 21, 22, 23, 26, 27, 28, 32, 33, 36, 39, 44, 49, 62, 88, 89, 90, 91, 92, 93, 94, 95, 96, 106, 108, 114, 121, 130, 132
Atlantis, 7, 14, 17, 19, 20, 21, 22, 23, 26, 32, 83, 101
autochthony, 39, 62, 63

banquet, 15, 16, 17, 25, 26, 34
Bardesanes, 42, 43, 44, 52, 78
beauty, 65, 67, 69, 75, 76, 77, 78, 96
Bendis, 18, 126
body, 29, 30, 38, 52, 53, 54, 68, 69, 70, 73, 77, 78, 126, 127, 129

carding, 91, 94, 95
Chalkeia, 36, 89
chôra, 62, 63
chorus, 114, 127, 128, 129, 132, 133, 134
circle, 43, 72, 74, 78, 80, 119, 123, 133
Cleinias, 44, 47, 106, 107, 108, 109, 110, 112, 115, 117, 119, 124, 127, 129, 132
commensurable, 61, 71, 128
common good, 109
complete (*teleios*), 51, 68, 69
constitution, 43, 45, 89, 93, 95, 101, 102, 106, 108, 110, 111, 131

cosmos, 27, 34, 36, 37, 48, 56, 68, 69, 93, 102, 103, 118, 123, 124
courage, 108, 109, 127
craft (*technê*), 25, 26, 29, 35, 36, 39, 41, 44, 50, 54, 57, 58, 90, 91, 93, 96, 97
Crete, 44, 47, 106, 107, 108, 109, 110, 113, 117, 119, 127
Critias, 14, 15, 16, 17, 18, 19, 20, 21, 22, 23, 26, 27, 39, 62, 83

dancing, 13, 114, 118, 122, 125, 127, 128, 129, 133
dêmiourgos, 28, 35, 47, 48, 68
demiurge, 25, 26, 27, 28, 29, 30, 31, 32, 33, 34, 35, 36, 37, 38, 39, 41, 42, 43, 44, 51, 52, 53, 54, 57, 58, 59, 63, 65, 66, 67, 68, 77, 98
democracy, 108
desmos, 52, 54
dialectic, 9, 96, 97, 100
Didyma, 49
difference, 70, 73, 77, 78, 80, 97, 124
Dionysia, 114, 120, 122, 129
Dionysus, 113, 114, 126, 129
dramatic date, 4
    Laws, 106, 107
    Statesman, 87, 88, 90, 93
    Timaeus, 13, 14, 16, 18, 20, 27

elements (four), 30, 52, 53, 54, 55, 56, 57, 59, 60, 61, 73, 74, 75, 77, 102, 123, 124, 130
equality, 53, 71, 72, 73, 75, 77, 78, 80, 124, 125
    arithmetic, 71, 78
    geometrical, 55, 56, 71, 78, 79, 120
    harmonic, 71, 78
exemplar, 50, 54, 57, 91, 109
exemplum, 91, 95

fabric, 92, 93, 94, 95, 96, 97
family, 46, 120
father, 27, 28, 29, 30, 31, 32, 33, 39
festival, 13, 14, 16, 27, 36, 87, 88, 89, 90, 113, 114, 118, 121, 122, 126, 129, 133

155

General Index

Forms, 10, 41, 42, 44, 50, 51, 52, 53, 57, 58, 59, 60, 61, 78, 96, 97, 98, 124, 125
freedom, 109
friendship, 44, 45, 51, 52, 56, 92
frieze, 27, 36, 58, 123, 129

gegone, 38, 39
genesis, 38, 39, 62
geometrical shape, 52, 53, 55, 56, 59, 60, 61, 74
Giants, 32, 89, 90
gigantomachia, 32, 90
goal, 47, 50, 51, 55, 56, 57, 67, 76, 78, 98, 109, 111, 112, 124, 128, 131
gods, 30, 31, 32, 33, 34, 120, 121, 122, 123, 129
 astral gods, 31, 126, 129
 existence of, 112, 130
 Olympian gods, 32, 34, 120, 129
 regional/tribal gods, 120, 121, 129, 130, 131, 132
 traditional gods, 28, 29, 31, 34, 39, 129, 130, 131, 132
 young gods, 31, 54, 57
gomphos, 54
good, 30, 33, 34, 35, 36, 37, 38, 41, 44, 46, 47, 51, 66, 67, 68, 69, 72, 75, 76, 77, 92, 99, 105, 106, 107, 108, 109, 110, 111, 112, 114
Guardians of the Laws, 110, 111, 117
guest (*xenos*), 14, 15, 87, 107

Hagia Sophia, 79, 80, 82
happiness, 27, 43, 44, 46, 56, 98, 118
harmony, 37, 44, 45, 47, 51, 67, 71, 75, 78, 92, 93, 94, 127, 128, 133
hedra, 62
Hephaistos, 19, 36, 39, 62, 90, 91
Heraclitus, 28, 65
Hermocrates, 14, 15, 17, 19, 20, 22, 23, 26, 83
Hestia, 120, 121, 130
hupodochê, 62
hupographê, 109
hymn, 16, 34, 36, 122, 128, 132

Ibn Tufayl, 133
ichnos, 60, 61, 102
identity, 53, 70, 71, 72, 73, 77, 78, 79, 80, 97, 124
impiety, 131
inequality, 46, 71, 73, 75, 77, 80, 120

Julian the Emperor, 131
jurisdiction, 100
justice, 32, 43, 44, 55, 56, 57, 96, 97, 109, 120, 130

kalos, 66, 127
knowledge, 27, 29, 70, 87, 96, 97, 99, 105, 109, 112, 113, 115, 117, 125, 127, 128, 132

law, 22, 37, 45, 46, 55, 56, 57, 58, 76, 100, 101, 102, 106, 107, 108, 110, 111, 112, 115, 117, 128, 132
lawgiver, 17, 19, 35, 45, 79
legislation, 45, 46, 47, 99, 100, 101, 102, 105, 106, 107, 108, 109, 110, 111, 115
Lycurgos, 107, 108, 128, 132

Magnesia, 118, 119
measure, 60, 61, 65, 68, 69, 70, 71, 73, 75, 78
Megillos, 44, 106, 107, 108, 109, 112, 113, 132
Minos, 106, 107, 108, 110, 111, 132
model, 21, 25, 26, 28, 29, 30, 35, 41, 42, 43, 44, 45, 46, 47, 48, 49, 50, 51, 52, 53, 54, 55, 56, 57, 58, 59, 60, 61, 65, 66, 67, 69, 72, 73, 77, 78, 95, 97, 98, 117, 124, 125, 128
moderation, 44, 45, 56, 97, 109, 127
moira, 70
mother, 39
Muse, 113, 115, 126, 129
muthologia, 129

Nocturnal Council, 110, 111, 112, 113
nomos, 128, 132

oikêsis, 68, 103
oikos, 103
open interpretation, 3, 4, 6, 8, 9, 105

painters, 43, 44, 59, 96, 109
Panathenaea, 13, 14, 18, 27, 34, 36, 39, 87, 88, 90, 94, 100, 114, 122
panêguris, 16, 122
paradeigma, 41, 42, 43, 44, 46, 47, 48, 49, 50, 54, 57, 66, 89, 90, 91, 95, 97, 98, 109, 128
Parmenides, 14, 87, 88, 90, 100, 106, 107
Parthenon, 13, 22, 27, 32, 36, 58, 79, 82, 89, 90, 103, 129
pattern, 57, 97, 98
peace, 32, 44, 45, 47, 68, 93, 94, 109, 124, 127
peplos, 13, 27, 32, 36, 88, 89, 90, 93, 94, 95, 96, 97
perigraphê, 109
perpetuity, 56
Philolaus, 14
philosopher, 20, 21, 29, 43, 44, 53, 87, 96, 97, 98, 99, 112, 113, 131, 132, 133
plans (architectural), 49, 50, 57, 65, 75, 78
pleonexia, 22, 56
poets, 20, 29, 31, 33, 34, 57, 93, 94, 114, 128, 129, 132
political science (political art), 50, 91, 96, 97, 98, 99, 100, 101, 102, 109, 110, 111, 125
politikos, 99, 111
Poseidon, 22
preambles, 128
pre-elements, 52, 53, 59, 60, 61, 74
Priene, 49, 109

General Index

private property, 46
proportion, 30, 49, 50, 57, 60, 61, 71, 72, 73, 74,
    75, 77, 78, 120, 123, 127
  arithmetic, 55, 71
  geometrical, 52, 53, 55, 56, 71, 73, 75, 78, 123, 124
  harmonic, 71
propulaia, 69, 103
prothuron, 68, 103

region, 120, 121, 123
religion, 28, 118, 120, 122, 125, 129, 130, 131, 132
rhetoric, 99, 100, 123, 132
royal art, 92, 99, 101

Sais, 17, 19, 27, 37
self-sufficiency, 56, 63, 119, 123, 124
Socrates, 8, 13, 14, 18, 19, 21, 32, 57, 83, 87, 90, 96,
    106, 107, 126, 127
Socrates (Young), 87, 90, 94, 95, 96, 97, 98, 100
Solon, 17, 19, 100, 101, 107, 108, 115, 128
song, 34, 125, 127, 128, 129
sophist, 20, 87, 97, 99, 100
soul, 30, 38, 44, 48, 51, 54, 55, 56, 57, 68, 69, 70, 71,
    72, 73, 74, 75, 77, 78, 92, 99, 109, 112, 122,
    123, 131, 132
space, 121, 122, 123
spherical shape, 54, 57, 123, 124
spinning, 91, 95, 133
square, 74, 75, 79, 80, 82

statesman, 21, 35, 36, 87, 91, 92, 93, 94, 95, 96, 97,
    98, 99, 100, 101, 102, 105, 110, 111
summetria, 68, 69, 70, 72, 77
symposiarch, 15

technê, 99, 130
Timaeus, 17, 21, 29, 30, 35, 38, 51, 52, 53, 54, 59, 60
time, 30, 37, 38, 60, 72, 77, 87, 121, 122, 123,
    124, 132
tithênê, 62
topos, 19
trainer, 99, 100
triangles, 53, 74, 75, 78, 80, 82
tupos, 48, 49, 57, 68, 69, 109

unity, 44, 46, 47, 51, 54, 56, 71, 72, 73, 74, 78, 80,
    119, 121, 124

Vitruvius, 49, 50

war, 15, 17, 19, 45, 93, 108, 109, 127, 131
wax, 46, 48, 49
wealth, 22, 45, 46, 79, 120
weaving, 35, 36, 50, 88, 89, 90, 91, 92, 93, 94, 95,
    96, 97, 101, 134

Zeus, 26, 27, 28, 31, 32, 33, 34, 35, 36, 39, 43, 58, 68,
    89, 91, 94, 95, 98, 102, 106, 107, 108, 110, 113,
    114, 121, 130, 132